The Philosophy of Edmund Burke

THE PHILOSOPHY OF EDMUND BURKE

A Selection from His Speeches and Writings

Edited with an Introduction
by Louis I. Bredvold and Ralph G. Ross

Ann Arbor Paperbacks
The University of Michigan Press

First edition as an Ann Arbor Paperback 1967
Copyright © by The University of Michigan 1960
All rights reserved
ISBN 0-472-06121-6
Published in the United States of America by
The University of Michigan Press and
in Rexdale, Canada, by John Wiley & Sons Canada, Limited
Manufactured in the United States of America

1983   1982   1981   1980   7   6   5   4

Contents

Introduction 1

CHAPTER I Theory of Law and Legislation 13
1 Positive Law and Economic Law 27
2 International Law and Interference in a Foreign Nation 31

CHAPTER II Prudence as a Political Virtue 35

CHAPTER III The State and Society 43
1 The Nature of Society 43
2 What Is a "People"? 49
3 Liberty and Natural Rights 64
4 Liberty within the Social Order 67

CHAPTER IV Government and Human Nature 82
1 On Conciliation with the American Colonies 82
2 Religion and the State 104
3 Manners 125

CHAPTER V Practical Politics 132
1 Political Parties 132
2 Aristocracy and Leadership 139
3 The Duties of Popular Representatives 146
4 Elections and Parliamentary Reform 150

CHAPTER VI Reform and Tradition 156
1 Tradition and Change 156
2 Principles of Reform 165

CHAPTER VII Tradition in the English Establishment 176
1 The English Constitution 176
2 Prescription and Property 208

CHAPTER VIII   Jacobinism   231
          1   The New Morality of France and
              Rousseau   246
CHAPTER IX   Aesthetics: The Psychology of the Sublime   256
              Appendix: Leading Dates of Burke's Life   268
              Suggestions for Further Reading   269
              Index   270

The materials of his thought never reappear in the same form in which he obtained them. They have been smelted and recoined. They have come under the drill and inspiration of a great constructive mind, have caught life and taken structure from it. Burke is not literary because he takes from books, but because he makes books, transmuting what he writes upon into literature. It is this inevitable literary quality, this sure mastery of style, that mark the man, as much as his thought itself. He is a master in the use of the great style. Every sentence, too, is steeped in the colors of his extraordinary imagination. The movement takes your breath and quickens your pulses. The glow and power of the matter rejuvenate your faculties.

—*Woodrow Wilson*

What makes Burke stand out so splendidly among politicians is that he treats politics with his thought and imagination; therefore whether one agrees with him or not, he always interests you, stimulates you, and does you good.

—*Matthew Arnold*

Introduction

Politics, more than other sciences, has attracted the literary artist. That is reasonable, for politics is basic to human life and to the moral order, and these are the great subjects of the literary artist. Political thought, like history, is no less one of the humanities for being a social science. Coleridge and Shelley were devoted to politics. Dostoevsky and Conrad were so much more acute about great political issues than most "politicians" that, had we learned their lessons in time, we could have been saved at the very least many agonies of indecision. But Burke is less of their company than that of artists whose art was in the way they wrote and spoke of politics. His company is made of those like Plato and Rousseau. And like them, he knew many other things and knew them well. Politics, like morals, is not a subject to be learned alone. It should be a result of ripeness and wisdom. Samuel Johnson said of Burke, "Take up whatever topick you please, he is ready to meet you."

Burke started his literary career young. He was twenty-seven in 1756 when he published *A Vindication of Natural Society* and *A Philosophical Enquiry into The Origin of Our Ideas of The Sublime and Beautiful.* He was sixty-seven in 1796 and only a year from death when he published his last work, *Letters on a Regicide Peace.* In those forty years he wrote and spoke mostly on politics, but he managed to include *Hints for an Essay on the Drama* and *An Abridgment of English History.* Some of his ideas changed, especially as a result of the most shattering political event of his time, the French Revolution. And he never put them down in a systematic treatise where their relations show clearly. So it is remarkable, as one searches his works for his philosophy, how consistent and firm the outline is from youth to age.

Today Burke is called a conservative. And he is one, by most definitions. But he devoted his political career to reform. He was one of the two great European publicists of the American cause (the other was Thomas Paine), he was eloquent and formidable in defense of religious toleration, he damned the African slave trade, and he took enormous pains to fight corruption and mismanagement in the government of British India. He attacked the aristocracy, opposing to an aristocracy of birth a natural aristocracy (as did Jefferson and John Adams). "You do not imagine," Burke wrote, "that I wish to confine power, authority, and distinction to blood and names and titles. No, sir. There is no qualification for government but virtue and wisdom, actual or presumptive." He denounced the meddling of the king and the "King's friends" in politics, and pushed through his Bill for Economical Reform, which has been called "probably the most important single act of reform achieved in England in the eighteenth century," against the determined opposition of George III.

Burke was also a romantic. In politics, his disciples included many of the Lake poets. His romanticism was a corrective of the often thin and artificial neoclassicism of the enlightenment. His sensibility and his experience made him aware of the complexities of circumstance and the painful nuances of judgment and practice that are necessary if we are to have and to do justice. How could he not be suspicious of the amateurs and *ideologues* who presumed to govern the new French Republic?

Burke's value to us depends on how we use him. When he is used as a critic of our own government, or of some of its tendencies, he must be used as a critic from within. The critics of democracy can be its greatest friends, but only when they are within the fold, for then they criticize the existent by the standards of the ideal; they don't oppose the ideal itself. Those who do are enemies who want to curtail liberty, not to make it more responsible, to enslave, not to free.

Burke's understanding of the French Revolution is so valuable in application to the Russian Revolution, that that may be one of the best uses we can make of him. All his ideas then came together, were rethought and extended, and then marshalled to fight for justice and freedom. In his mortal combat, he was sometimes ungenerous and he sometimes exaggerated. He saw some things badly. He thought the French Revolution an enemy of property, for it confiscated the property of aristocrats, yet in fact it gave property into the hands of those whose grip was most relentless.

He overlooked the appeal of the Revolution to the most ardent and purest of the young men. He modified his earlier belief about the just powers of the people. And he minimized, absurdly, the abuses of the *ancien régime*, as some today minimize the abuses of Czarism.* But he was at war, at war with an idea that he thought deadly to civilization. The astonishing thing is how much he saw and how well he predicted. One need only be reminded that he even foresaw Bonapartism:

> Some popular general, who understands the art of conciliating the soldiery, and who possesses the true spirit of command, shall draw the eyes of all men on himself. Armies will obey him on his personal account. . . . But the moment in which that event will happen, the person who really commands the army is your master; the master . . . of your whole republic.

Burke seemed able to predict too well, to know exactly where the stream of the Revolution was flowing. It has been suggested, perhaps correctly, that Paine, before he turned against Burke, thought he could win him to the French cause, and kept him informed of the private decisions of the Revolutionary leaders. Apparently he did show Burke a letter of Jefferson's, and Jefferson, then Ambassador to the court of Louis XVI, was privy to some of the Revolutionary leaders' plans. But Burke, no matter how much special information was given to him, still grasped the essence of the Revolution, or one important aspect of it, as no one else did, and grasped it early. His quickness hurt his reputation. He was a premature anti-Revolutionary, as others have been "premature anti-Communists" or "premature anti-Fascists."

The French Revolution developed much as Burke expected. On May 5, 1789, Louis XVI opened the session of the States General, in which the three estates met together, and next morning the deputies of the Third Estate held their first meeting alone, the decisive step toward revolution. In October of the same year,

*Burke's passage in the *Reflections* on Marie Antoinette and the chivalry that should have been accorded her was so extravagant that it enabled Paine to score effectively for once, by remarking: "He pities the plumage but forgets the dying bird."

Burke wrote critically of what was taking place.° And in November of 1790, his thoughts on the subject ordered, he published the *Reflections on the Revolution in France.* On February 5, 1794, eleven months after the beginning of the Reign of Terror, Robespierre addressed the National Convention thus:

> They say that terrorism is the resort of despotic government. Is our government then like despotism? Yes, as the sword that flashes in the hand of the hero of liberty is like that with which the satellites of tyranny are armed. . . . The government of the Revolution is the despotism of liberty against tyranny.†

And in 1799, two years after Burke's death, Bonaparte became First Consul.

What Burke saw in the eighteenth-century French Revolution was not quite the kind of thing that the Nazis brought in the twentieth century. Aurel Kolnai called that "the war against the west" and it was an attack (intellectually, if not technologically) from outside the Western tradition, with a base partly in ancient Egypt and partly in the jungle. The French Revolution, as Burke understood it, was an attack on the West based on some of the best aspects of its own civilization, but wrenching those aspects from context and transforming them into an entire philosophy, arrogant and rootless. The analogy is to the Russian Revolution, blinded by ideology, invoking "science" as the French Revolution invoked "reason," and announcing, as the French had, its devotion to the age-old aspirations of man. Just as Napoleon's troops still bore the banner "Liberty, Equality, Fraternity," so Stalin's figuratively bore "The Classless Society"; the revolutionary labels were pasted on counter-revolutionary bottles.

Because Burke is a conservative, it is sometimes falsely assumed that he was a natural enemy of all revolution. That is not so. He was not an enemy of revolution if it was a last resort and there

---

° The French Revolution was no more Jacobin at first than the Russian Revolution was Bolshevik. Much of the world rejoiced, in both cases, at the overthrow of tyranny. But there was real danger, poorly seen and weakly met, of revolutionary tyranny; Mirabeau in France and Plekhanov in Russia probably understood.

† How many echoes of this sophistry are heard in Soviet polemics!

were no means of reform; although even then he wanted to know what new forms would succeed the old. "When tyranny is extreme," he wrote, "and abuses of government intolerable, men resort to the rights of Nature to shake it off." But revolution is justified only if it is also for, not against, the moral law. So Burke defended the Glorious Revolution of 1688 and the American Revolution, but distinguished them sharply from the French Revolution. The first two built on their heritage and their ideals; the third wanted a universal conflagration so it could build on the ashes.

The French Revolution was, in its ideas, an offshoot of several important beliefs of the Enlightenment, among them that man per se had natural rights and that all men were equal, that the reason with which man was endowed was sufficient to solve his problems, that if men understood what was right they would do it, for no man willed evil. Sovereign Reason was enthroned. History was the realm of the contingent and irrational; by taking thought man could find the truth, and by action guided by truth, he could overthrow the result of centuries of greed and accident. Then he could build anew, with laws that were just. (Some of the arguments are different from the Communists', but the temper is the same.)

Burke's attack was not, as is often stated, a defense of history against reason. He was, perhaps above all else, a defender of reason. What he hated was rationalism, the derivation of a whole system of ideas from a priori or postulated grounds. Nor was Burke an enemy of generalization; he was an empiricist who demanded that social principles be grounded in social experience (including past experience, or history). He even thought that constant concern with abstraction was temperamental, in part a device of the "slothful" to evade the labors of experience. And impatience with reality leads to blood.

Abstraction, to Burke, is the seedbed of fanaticism. If one keeps thinking in terms of categories he will finally overlook their members. The French *ideologues*, Burke said, loved mankind dearly but could not abide men. Still, it is bad enough just to forget them. The fanatic resorts to the bullet and bayonet because a principle requires the extermination of members of a class. Abstraction classifies men and then forgets they are human. "Let us destroy the aristocracy," someone says (or "liquidate the bourgeoisie") and people are killed. "Nothing can be conceived more hard than the heart of a thoroughbred metaphysician. It comes nearer to the cold malignity of a wicked spirit than to the frailty and passion of a man." For "metaphysician" read "rationalist social philosopher" and Burke's meaning becomes clear. Such men would wipe out whole groups (why is genocide worse than killing all aristocrats or all bourgeois or, for that matter, all lawyers?) or sacrifice the present generation to the future. To suggest the latter presupposes that we are not so important as they (or that a bird in the bush is worth two in the hand). That is like the pacifist who refuses to fight because life is sacred, but will offer his own life nobly to save someone else, presumably because all life is sacred except his own.

There is also a peculiarly Burkean objection to the fanatical sacrifice of the present to the future: today is tomorrow's past. What tomorrow will be is largely determined by what today is. The national heritage will in part be one of shame, and the consequences of today's actions will not easily be wiped out. The danger of rationalism is that one confronts experience with antecedent principles assumed a priori and in no way the fruits of past experience. With all his devotion to the natural law, Burke knew that its principles could be only a general guide, and that consequences as well as antecedents were involved in moral decision. "In all moral machinery," he said, "the moral results are its test." A proper concern for the consequences of action is indispensable to statesmanship, as to private life, and it can prevent the follies of rigidity as well as the horrors of fanaticism.

Burke's very concern with history was based on his understanding of the relation between theory and practice. He wanted theory based on practice and practice guided by theory, but only by theory that had itself been tested in practice. The arena of social and political test was, and could only be, history. Our institutions are the results of a kind of natural selection: they are the ones that continue to work. If they falter in our time, they need reform. Only if they collapse totally or work iniquity under these new circumstances should they be replaced, for total innovation is a chancy business, and men's lives are at stake. In guiding and reforming institutions, and in innovating, if it comes to that, we must be guided by reflection on history, for that is the way to learn the lessons of the human race. French rationalism simply refused to do this because it denied there was reason in history, and found it solely in the mind. Burke's defense of history is easily misunderstood. He did not defend history against reason as the rationalists defended reason against history; he used history for the sake of reason, not for its own sake. "God forbid," he said, "that we should attempt to be wise by precedent."

In the rationalist's emphasis on abstract reason, Burke found, one may suspect, the beginning of that fragmentation of personality which has developed so rapidly in the modern world. He trusted reason when it was allied to feeling and instinct, quickened by sensibility, and nurtured by civilization. He distrusted reason without feeling and morals as he distrusted reason without experience. Indeed, if he had to choose, he preferred habit and "prejudice" alone to abstract reason alone, for customs are "the standing wisdom of the country" and abstract reason is unlikely to do better. Reason properly employed, in alliance with feeling and experience, considers the variety and complexity of existence. It is humble, because it tries to understand the moral order (for Burke a part of the divine order) as much as it possibly can, but realizes how little that is. And it is humble, too, because it recognizes that without regard for circumstance the greatest abstract good readily becomes evil.

Abstract reason, rationalism, is like imagination in having almost no bounds; it is not like feeling which is rooted in things and limited by our reactions to them. Its arrogance rejects the ordinary feelings of men as untutored or unimportant, and is always in danger of becoming a rationalization for strange or unrecognized feelings. Man is not only a rational animal; reason when it is not tied to feeling and enlisted by morals, can be captured by strong and ruthless emotions. There are always the drive for power, the lust for glory, the hidden demands of egoism, to control our actions while we explain them piously in terms of abstract rights and abstract good.

Indeed, the abstract rights of man, as enunciated by the French, sound suspicious to Burke. The liberty they proclaim "consists, and consists alone, in being free from those restraints, which are imposed by the virtues upon the passions." Against it Burke poses "social freedom," which is "that state of things in which liberty is secured by the equality of restraint"; and restraint comes from both society and self-discipline. Here we approach the core of Burke's view of man. Man is not a creature who moved from his original state, that of nature, into society and the state because he found it advantageous. On the contrary, man's nature is fulfilled only in civil society, and he cannot exist as a fully developed creature outside of it.

The state of civil society . . . is a state of nature; and much more truly so than a savage and incoherent mode of life. For man is by nature reasonable; and he is never perfectly in his natural state, but when he is placed where reason may be best cultivated, and most predominate. Art is man's nature. We are as much, at least, in a state of nature in formed manhood, as in immature and helpless infancy.

As usual, Burke is Aristotelian in his thought, although with an admixture of Thomism. His words have some of the ring of Thomas' dictum: "Grace does not abolish Nature but perfects it."

The Russian Revolution did not appeal to abstract reason as the French Revolution did. Its guide is "History," which is history interpreted rigidly by principles labeled "scientific" but bearing the clear mark of the a priori. Yet the result is the same in essence: reason is separated from experience and becomes the enemy of morals. A nation is created which is not just a nation but the center of a world-wide revolution, which exists to foment civil war everywhere. Its end is a new social organization opposed to the spirit—moral, social, religious—of Western civilization as it has developed up to now. Its means are any that will serve its purposes—whatever is good for the "proletariat" is good—and they are forged deftly, without the hindrance of scruple. To confront the U.S.S.R. as though it were just another powerful state bidding for still more power and to try to defeat it by nineteenth-century means would be suicidal folly; but we are tyros at this sort of politics.

Burke found England equally unprepared to cope with the Jacobins.

It is a dreadful truth, but it is a truth that cannot be concealed; in ability, in dexterity, in the distinctness of their views, the Jacobins are our superiors. They saw the thing right from the very beginning. Whatever were the first motives to the war among politicians, they saw that in its spirit, and for its objects, it was a *civil war;* and as such they pursued it. It is a war between the partisans of the ancient, civil, moral, and political order of Europe, against a sect of fanatical and ambitious atheists which means to change them all. It is not France extending a foreign empire over other nations; it is a sect aiming at universal empire, and beginning with the conquest of France.

Burke sounds as though he were talking of Communists, not Jacobins, and he sounds that way over and over because he is talking about the same issue. What of religion? Communism is opposed to it; those who worship the state will tolerate no rival faith. Jacobinism, too, was opposed to religion, despite some words in its favor. Burke suggested a reason. "Your despots govern by terror. They know that he who fears God fears nothing else; and therefore they eradicate from the mind . . . that only sort of fear which generates true courage."

Communism is totalitarian; it differs from ordinary despotism because it enters every area of life. Every problem, then, has a political aspect and every person a political role. This is not just for the sake of efficiency; it is often wasteful and inefficient. It is because their politics are based on a total system of belief, taking precedence over all other commitments, if there is room for them at all. It is usually assumed that totalitarianism is a twentieth-century creation. Yet Burke found that Jacobinism governed too much, that its hand was on every aspect of life, that it interfered even with the family. From "the day of the Revolution, France," he said, "has been of all governments the most absolute, despotic, and effective that has hitherto appeared on earth." In a word, he found it totalitarian.

Individuality is left out of their scheme of government. The state is all in all. . . . The state has dominion and conquest for its sole objects,—dominion over minds by proselytism, over bodies by arms.

Is there even in detail an attempt to live up to the ideals proclaimed so bravely? One example to the contrary should suffice. The 1936 constitution of the U.S.S.R. stipulated "free education including higher education" for all citizens, but in 1940 stipends for students in secondary schools and universities were withdrawn and very high fees were introduced for secondary schools in their upper classes and for all higher institutions of learning. Those whose parents could not pay were drafted in large numbers into the labor force. In Jacobin France, which boasted of its base in the Rights of Man, a property qualification was reintroduced for the vote itself. "You order him to buy the right," Burke put it, "which you before told him nature had given to him gratuitously at his birth, and of which no authority on earth could legally deprive him."

In the end, the indictment against such revolution comes as readily to a liberal as to a conservative pen. One has only to believe in Western civilization, in justice, and in what we call democracy and Burke might have called representation. The indictment in brief is that a hard-won product of our civilization is separated from the conditions that nurtured it and the proper context of its use, and is proclaimed *The Way* to realization of the ancient goals of our tradition. How else, it is asked, can we attain peace, equality, abundance, and the brotherhood of man? They have not been attained yet, but a method ("abstract reason," "science") at last exists. If we destroy all that has existed before this new dispensation, we can even make a new kind of man (Burke knew that to reject man was to rebuke God). So we must destroy the conditions under which our method came into being without asking whether they, or some of them, are necessary for its survival; and in seeking the as yet unattained goals of man we destroy what we have so far won. Whether, with scorn, you denounce them as aristocratic, or with equal scorn you call them bourgeois, you oppose the dominant ideals of our civilization which were proclaimed, not surprisingly, by a dominant class. Whatever there was of community, observance, humility, moral order, and independence of mind and spirit must go.

There is a quality of the Western tradition (and the Eastern, for that matter) which such revolutionists do not understand. Christianity did not destroy but tried to build on Judaism; Islam accepted both in its own revolution. And, though many have tried to alter this situation by arms, each of these religions still develops its own tradition in its own ways, secure in the common beliefs that permit ordinary intercourse with the others and with the irreligious inheritors of the tradition. That is not the spirit of the war against the West; it wants nothing else to survive. Burke wrote:

I never thought we could make peace with the system; because it was not for the sake of an object we pursued in rivalry with each other, but with the system itself that we were at war. As I understood the matter, we were at war, not with its conduct, but with its existence,—convinced that its existence and its hostility were the same.

There is much in all the countries of the West that resonates to Russian words, for they are our words; as it still resonates to Jacobin words, for they are our words, too. And because the words are so often our words, the threat of civil war has always been real (even when it is called "the social revolution"). If we avoid civil war, we may still be plunged into national war. A great price can properly be paid to avoid that. But in the end, whatever the battlefield—intellect, spirit, or body—the last words are Burke's: ". . . with this republic nothing independent can coexist."

CHAPTER I

Theory of Law and Legislation

All theories of jurisprudence, from the earliest to the latest, must belong to one of two basic types, according to how they conceive of the source of law and the kind of submission it may expect to command from human nature. On the one hand law is simply and merely a command, issued of course by a governmental authority strong enough to enforce it. This definition would include every governmental directive, whatever its nature, whether the edicts of dictators or kings, the legislative acts of representative bodies, the regulations of administrative law, or the decisions by popular referendum. Law would accordingly be whatever has been promulgated by a superior power. The other type of theory desires to superimpose on the concept of command a higher concept of justice and right. This higher concept has taken many forms, from the will of God, as John Calvin held, to the Rights of Man. It permits appeal from the injustices of government to a higher court. The longest and most continuous tradition of this type of theory, with a complicated history from Stoic philosophy and Roman jurisprudence down to our own time, has been generally called by its exponents "the Law of Nature." Adherents of this theory insist that the moral law constitutes a basis, not purely utilitarian, for discriminating between good laws and bad. They contend that it is both possible and necessary to inquire whether the justice being administered is just. Consequently they appeal to "eternal principles of justice and morality." Among the eminent English champions of the first group may be mentioned Thomas Hobbes in the seventeenth century and John Austin in the nineteenth. Burke adhered to the Natural Law tradition, and he studied its great authorities from Cicero down to his contemporary French revolutionist Emmerich de Vattel. The principles he formulated in his early *Tract on the Popery Laws* he repeatedly appealed to throughout his life. Among the authoritative works on this subject may be mentioned Peter J. Stanlis, *Edmund Burke and the Natural Law* (Ann Arbor, 1958), A. P. d'Entrèves, *Natural Law, An Introduction to Legal Philosophy* (London, 1951), and a monumental work by R. W. and A. J. Carlyle, *A History of Medieval Political Theory in the West*, 6 vols. (London, 1903–36).

... power ... to be legitimate must be according to that eternal, immutable law in which will and reason are the same ...
Reflections (1790). III, 356.*

Civil laws are not all of them merely positive. Those which are rather conclusions of legal reason than matters of statutable provision belong to universal equity, and are universally applicable.
First Letter on a Regicide Peace (1796). V, 321.

As to the opinion of the people, which some think, in such cases, is to be implicity obeyed, . . . when we know that the opinions of even the greatest multitudes are the standard of rectitude, I shall think myself obliged to make those opinions the masters of my conscience. But if it may be doubted whether Omnipotence itself is competent to alter the essential constitution of right and wrong, sure I am that such *things* as they and I are possessed of no such power. No man carries further than I do the policy of making government pleasing to the people. But the widest range of this politic complaisance is confined within the limits of justice. I would not only consult the interest of the people, but I would cheerfully gratify their humors. We are all a sort of children that must be soothed and managed. I think I am not austere or formal in my nature. I would bear, I would even myself play my part in, any innocent buffooneries, to divert them. But I never will act the tyrant for their amusement. If they will mix malice in their sports, I shall never consent to throw them any living, sentient creature whatsoever, no, not so much as a kitling, to torment.
Speech at Bristol Previous to the Election (1780). II, 421.

Observe, Sir, that the apology for my undertaking (an apology which, though long, is no longer than necessary) is not grounded on my want of the fullest sense of the difficult and invidious nature of the task I undertake. I risk odium, if I succeed, and contempt, if I fail. My excuse must rest in mine and your conviction of the absolute, urgent *necessity* there is that something of the kind should be done. . . . But, indeed, it is necessary that the attempt should be made. It is necessary from our own political circumstances; it

* See bibliographical references in Suggestions for Further Reading.

is necessary from the operations of the enemy; it is necessary from the demands of the people, whose desires, when they do not militate with the stable and eternal rules of justice and reason, (rules which are above us and above them,) ought to be as a law to a House of Commons.

Speech on the Plan for Economical Reform (1780). II, 271.

What the law respects shall be sacred to me. If the barriers of law should be broken down, upon ideas of convenience, even of public convenience, we shall have no longer anything certain among us. If the discretion of power is once let loose upon property, we can be at no loss to determine whose power and what discretion it is that will prevail at last. It would be wise to attend upon the order of things, and not to attempt to outrun the slow, but smooth and even course of Nature. There are occasions, I admit, of public necessity, so vast, so clear, so evident, that they supersede all laws. Law, being only made for the benefit of the community, cannot in any one of its parts resist a demand which may comprehend the total of the public interest. To be sure, no law can set itself up against the cause and reason of all law; but such a case very rarely happens, and this most certainly is not such a case. The mere time of the reform is by no means worth the sacrifice of a principle of law. Individuals pass like shadows; but the commonwealth is fixed and stable. The difference, therefore, of to-day and to-morrow, which to private people is immense, to the state is nothing. At any rate, it is better, if possible, to reconcile our economy with our laws than to set them at variance,—a quarrel which in the end must be destructive to both.

Speech on the Plan for Economical Reform (1780). II, 329–30.

And first of all, the science of jurisprudence, the pride of the human intellect, which, with all its defects, redundancies, and errors, is the collected reason of ages, combining the principles of original justice with the infinite variety of human concerns, as a heap of old exploded errors, would be no longer studied. Personal self-sufficiency and arrogance (the certain attendants upon all those who have never experienced a wisdom greater than their own) would usurp the tribunal.

Reflections (1790). III, 357.

A government of the nature of that set up at our very door has never been hitherto seen or even imagined in Europe. What our relation to it will be cannot be judged by other relations. It is a serious thing to have a connection with a people who live only under positive, arbitrary, and changeable institutions,—and those not perfected nor supplied nor explained by any common, acknowledged rule of moral science. I remember, that, in one of my last conversations with the late Lord Camden, we were struck much in the same manner with the abolition in France of the law as a science of methodized and artificial equity. France, since her Revolution, is under the sway of a sect whose leaders have deliberately, at one stroke, demolished the whole body of that jurisprudence which France had pretty nearly in common with other civilized countries. In that jurisprudence were contained the elements and principles of the law of nations, the great ligament of mankind. With the law they have of course destroyed all seminaries in which jurisprudence was taught, as well as all the corporations established for its conservation. I have not heard of any country, whether in Europe or Asia, or even in Africa on this side of Mount Atlas, which is wholly without some such colleges and such corporations, except France. No man, in a public or private concern, can divine by what rule or principle her judgments are to be directed: nor is there to be found a professor in any university, or a practitioner in any court, who will hazard an opinion of what is or is not law in France, in any case whatever. They have not only annulled all their old treaties, but they have renounced the law of nations, from whence treaties have their force. With a fixed design they have outlawed themselves, and to their power outlawed all other nations.

First Letter on a Regicide Peace (1796). V, 307–8.

Sir John Seeley is responsible for a well-known jingle: "History without Political Science has no fruit: Political Science without History has no root."

My principles enable me to form my judgment upon men and actions in history, just as they do in common life, and are not formed out of events and characters, either present or past. History is a preceptor of prudence, not of principles. The principles of true politics are those of morality enlarged; and I neither now do, nor ever will, admit of any other. . . . The principles that guide us in public and private, as they are not of our devising, but moulded into the nature and essence of things, will endure with the sun and moon,—long, very long after whig and tory, Stuart and Brunswick, and all such miserable bubbles and playthings of the hour, are vanished from existence and from memory.

Draft of Letter to the Bishop of Chester, 1771.
Correspondence. I, 332–33.

Nothing in Mr. Hasting's proceedings is so curious as his several defences; and nothing in the defences is so singular as the principles upon which he proceeds. Your Lordships will have to decide not only upon a large, connected, systematic train of misdemeanors, but an equally connected system of principles and maxims of government, invented to justify those misdemeanors. He has brought them forward and avowed them in the face of day. . . .

He has told your Lordships, in his defence, that actions in Asia do not bear the same moral qualities which the same actions would bear in Europe. My Lords, we positively deny that principle. . . . These gentlemen have formed a plan of *geographical morality*, by which the duties of men, in public and in private situations, are not to be governed by their relation to the great Governor of the Universe, or by their relation to mankind, but by climates, degrees of longitude, parallels, not of life, but of latitudes: as if, when you have crossed the equinoctial, all the virtues die, as they say some insects die when they cross the line. . . . This geographical morality we do protest against; Mr. Hastings shall not screen himself under it. . . . We think it necessary, in justification of ourselves, to declare that the laws of morality are the same everywhere, and that there is no action which would pass for an act of extortion, of peculation, of bribery, and of oppression in England, that is not an act of extortion, of peculation, of bribery, and oppression in Europe, Asia, Africa, and all the world over. This I contend for not in the technical forms of it, but I contend for it in the substance.

Mr. Hastings comes before your Lordships not as a British governor answering to a British tribunal, but as a subahdar, as a bashaw of three tails. He says, "I had an arbitrary power to exercise: I exercised it. Slaves I found the people: slaves they are,—they are so by their constitution; and if they are, I did not make it for them. I was unfortunately bound to exercise this arbitrary power, and accordingly I did exercise it. It was disagreeable to me, but I did exercise it; and no other power can be exercised in that country." . . . Will your Lordships submit to hear the corrupt practices of mankind made the principles of government? No! it will be your pride and glory to teach men intrusted with power, that, in their use of it, they are to conform to principles, and not to draw their principles from the corrupt practice of any man whatever. Was there ever heard, or could it be conceived, that a governor would dare to heap up all the evil practices, all the cruelties, oppressions, extortions, corruptions, briberies, of all the ferocious usurpers, desperate robbers, thieves, cheats, and jugglers, that ever had office, from one end of Asia to another, and, consolidating all this mass of the crimes and absurdities of barbarous domination into one code, establish it as the whole duty of an English governor? I believe that till this time so audacious a thing was never attempted by man.

He have arbitrary power! My Lords, the East India Company have not arbitrary power to give him; the king has no arbitrary power to give him; your Lordships have not; nor the Commons, nor the whole legislature. We have no arbitrary power to give, because arbitrary power is a thing which neither any man can hold nor any man can give. No man can lawfully govern himself according to his own will; much less can one person be governed by the will of another. We are all born in subjection,—all born equally, high and low, governors and governed, in subjection to one great, immutable, pre-existent law, prior to all our devices and prior to all our contrivances, paramount to all our ideas and all our sensations, antecedent to our very existence, by which we are knit and connected in the eternal frame of the universe, out of which we cannot stir.

This great law does not arise from our conventions or compacts; on the contrary, it gives to our conventions and compacts all the force and sanction they can have. It does not arise from our vain institutions. Every good gift is of God; all power is of God; and He who has given the power, and from whom alone it originates, will never suffer the exercise of it to be practised upon any less solid foundation than the power itself. If, then, all dominion of man over man is the effect of the Divine disposition, it is bound by the eternal laws of Him that gave it, with which no human authority can dispense,—neither he that exercises it, nor even those who are subject to it; and if they were mad enough to make an express compact that should release their magistrate from his duty, and should declare their lives, liberties, and properties dependent upon, not rules and laws, but his mere capricious will, that covenant would be void. The acceptor of it has not his authority increased, but he has his crime doubled. Therefore can it be imagined, if this be true, that He will suffer this great gift of government, the greatest, the best, that was ever given by God to mankind, to be the plaything and the sport of the feeble will of a man, who, by a blasphemous, absurd, and petulant usurpation, would place his own feeble, contemptible, ridiculous will in the place of Divine wisdom and justice? . . .

Law and arbitrary power are in eternal enmity. Name me a magistrate, and I will name property; name me power, and I will name protection. It is a contradiction in terms, it is blasphemy in religion, it is wickedness in politics, to say that any man can have arbitrary power. In every patent of office the duty is included. For what else does a magistrate exist? To suppose for power is an absurdity in idea. Judges are guided and governed by the eternal laws of justice, to which we are all subject. We may bite our chains, if we will, but we shall be made to know ourselves, and be taught that man is born to be governed by law; and he that will substitute *will* in the place of it is an enemy to God.

Despotism does not in the smallest degree abrogate, alter, or lessen any one duty of any one relation of life, or weaken the force or obligation of any one engagement or contract whatsoever. Despotism, if it means anything at all defensible, means a mode of government bound by no written rules, and coerced by no controlling magistracies or well-settled orders in the state. But if it has no written law, it neither does nor can cancel the primeval, indefeasible, unalterable law of Nature and of nations; and if no magistracies control its exertions, those exertions must derive their limitation and direction either from the equity and moderation of the ruler, or from downright revolt on the part of the subject by rebellion, divested of all its criminal qualities. The moment a sovereign removes the idea of security and protection from his subjects, and declares that he is everything and they nothing, when he declares that no contract he makes with them can or ought to bind him, he then declares war upon them: he is no longer sovereign; they are no longer subjects.

Speech on Impeachment of Warren Hastings, February 16, 1788.
IX, 446–59.

After Burke died there was found among his papers a fragmentary sketch, written before his political career began, in which he examined the several penal laws under which Catholics then suffered in Ireland. Catholics were excluded from civil and military service, even from the practice of law. They were, said Burke, "disabled from taking or purchasing . . . any lands, any mortgage upon land, any rents or profits from land, any lease, interest, or term of any land, any annuity for life or lives or years, or any estate whatsoever, chargeable upon, or which may in any manner affect, any lands." He based his criticism on the principles of Natural Law.

The system which we have just reviewed, and the manner in which religious influence on the public is made to operate upon the laws concerning property in Ireland, is in its nature very singular, and differs, I apprehend, essentially, and perhaps to its disadvantage, from any scheme of religious persecution now existing in any other country in Europe, or which has prevailed in any time or nation with which history has made us acquainted. I believe it will not be difficult to show that it is unjust, impolitic, and inefficacious; that it has the most unhappy influence on the prosperity, the morals, and the safety of that country; that this influence is not accidental, but has flowed as the necessary and direct consequence of the laws themselves, first on account of the object which they affect, and next by the quality of the greatest part of the instruments they employ. Upon all these points, first upon the general, and then on the particular, this question will be considered with as much order as can be followed in a matter of itself as involved and intricate as it is important.

The first and most capital consideration with regard to this, as to every object, is the extent of it. And here it is necessary to premise, this system of penalty and incapacity has for its object no small sect or obscure party, but a very numerous body of men,—a body which comprehends at least two thirds of that whole nation: it amounts to 2,800,000 souls, a number sufficient for the materials constituent of a great people. Now it is well worthy of a serious and dispassionate examination, whether such a system, respecting such an object, be in reality agreeable to any sound principles of legislation or any authorized definition of law; for if our reasons or practices differ from the general informed sense of mankind, it is very moderate to say that they are at least suspicious.

This consideration of the magnitude of the object ought to attend us through the whole inquiry: if it does not always affect the reason, it is always decisive on the importance of the question. It not only makes in itself a more leading point, but complicates itself with every other part of the matter, giving every error, minute in itself, a character and significance from its application. It is therefore not to be wondered at, if we perpetually recur to it in the course of this essay.

In the making of a new law it is undoubtedly the duty of the legislator to see that no injustice be done even to an individual: for there is then nothing to be unsettled, and the matter is under his hands to mould it as he pleases; and if he finds it untractable in the working, he may abandon it without incurring any new inconvenience. But in the question concerning the repeal of an old one, the work is of more difficulty; because laws, like houses, lean on one another, and the operation is delicate, and should be necessary: the objection, in such a case, ought not to arise from the natural infirmity of human institutions, but from substantial faults which contradict the nature and end of law itself,—faults not arising from the imperfection, but from the misapplication and abuse of our reason. As no legislators can regard the *minima* of equity, a law may in some instances be a just subject of censure without being at all an object of repeal. But if its transgressions against common right and the ends of just government should be considerable in their nature and spreading in their effects, as this objection goes to the root and principle of the law, it renders it void in its obligatory quality on the mind, and therefore determines it as the proper object of abrogation and repeal, so far as regards its civil existence. The objection here is, as we observed, by no means on account of the imperfection of the law; it is on account of its erroneous principle: for if this be fundamentally wrong, the more perfect the law is made, the worse it becomes. It cannot be said to have the properties of genuine law, even in its imperfections and defects. The true weakness and opprobrium of our best general constitutions is, that they cannot provide beneficially for every particular case, and thus fill, adequately to their intentions, the circle of universal justice. But where the principle is faulty, the erroneous part of the law is the beneficial, and justice only finds refuge in those holes and corners which had escaped the sagacity and inquisition of the legislator. The happiness or misery of multitudes can never be a thing indifferent. A law against the majority of the people is in substance a law against the people itself; its extent determines its invalidity; it even changes its character as it enlarges its operation: it is not particular injustice, but general oppression; and can no longer be considered as a private hardship, which might be borne, but spreads and grows up into the unfortunate importance of a national calamity.

Now as a law directed against the mass of the nation has not the nature of a reasonable institution, so neither has it the authority: for in all forms of government the people is the true legislator; and whether the immediate and instrumental cause of the law be a single person or many, the remote and efficient cause is the consent of the people, either actual or implied; and such consent is absolutely essential to its validity. To the solid establishment of every law two things are essentially requisite: first, a proper and sufficient human power to declare and modify the matter of the law; and next, such a fit and equitable constitution as they have a right to declare and render binding. With regard to the first requisite, the human authority, it is their judgment they give up, not their right. The people, indeed, are presumed to consent to whatever the legislature ordains for their benefit; and they are to acquiesce in it, though they do not clearly see into the propriety of the means by which they are conducted to that desirable end. This they owe as an act of homage and just deference to a reason which the necessity of government has made superior to their own. But though the means, and indeed the nature, of a public advantage may not always be evident to the understanding of the subject, no one is so gross and stupid as not to distinguish between a benefit and an injury. No one can imagine, then, an exclusion of a great body of men, not from favors, privileges, and trusts, but from the common advantages of society, can ever be a thing intended for their good, or can ever be ratified by any implied consent of theirs. If, therefore, at least an implied human consent is necessary to the existence of a law, such a constitution cannot in propriety be a law at all.

But if we could suppose that such a ratification was made, not virtually, but actually, by the people, not representatively, but even collectively, still it would be null and void. They have no right to make a law prejudicial to the whole community, even though the delinquents in making such an act should be themselves the chief sufferers by it; because it would be made against the principle of a superior law, which it is not in the power of any community, or of the whole race of man, to alter,—I mean the will of Him who gave us our nature, and in giving impressed an invariable law upon it. It would be hard to point out any error more truly subversive of all the order and beauty, of all the peace and happiness of human society, than the position, that any body of men have a right to make what laws they please,—or that laws can derive any authority from their institution merely, and independent of the quality of the subject-matter. No arguments of policy, reason of state, or preservation of the constitution can be pleaded in favor of such a practice. They may, indeed, impeach the frame of that constitution, but can never touch this immovable principle. This seems to be, indeed, the doctrine which Hobbes broached in the last century, and which was then so frequently and so ably refuted. Cicero exclaims with the utmost indignation and contempt against such a notion: [1] he considers it not only as unworthy of a philosopher, but of an illiterate peasant; that of all things this was the most truly absurd, to fancy that the rule of justice was to be taken from the

---

[1] "O rem dignam, in qua non modo docti, verum etiam agrestes erubescant! Jam vero illud stultissimum existimare omnia justa esse, quæ scita sint in populorum institutis aut legibus," etc. "Quod si populorum jussis, si principum decretis, si sententiis judicum jura constituerentur, jus esset latrocinari, jus adulterare, jus testamenta falsa supponere, si hæc suffragiis aut scitis multitudinis probarentur." Cicero de Legibus, Lib. I. 14, 15 et 16. [Burke].

Obedience to laws only through fear is a motive "that might bring a blush of shame not only to the enlightened person, but even to a simple rustic. But indeed the most foolish idea of all is the belief that everything found in the laws and customs of peoples is just. . . . For if the principles of justice are to be constituted from the decrees of peoples, the edicts of princes, the opinions of judges, then Justice would sanction robbery, adultery, and the forging of wills, in case such acts were approved by popular vote or decree."

constitutions of commonwealths, or that laws derived their authority from the statutes of the people, the edicts of princes, or the decrees of judges. If it be admitted that it is not the black-letter and
the king's arms that makes the law, we are to look for it elsewhere.

In reality there are two, and only two, foundations of law; and
they are both of them conditions without which nothing can give
it any force: I mean equity and utility. With respect to the former,
it grows out of the great rule of equality, which is grounded upon
our common nature, and which Philo, with propriety and beauty,
calls the mother of justice. All human laws are, properly speaking,
only declaratory; they may alter the mode and application, but
have no power over the substance of original justice. The other
foundation of law, which is utility, must be understood, not of
partial or limited, but of general and public utility, connected in
the same manner with, and derived directly from, our rational nature: for any other utility may be the utility of a robber, but cannot be that of a citizen,—the interest of the domestic enemy, and
not that of a member of the commonwealth. This present equality
can never be the foundation of statutes which create an artificial
difference between men, as the laws before us do, in order to induce a consequential inequality in the distribution of justice. Law
is a mode of human action respecting society, and must be governed by the same rules of equity which govern every private action; and so Tully considers it in his Offices as the only utility
agreeable to that nature: 'Unum debet esse omnibus propositum,
ut eadem sit utilitas uniuscujusque et universorum; quam si ad se
quisque rapiat, dissolvetur omnis humana consortio." ["We should
all of us propose the same end, so that everyone should think his
own particular interest to be the same as that of the whole people;
which, if each person tries to snatch with pure selfishness, all union and agreement among men will be dissolved." Cicero De Officiis iii. 6.]

If any proposition can be clear in itself, it is this: that a law
which shuts out from all secure and valuable property the bulk of
the people cannot be made for the utility of the party so excluded.
This, therefore, is not the utility which Tully mentions. But if it
were true (as it is not) that the real interest of any part of the community could be separated from the happiness of the rest, still it
would afford no just foundation for a statute providing exclusively

for that interest at the expense of the other; because it would be repugnant to the essence of law, which requires that it be made as much as possible for the benefit of the whole. If this principle be denied or evaded, what ground have we left to reason on? We must at once make a total change in all our ideas, and look for a new definition of law. Where to find it I confess myself at a loss. If we resort to the fountains of jurisprudence, they will not supply us with any that is for our purpose. *"Jus"* (says Paulus) *"pluribus modis dicitur: uno modo, cum id, quod semper æquum et bonum est, jus dicitur, ut est jus naturale";*—this sense of the word will not be thought, I imagine, very applicable to our penal laws;—*"altero modo, quod omnibus aut pluribus in unaquaque civitate utile est, ut est jus civile."* ["We can speak of law in different senses; in one sense, when we call law what is always equitable and good, as is natural law. In another sense, what in each particular city is profitable to all or to many, as is civil law." Paulus, a Roman jurist, quoted in the Justinian *Digest* I.i.11.] Perhaps this latter will be as insufficient, and would rather seem a censure and condemnation of the Popery Acts than a definition that includes them; and there is no other to be found in the whole Digest; neither are there any modern writers whose ideas of law are at all narrower.

It would be far more easy to heap up authorities on this article than to excuse the prolixity and tediousness of producing any at all in proof of a point which, though too often practically denied, is in its theory almost self-evident. . . . Partiality and law are contradictory terms. Neither the merits nor the ill deserts, neither the wealth and importance nor the indigence and obscurity, of the one part or of the other, can make any alteration in this fundamental truth. On any other scheme, I defy any man living to settle a correct standard which may discriminate between equitable rule and the most direct tyranny. For if we can once prevail upon ourselves to depart from the strictness and integrity of this principle in favor even of a considerable party, the argument will hold for one that is less so; and thus we shall go on, narrowing the bottom of public right, until step by step we arrive, though after no very long or very forced deduction, at what one of our poets calls the *enormous faith*,—the faith of the many, created for the advantage of a single person. I cannot see a glimmering of distinction to evade it; nor is it possible to allege any reason for the proscription of so large a part of the kingdom, which would not hold equally to support, under parallel circumstances, the proscription of the whole.

I am sensible that these principles, in their abstract light, will not be very strenuously opposed. Reason is never inconvenient, but when it comes to be applied. Mere general truths interfere very little with the passions. They can, until they are roused by a troublesome application, rest in great tranquillity, side by side with tempers and proceedings the most directly opposite to them. Men want to be reminded, who do not want to be taught; because those original ideas of rectitude, to which the mind is compelled to assent when they are proposed, are not always as present to it as they ought to be. When people are gone, if not into a denial, at least into a sort of oblivion of those ideas, when they know them only as barren speculations, and not as practical motives for conduct, it will be proper to press, as well as to offer them to the understanding; and when one is attacked by prejudices which aim to intrude themselves into the place of law, what is left for us but to vouch and call to warranty those principles of original justice from whence alone our title to everything valuable in society is derived? Can it be thought to arise from a superfluous, vain parade of displaying general and uncontroverted maxims, that we should revert at this time to the first principles of law, when we have directly under our consideration a whole body of statutes, which, I say, are so many contradictions, which their advocates allow to be so many exceptions from those very principles? Take them in the most favorable light, every exception from the original and fixed rule of equality and justice ought surely to be very well authorized in the reason of their deviation, and very rare in their use. For, if they should grow to be frequent, in what would they differ from an abrogation of the rule itself? By becoming thus frequent, they might even go further, and, establishing themselves into a principle, convert the rule into the exception. It cannot be dissembled that this is not at all remote from the case before us, where the great body of the people are excluded from all valuable property, —where the greatest and most ordinary benefits of society are conferred as privileges, and not enjoyed on the footing of common rights.

Tract on the Popery Laws. VI, 317–27.

1. Positive Law and Economic Law

Like his friend Adam Smith, Burke opposed government interference with the free operation of supply and demand in establishing prices. In 1795, when the harvests had been somewhat short, he wrote a memorandum for the Prime Minister in which he warned against agitation for fixing agricultural prices and wages by law. He referred to his own experience during "the seven-and-twenty years during which I have been a farmer."

To provide for us in our necessities is not in the power of government. It would be a vain presumption in statesmen to think they can do it. The people maintain them, and not they the people. It is in the power of government to prevent much evil; it can do very little positive good in this, or perhaps in anything else. It is not only so of the state and statesman, but of all the classes and descriptions of the rich: they are the pensioners of the poor, and are maintained by their superfluity. They are under an absolute, hereditary, and indefeasible dependence on those who labor and are miscalled the poor.

The laboring people are only poor because they are numerous. Numbers in their nature imply poverty. In a fair distribution among a vast multitude none can have much. That class of dependent pensioners called the rich is so extremely small, that, if all their throats were cut, and a distribution made of all they consume in a year, it would not give a bit of bread and cheese for one night's supper to those who labor, and who in reality feed both the pensioners and themselves.

But the throats of the rich ought not to be cut, nor their magazines plundered; because, in their persons, they are trustees for those who labor, and their hoards are the banking-houses of these latter. Whether they mean it or not, they do, in effect, execute their trust,—some with more, some with less fidelity and judgment. But, on the whole, the duty is performed, and everything returns, deducting some very trifling commission and discount, to the place from whence it arose. When the poor rise to destroy the rich, they act as wisely for their own purposes as when they burn mills and throw corn into the river to make bread cheap.

When I say that we of the people ought to be informed, inclusively I say we ought not to be flattered; flattery is the reverse of instruction. The *poor* in that case would be rendered as improvident as the rich, which would not be at all good for them.

Nothing can be so base and so wicked as the political canting language, "the laboring *poor*." Let compassion be shown in action, —the more, the better,—according to every man's ability; but let there be no lamentation of their condition. It is no relief to their miserable circumstances; it is only an insult to their miserable understandings. It arises from a total want of charity or a total want of thought. Want of one kind was never relieved by want of any other kind. Patience, labor, sobriety, frugality, and religion should be recommended to them; all the rest is downright *fraud.* It is horrible to call them "the *once happy* laborer."

Whether what may be called the moral or philosophical happiness of the laborious classes is increased or not, I cannot say. The seat of that species of happiness is in the mind; and there are few data to ascertain the comparative state of the mind at any two periods. Philosophical happiness is to want little. Civil or vulgar happiness is to want much and to enjoy much. . . .

Labor is a commodity like every other, and rises or falls according to the demand. This is in the nature of things; however, the nature of things has provided for their necessities. . . .

When a man cannot live and maintain his family by the natural hire of his labor, ought it not to be raised by authority?

On this head I must be allowed to submit what my opinions have ever been, and somewhat at large.

And, first, I premise that labor is, as I have already intimated, a commodity, and, as such, an article of trade. If I am right in this notion, then labor must be subject to all the laws and principles of trade, and not to regulations foreign to them, and that may be totally inconsistent with those principles and those laws. When any commodity is carried to market, it is not the necessity of the vendor, but the necessity of the purchaser, that raises the price. The extreme want of the seller has rather (by the nature of things with which we shall in vain contend) the direct contrary operation. If the goods at market are beyond the demand, they fall in their value; if below it, they rise. The impossibility of the subsistence of a man who carries his labor to a market is totally beside the question, in this way of viewing it. The only question is, *What* is it worth to the buyer?

But if authority comes in and forces the buyer to a price, what is this in the case (say) of a farmer who buys the labor of ten or twelve laboring men, and three or four handicrafts,—what is it but to make an arbitrary division of his property among them?

The whole of his gains (I say it with the most certain conviction) never do amount anything like in value to what he pays to his laborers and artificers; so that a very small advance upon what *one* man pays to *many* may absorb the whole of what he possesses, and amount to an actual partition of all his substance among them. A perfect equality will, indeed, be produced,—that is to say, equal want, equal wretchedness, equal beggary, and, on the part of the partitioners, a woeful, helpless, and desperate disappointment. Such is the event of all compulsory equalizations. They pull down what is above; they never raise what is below; and they depress high and low together beneath the level of what was originally the lowest.

If a commodity is raised by authority above what it will yield with a profit to the buyer, that commodity will be the less dealt in. If a second blundering interposition be used to correct the blunder of the first and an attempt is made to force the purchase of the commodity, (of labor, for instance,) the one of these two things must happen: either that the forced buyer is ruined, or the price of the product of the labor in that proportion is raised. Then the wheel turns round, and the evil complained of falls with aggravated weight on the complainant. The price of corn, which is the result of the expense of all the operations of husbandry taken together, and for some time combined, will rise on the laborer, considered as a consumer. The very best will be, that he remains where he was. But if the price of the corn should not compensate the price of labor, what is far more to be feared, the most serious evil, the very destruction of agriculture itself, is to be apprehended . . .

A greater and more ruinous mistake cannot be fallen into than that the trades of agriculture and grazing can be conducted upon any other than the common principles of commerce: namely, that the producer should be permitted, and even expected, to look to all possible profit which without fraud or violence he can make; to turn plenty or scarcity to the best advantage he can; to keep back or to bring forward his commodities at his pleasure; to account to no one for his stock or for his gain. On any other terms he is the slave of the consumer: and that he should be so is of no benefit to the consumer. No slave was ever so beneficial to the master as a freeman that deals with him on an equal footing by convention, formed on the rules and principles of contending interests and compromised advantages. The consumer, if he were suffered, would in the end always be the dupe of his own tyranny and injustice. The landed gentleman is never to forget that the farmer is his representative. . . .

I beseech the government (which I take in the largest sense of the word, comprehending the two Houses of Parliament) seriously to consider that years of scarcity or plenty do not come alternately or at short intervals, but in pretty long cycles and irregularly, and consequently that we cannot assure ourselves, if we take a wrong measure, from the temporary necessities of one season, but that the next, and probably more, will drive us to the continuance of it; so that, in my opinion, there is no way of preventing this evil, which goes to the destruction of all our agriculture, and of that part of our internal commerce which touches our agriculture the most nearly, as well as the safety and very being of government, but manfully to resist the very first idea, speculative or practical, that it is within the competence of government, taken as government, or even of the rich, as rich, to supply to the poor those necessaries which it has pleased the Divine Providence for a while to withhold from them. We, the people, ought to be made sensible that it is not in breaking the laws of commerce, which are the laws of Nature, and consequently the laws of God, that we are to place our hope of softening the Divine displeasure to remove any calamity under which we suffer or which hangs over us.

Thoughts on Scarcity (1795). V, 133–57.

It is one of the finest problems in legislation, and what has often engaged my thoughts whilst I followed that profession,— What the state ought to take upon itself to direct by the public wisdom, and what it ought to leave, with as little interference as possible, to individual discretion. Nothing, certainly, can be laid down on the subject that will not admit of exceptions,—many permanent, some occasional. But the clearest line of distinction which I could draw, whilst I had my chalk to draw any line, was this: that the state ought to confine itself to what regards the state or the creatures of the state: namely, the exterior establishment of its religion; its magistracy; its revenue; its military force by sea and land; the corporations that owe their existence to its fiat; in a word, to everything that is *truly and properly* public,—to the public peace, to the public safety, to the public prosperity. In its preventive police it ought to be sparing of its efforts, and to employ means, rather few, unfrequent, and strong, than many, and frequent, and, of course, as they multiply their puny politic race and dwindle, small and feeble. Statesmen who know themselves will, with the dignity which belongs to wisdom, proceed only in this the superior orb and first mover of their duty, steadily, vigilantly, severely, courageously: whatever remains will, in a manner, provide for itself. But as they descend from the state to a province, from a province to a parish, and from a parish to a private house, they go on accelerated in their fall. They *cannot* do the lower duty; and in proportion as they try it, they will certainly fail in the higher. They ought to know the different departments of things,—what belongs to laws, and what manners alone can regulate. To these great politicians may give a leaning, but they cannot give a law.

Thoughts on Scarcity (1795). V, 166–67.

2. International Law and Interference in a Foreign Nation

Burke argued that England and her allies would be justified under international law in sending forces to assist the counterrevolutionary elements in France.

By the law of nations, when any country is divided, the other powers are free to take which side they please. For this, consult a very republican writer, Vattel.

Letter to Richard Burke, August 5, 1791.
Correspondence. III, 226.

I perceive that much pains are taken by the Jacobins of England to propagate a notion, that one state has not a right to interfere according to its discretion in the interior affairs of another. . . . To interfere in such dissensions requires great prudence and circumspection, and a serious attention to justice, and to the policy of one's own country, as well as to that of Europe. But an abstract principle of public law, forbidding such interference, is not supported by the reason of that law, nor by the authorities on the subject, nor by the practice of this kingdom, nor by that of any civilized nation in the world. This nation owes its laws and liberties, his Majesty owes the throne on which he sits, to the contrary principle. The several treaties of guarantee to the Protestant succession more than once reclaimed, affirm the principle of interference, which in a manner forms the basis of the public law in Europe.

Letter to Lord Grenville, August 18, 1792.
Correspondence. III, 508–9.

I think I have myself studied France as much as most of those whom the allied courts are likely to employ in such a work. I have likewise of myself as partial and as vain an opinion as men commonly have of themselves. But if I could command the whole military arm of Europe, I am sure that a bribe of the best province in that kingdom would not tempt me to intermeddle in their affairs, except in perfect concurrence and concert with the natural, legal interests of the country, composed of the ecclesiastical, the military, the several corporate bodies of justice and of burghership, making under a monarch (I repeat it again and again) *the French nation according to its fundamental Constitution.* No considerate statesman would undertake to meddle with it upon any other condition.

The government of that kingdom is fundamentally monarchical. The public law of Europe has never recognized in it any other form of government. The potentates of Europe have, by that law, a right, an interest, and a duty to know with what government they are to treat, and what they are to admit into the federative society, —or, in other words, into the diplomatic republic of Europe. This right is clear and indisputable.

What other and further interference they have a right to in the interior of the concerns of another people is a matter on which, as on every political subject, no very definite or positive rule can well be laid down. Our neighbors are men; and who will attempt to dictate the laws under which it is allowable or forbidden to take a part in the concerns of men, whether they are considered individually or in a collective capacity, whenever charity to them, or a care of my own safety, calls forth my activity? Circumstances perpetually variable, directing a moral prudence and discretion, the *general* principles of which never vary, must alone prescribe a conduct fitting on such occasions. The latest casuists of public law are rather of a republican cast, and, in my mind, by no means so averse as they ought to be to a right in the people (a word which, ill defined, is of the most dangerous use) to make changes at their pleasure in the fundamental laws of their country. These writers, however, when a country is divided, leave abundant liberty for a neighbor to support any of the parties according to his choice.[2] This interference must, indeed, always be a right, whilst the privilege of doing good to others, and of averting from them every sort of evil, is a right: circumstances may render that right a duty. It depends wholly on this, whether it be a *bonâ fide* charity to a party, and a prudent precaution with regard to yourself, or whether, under the pretence of aiding one of the parties in a nation, you act in such a manner as to aggravate its calamities and accomplish its final destruction. In truth, it is not the interfering or keeping aloof, but iniquitous intermeddling, or treacherous inaction, which is praised or blamed by the decision of an equitable judge.

It will be a just and irresistible presumption against the fairness of the interposing power, that he takes with him no party or description of men in the divided state. It is not probable that these parties should all, and all alike, be more adverse to the true interests of their country, and less capable of forming a judgment upon them, than those who are absolute strangers to their affairs, and to the character of the actors in them, and have but a remote, feeble, and secondary sympathy with their interest. Sometimes a calm and healing arbiter may be necessary; but he is to compose differences, not to give laws. It is impossible that any one should not feel the full force of that presumption. Even people, whose politics for the supposed good of their own country lead them to take advantage of the dissensions of a neighboring nation in order to ruin it, will not directly propose to exclude the natives, but they will take that mode of consulting and employing them which most nearly approaches to an exclusion. In some particulars they propose what

[2] Burke refers to Emmerich de Vattel, *Droit de Gens ou Principes du Droit Naturel* (1758).

amounts to that exclusion, in others they do much worse. They recommend to ministry, "that no Frenchman who has given a decided opinion or acted a decided part in this great Revolution, for or against it, should be countenanced, brought forward, trusted, or employed, even in the strictest subordination to the ministers of the allied powers." Although one would think that this advice would stand condemned on the first proposition, yet, as it has been made popular, and has been proceeded upon practically, I think it right to give it a full consideration.

Remarks on the Policy of the Allies (1793). IV, 433–35.

CHAPTER II

Prudence as a Political Virtue

Cicero, who was one of Burke's favorite authors, used the words *prudentia* and *sapientia*, or *wisdom*, interchangeably. The Greeks called this virtue *phronesis*, etymologically meaning "fore-thought." By *prudence* Burke does not mean a mere utilitarian calculation of benefits, though his language often includes that meaning. He refers to the necessity of intimate knowledge of a situation in its concreteness, and an insight into its potentialities, before an attempt is made to apply general principles or abstract theories to it. He repeatedly criticized the revolutionary "philosophes" of the eighteenth century for their belief that theories of man and society should be generated logically from a priori axioms, and thus have the certainty and absoluteness or geometrical theorems. These theorists often expressed their ambition to be "the Newtons of political science."

No lines can be laid down for civil or political wisdom. They are a matter incapable of exact definition. But, though no man can draw a stroke between the confines of day and night, yet light and darkness are upon the whole tolerably distinguishable. Nor will it be impossible for a prince to find out such a mode of government, and such persons to administer it, as will give a great degree of content to his people; without any curious and anxious research for that abstract, universal, perfect harmony, which while he is seeking, he abandons those means of ordinary tranquillity which are in his power without any research at all.

Thoughts on the Cause of the Present Discontents (1770). I, 477.

The rules and definitions of prudence can rarely be exact, never universal.

First Letter on a Regicide Peace (1796). V, 241.

The condition of our nature is such that we buy our blessings at a price.

Speech at Bristol Previous to the Election (1780). II, 389.

35

As to the right of men to act anywhere according to their pleasure, without any moral tie, no such right exists. Men are never in a state of *total* independence of each other. It is not the condition of our nature: nor is it conceivable how any man can pursue a considerable course of action without its having some effect upon others, or, of course, without producing some degree of responsibility for his conduct. The *situations* in which men relatively stand produce the rules and principles of that responsibility, and afford directions to prudence in exacting it.

First Letter on a Regicide Peace (1796). V, 321.

[My idea is nothing more.] Refined policy ever has been the parent of confusion,—and ever will be so, as long as the world endures. Plain good intention, which is as easily discovered at the first view as fraud is surely detected at last, is, let me say, of no mean force in the government of mankind. Genuine simplicity of heart is an healing and cementing principle.

Speech on Conciliation with America (1775). II, 106.

Your ministers, in their own and his Majesty's name, have already adopted the American distinction of internal and external duties. It is a distinction, whatever merit it may have, that was originally moved by the Americans themselves; and I think they will acquiesce in it, if they are not pushed with too much logic and too little sense, in all the consequences: that is, if external taxation be understood, as they and you understand it, when you please, to be not a distinction of geography, but of policy; that it is a power for regulating trade, and not for supporting establishments. The distinction, which is as nothing with regard to right, is of most weighty consideration in practice. Recover your old ground, and your old tranquillity; try it; I am persuaded the Americans will compromise with you. When confidence is once restored, the odious and suspicious *summum jus* will perish of course. The spirit of practicability, of moderation, and mutual convenience will never call in geometrical exactness as the arbitrator of an amicable settlement. Consult and follow your experience.

Speech on American Taxation (1774). II, 71.

It looks to me to be narrow and pedantic to apply the ordinary ideas of criminal justice to this great public contest. I do not know the method of drawing up an indictment against an whole people. I cannot insult and ridicule the feelings of millions of my fellow-creatures as Sir Edward Coke insulted one excellent individual (Sir Walter Raleigh) at the bar. I am not ripe to pass sentence on the gravest public bodies, intrusted with magistracies of great authority and dignity, and charged with the safety of their fellow-citizens, upon the very same title that I am. I really think that for wise men this is not judicious, for sober men not decent, for minds tinctured with humanity not mild and merciful.

Speech on Conciliation with America (1775). II, 136.

I do not know that the colonies have, in any general way, or in any cool hour, gone much beyond the demand of immunity in relation to taxes. It is not fair to judge of the temper or dispositions of any man or any set of men, when they are composed and at rest, from their conduct or their expressions in a state of disturbance and irritation. It is, besides, a very great mistake to imagine that mankind follow up practically any speculative principle, either of government or of freedom, as far as it will go in argument and logical illation. We Englishmen stop very short of the principles upon which we support any given part of our Constitution, or even the whole of it together. I could easily, if I had not already tired you, give you very striking and convincing instances of it. This is nothing but what is natural and proper. All government, indeed every human benefit and enjoyment, every virtue and every prudent act, is founded on compromise and barter. We balance inconveniences; we give and take; we remit some rights, that we may enjoy others; and we choose rather to be happy citizens than subtle disputants. As we must give away some natural liberty, to enjoy civil advantages, so we must sacrifice some civil liberties, for the advantages to be derived from the communion and fellowship of a great empire. But, in all fair dealings, the thing bought must bear some proportion to the purchase paid. None will barter away the immediate jewel of his soul. Though a great house is apt to makes slaves haughty, yet it is purchasing a part of the artificial importance of a great empire too dear, to pay for it all essential rights, and all the intrinsic dignity of human nature. None of us who would not risk his life rather than fall under a government purely arbitrary. But although there are some amongst us who think our Constitution wants many improvements to make it a complete system of liberty, perhaps none who are of that opinion would think it right to aim at such improvement by disturbing his country and risking everything that is dear to him. In every arduous enterprise, we consider what we are to lose, as well as what we are to gain; and the more and better stake of liberty every people possess, the less they will hazard in a vain attempt to make it more. These are *the cords of man*. Man acts from adequate motives relative to his interest, and not on metaphysical speculations. Aristotle, the great master of reasoning, cautions us, and with great weight and propriety, against this species of delusive geometrical accuracy in moral arguments, as the most fallacious of all sophistry.

Speech on Conciliation with America (1775). II, 168–70.

Prudence (in all things a virtue, in politics the first of virtues,) will lead us rather to acquiesce in some qualified plan that does not come up to the full perfection of the abstract idea, than to push for the more perfect, which cannot be attained without tearing to pieces the whole contexture of the commonwealth. . . . In all changes in the state, moderation is a virtue, not only amiable, but powerful. It is a disposing, arranging, conciliating, cementing, virtue. . . . Moderation (which times and situations will clearly distinguish from the counterfeits of pusillanimity and indecision) is the virtue only of superior minds. It requires a deep courage, and full of reflection, to be temperate when the voice of multitudes (the specious mimic of fame and reputation) passes judgment against you. The impetuous desire of an unthinking public will endure no course, but what conducts to splendid and perilous extremes. Then to dare to be fearful, when all about you are full of presumption and confidence, and when those who are bold at the hazard of others would push your caution and disaffection, is to show a mind prepared for its trial; it discovers, in the midst of general levity, a self-possessing and collected character, which, sooner or later, bids to attract every thing to it, as to a centre.

Letter to Mons. Dupont, October, 1789.
Correspondence. III, 118–20.

By these theorists the right of the people is almost always sophistically confounded with their power. The body of the community, whenever it can come to act, can meet with no effectual resistance; but till power and right are the same, the whole body of them has no right inconsistent with virtue, and the first of all virtues, prudence. Men have no right to what is not reasonable, and to what is not for their benefit.

Reflections (1790). III, 311.

The object of the state is (as far as may be) the happiness of the whole. Whatever makes multitudes of men utterly miserable can never answer that object; indeed, it contradicts it wholly and entirely; and the happiness or misery of mankind, estimated by their feelings and sentiments, and not by any theories of their rights, is, and ought to be, the standard for the conduct of legislators towards the people. This naturally and necessarily conducts us to the peculiar and characteristic situation of a people, and to a knowledge of their opinions, prejudices, habits, and all the circumstances that diversify and color life. The first question a good statesman would ask himself, therefore, would be, How and in what circumstances do you find society? and to act upon them.

Speech on the Petition of the Unitarians (1792). VII, 45.

That a man should rejoice and triumph in the destruction of an absolute monarchy,—that in such an event he should overlook the captivity, disgrace, and degradation of an unfortunate prince, and the continual danger to a life which exists only to be endangered, —that he should overlook the utter ruin of whole orders and classes of men, extending itself directly, or in its nearest consequences, to at least a million of our kind, and to at least the temporary wretchedness of a whole community,—I do not deny to be in some sort natural; because, when people see a political object which they ardently desire but in one point of view, they are apt extremely to palliate or underrate the evils which may arise in obtaining it. This is no reflection on the humanity of those persons. Their good-nature I am the last man in the world to dispute. It only shows that they are not sufficiently informed or sufficiently considerate. When they come to reflect seriously on the transaction, they will think themselves bound to examine what the object is that has been acquired by all this havoc. They will hardly assert that the destruction of an absolute monarchy is a thing good in itself, without any sort of reference to the antecedent state of things, or to consequences which result from the change,—without any consideration whether under its ancient rule a country was to a considerable degree flourishing and populous, highly cultivated and highly commercial, and whether, under that domination, though personal liberty had been precarious and insecure, property at least was ever violated. They cannot take the moral sympathies of the human mind along with them, in abstractions separated from the good or evil condition of the state, from the quality of actions, and the character of the actors. None of us love absolute and uncontrolled monarchy; but we could not rejoice at the sufferings of a Marcus Aurelius or a Trajan, who were absolute monarchs, as we do when Nero is condemned by the Senate to be punished *more majorum;* nor, when that monster was obliged to fly with his wife Sporus, and to drink puddle, were men affected in the same manner as when the venerable Galba, with all his faults and errors, was murdered by a revolted mercenary soldiery. With such things before our eyes, our feelings contradict our theories; and when this is the case, the feelings are true, and the theory is false. What I contend for is, that, in commending the destruction of an absolute monarchy, *all the circumstances* ought not to be wholly overlooked, as "considerations fit only for shallow and superficial minds." (The words of Mr. Fox, or to that effect.)

The subversion of a government, to deserve any praise, must be considered but as a step preparatory to the formation of something better, either in the scheme of the government itself, or in the persons who administer it, or in both. These events cannot in reason be separated. For instance, when we praise our Revolution of 1688, though the nation in that act was on the defensive, and was justified in incurring all the evils of a defensive war, we do not rest there. We always combine with the subversion of the old government the happy settlement which followed. When we estimate that Revolution, we mean to comprehend in our calculation both the value of the thing parted with and the value of the thing received in exchange.

The burden of proof lies heavily on those who tear to pieces the whole frame and contexture of their country, that they could find no other way of settling a government fit to obtain its rational ends, except that which they have pursued by means unfavorable to all the present happiness of millions of people, and to the utter ruin of several hundreds of thousands. In their political arrangements, men have no right to put the well-being of the present generation wholly out of the question. Perhaps the only moral trust with any certainty in our hands is the care of our own time. With regard to futurity, we are to treat it like a ward. We are not so to attempt an improvement of his fortune as to put the capital of his estate to any hazard.

It is not worth our while to discuss, like sophisters, whether in no case some evil for the sake of some benefit is to be tolerated. Nothing universal can be rationally affirmed on any moral or any political subject. Pure metaphysical abstraction does not belong to these matters. The lines of morality are not like the ideal lines of mathematics. They are broad and deep as well as long. They admit of exceptions; they demand modifications. These exceptions and modifications are not made by the process of logic, but by the rules of prudence. Prudence is not only the first in rank of the virtues political and moral, but she is the director, the regulator, the standard of them all. Metaphysics cannot live without definition; but Prudence is cautious how she defines. Our courts cannot be more fearful in suffering fictitious cases to be brought before them for eliciting their determination on a point of law than prudent moralists are in putting extreme and hazardous cases of conscience upon emergencies not existing. Without attempting, therefore, to define, what never can be defined, the case of a revolution in government, this, I think, may be safely affirmed,—that a sore and pressing evil is to be removed, and that a good, great in its amount and unequivocal in its nature, must be probable almost to certainty, before the inestimable price of our own morals and the well-being of a number of our fellow-citizens is paid for a revolution. If ever we ought to be economists even to parsimony, it is in the voluntary production of evil. Every revolution contains in it something of evil.

Appeal from the New to the Old Whigs (1791). IV, 78–81.

I never govern myself, no rational man ever did govern himself, by abstractions and universals. I do not put abstract ideas wholly out of any question; because I well know that under that name I should dismiss principles, and that without the guide and light of sound, well-understood principles, all reasonings in politics, as in everything else, would be only a confused jumble of particular facts and details, without the means of drawing out any sort of theoretical or practical conclusion. A statesman differs from a professor in an university: the latter has only the general view of society; the former, the statesman, has a number of circumstances to combine with those general ideas, and to take into his consideration. Circumstances are infinite, are infinitely combined, are variable and transient: he who does not take them into consideration is not erroneous, but stark mad; *dat operam ut cum ratione insaniat;* ["He labors to make his mind unsound by means of his reason." Adapted from Terence *Eunuch* I.i.18.] he is metaphysically mad. A statesman, never losing sight of principles, is to be guided by circumstances; and judging contrary to the exigencies of the moment, he may ruin his country forever.

I go on this ground,—that government, representing the society, has a general superintending control over all the actions and over all the publicly propagated doctrines of men, without which it never could provide adequately for all the wants of society: but then it is to use this power with an equitable discretion, the only bond of sovereign authority. For it is not, perhaps, so much by the assumption of unlawful powers as by the unwise or unwarrantable use of those which are most legal, that governments oppose their true end and object: for there is such a thing as tyranny, as well as usurpation. You can hardly state to me a case to which legislature is the most confessedly competent, in which, if the rules of benignity and prudence are not observed, the most mischievous and oppressive things may not be done. So that, after all, it is a moral and virtuous discretion, and not any abstract theory of right, which keeps governments faithful to their ends. Crude, unconnected truths are in the world of practice what falsehoods are in theory. A reasonable, prudent, provident, and moderate coercion may be a means of preventing acts of extreme ferocity and rigor: for by propagating excessive and extravagant doctrines, such extravagant disorders take place as require the most perilous and fierce corrections to oppose them.

Speech on the Petition of the Unitarians (1792). VII, 41–42.

CHAPTER III

The State and Society

1. The Nature of Society

The ancient theory of the social contract became after Locke the commonplace of European political thought. The attractive and liberating aspect of it was its implication that the failure of one party (the governors) to observe the contractual pact would justify the other party (the governed) in declaring the whole contract voided. The theory thus served well the purposes of a great era of political revolution. Burke qualified the theory by insisting that it be more realistic. The bonds of society are as complex as human nature and many of them are in the nature of things impossible to void. Society, Burke said, is neither exactly like a machine nor exactly like an organism; it partakes of some characteristics of each. As these analogies are only partially valid, they must be applied with judgment. Government is a corporate body, a matter of convention, but "the people" who make it and live under it are more than an aggregate of individuals. A nation, Burke said, is "a moral essence." A society or government constituted by such a nation is of course "made" by man, but it is nevertheless also "natural." For "art is man's nature."

Society is, indeed, a contract. Subordinate contracts for objects of mere occasional interest may be dissolved at pleasure; but the state ought not to be considered as nothing better than a partnership agreement in a trade of pepper and coffee, calico or tobacco, or some other such low concern, to be taken up for a little temporary interest, and to be dissolved by the fancy of the parties. It is to be looked on with other reverence; because it is not a partnership in things subservient only to the gross animal existence of a temporary and perishable nature. It is a partnership in all science, a partnership in all art, a partnership in every virtue and in all perfection. As the ends of such a partnership cannot be obtained in many generations, it becomes a partnership not only between those

43

who are living, but between those who are living, those who are dead, and those who are to be born. Each contract of each particular state is but a clause in the great primeval contract of eternal society, linking the lower with the higher natures, connecting the visible and invisible world, according to a fixed compact sanctioned by the inviolable oath which holds all physical and all moral natures each in their appointed place. This law is not subject to the will of those who, by an obligation above them, and infinitely superior, are bound to submit their will to that law. The municipal corporations of that universal kingdom are not morally at liberty, at their pleasure, and on their speculations of a contingent improvement, wholly to separate and tear asunder the bands of their subordinate community, and to dissolve it into an unsocial, uncivil, unconnected chaos of elementary principles. It is the first and supreme necessity only, a necessity that is not chosen, but chooses, a necessity paramount to deliberation, that admits no discussion and demands no evidence, which alone can justify a resort to anarchy. This necessity is no exception to the rule; because this necessity itself is a part, too, of that moral and physical disposition of things to which man must be obedient by consent or force: but if that which is only submission to necessity should be made the object of choice, the law is broken, Nature is disobeyed, and the rebellious are outlawed, cast forth, and exiled, from this world of reason, and order, and peace, and virtue, and fruitful penitence, into the antagonist world of madness, discord, vice, confusion, and unavailing sorrow.

Reflections (1790). III, 359–60.

It is no wonder, therefore, that, with these ideas of everything in their Constitution and government at home, either in Church or State, as illegitimate and usurped, or at best as a vain mockery, . . . [the revolutionists of France] look abroad with an eager and passionate enthusiasm. Whilst they are possessed by these notions, it is vain to talk to them of the practice of their ancestors, the fundamental laws of their country, the fixed form of a Constitution whose merits are confirmed by the solid test of long experience and an increasing public strength and national prosperity. They despise experience as the wisdom of unlettered men; and as for the rest, they have wrought under ground a mine that will blow up, at one grand explosion, all examples of antiquity, all precedents, charters, and acts of Parliament. They have "the rights of men." Against these there can be no prescription; against these no argument is binding: these admit no temperament and no compromise: anything withheld from their full demand is so much of fraud and injustice. Against these their rights of men let no government look for security in the length of its continuance, or in the justice and lenity of its administration. The objections of these speculatists, if its forms do not quadrate with their theories, are as valid against such an old and beneficent government as against the most violent tyranny or the greenest usurpation. They are always at issue with governments, not on a question of abuse, but a question of competency and a question of title. I have nothing to say to the clumsy subtilty of their political metaphysics. Let them be their amusement in the schools.

> *Illa* se jactet in aula
> Æolus, et clauso ventorum carcere regnet.

["In that hall let Aeolus, god of the winds, have the lordship and rule within the closed prison, the cave of the winds." Virgil *Aeneid* i.140–41.]
But let them not break prison to burst like a Levanter, to sweep the earth with their hurricane, and to break up the fountains of the great deep to overwhelm us!

Far am I from denying in theory, full as far is my heart from withholding in practice, (if I were of power to give or to withhold,) the *real* rights of men. In denying their false claims of right, I do not mean to injure those which are real, and are such as their pretended rights would totally destroy. If civil society be made for the advantage of man, all the advantages for which it is made become his right. It is an institution of beneficence; and law itself is only beneficence acting by a rule. Men have a right to live by that rule; they have a right to justice, as between their fellows, whether their fellows are in politic function or in ordinary occupation. They have a right to the fruits of their industry, and to the means of making their industry fruitful. They have a right to the acquisitions of their parents, to the nourishment and improvement of their offspring, to instruction in life and to consolation in death.

Whatever each man can separately do, without trespassing upon others, he has a right to do for himself; and he has a right to a fair portion of all which society, with all its combinations of skill and force, can do in his favor. In this partnership all men have equal rights; but not to equal things. He that has but five shillings in the partnership has as good a right to it as he that has five hundred pounds has to his larger proportion; but he has not a right to an equal dividend in the product of the joint stock. And as to the share of power, authority, and direction which each individual ought to have in the management of the state, that I must deny to be amongst the direct original rights of man in civil society; for I have in my contemplation the civil social man, and no other. It is a thing to be settled by convention.

If civil society be the offspring of convention, that convention must be its law. That convention must limit and modify all the descriptions of constitution which are formed under it. Every sort of legislative, judicial, or executory power are its creatures. They can have no being in any other state of things; and how can any man claim, under the conventions of civil society, rights which do not so much as suppose its existence,—rights which are absolutely repugnant to it? One of the first motives to civil society, and which becomes one of its fundamental rules, is, *that no man should be judge in his own cause*. By this each person has at once divested himself of the first fundamental right of uncovenanted man, that is, to judge for himself, and to assert his own cause. He abdicates all right to be his own governor. He inclusively, in a great measure, abandons the right of self-defence, the first law of Nature. Men cannot enjoy the rights of an uncivil and of a civil state together. That he may obtain justice, he gives up his right of determining what it is in points the most essential to him. That he may secure some liberty, he makes a surrender in trust of the whole of it.

Government is not made in virtue of natural rights, which may and do exist in total independence of it,—and exist in much greater clearness, and in a much greater degree of abstract perfection: but their abstract perfection is their practical defect. By having a right to everything they want everything. Government is a contrivance of human wisdom to provide for human *wants*. Men have a right that these wants should be provided for by this wisdom. Among these wants is to be reckoned the want, out of civil society, of a sufficient restraint upon their passions. Society requires not only that the passions of individuals should be subjected, but that even in the mass and body, as well as in the individuals, the inclinations of men should frequently be thwarted, their will controlled, and their passions brought into subjection. This can only be done *by a power out of themselves,* and not, in the exercise of its function, subject to that will and to those passions which it is its office to bridle and subdue. In this sense the restraints on men, as well as their liberties, are to be reckoned among their rights. But as the liberties and the restrictions vary with times and circumstances, and admit of infinite modifications, they cannot be settled upon any abstract rule; and nothing is so foolish as to discuss them upon that principle.

The moment you abate anything from the full rights of men each to govern himself, and suffer any artificial, positive limitation upon those rights, from that moment the whole organization of government becomes a consideration of convenience. This it is which makes the constitution of a state, and the due distribution of its powers, a matter of the most delicate and complicated skill. It requires a deep knowledge of human nature and human necessities, and of the things which facilitate or obstruct the various ends which are to be pursued by the mechanism of civil institutions. The state is to have recruits to its strength and remedies to its distempers. What is the use of discussing a man's abstract right to food or medicine? The question is upon the method of procuring and administering them. In that deliberation I shall always advise to call in the aid of the farmer and the physician, rather than the professor of metaphysics.

The science of constructing a commonwealth, or renovating it, or reforming it, is, like every other experimental science, not to be taught *a priori.* Nor is it a short experience that can instruct us in that practical science; because the real effects of moral causes are not always immediate, but that which in the first instance is prejudicial may be excellent in its remoter operation, and its excellence may arise even from the ill effects it produces in the beginning. The reverse also happens; and very plausible schemes, with very pleasing commencements, have often shameful and lamentable conclusions. In states there are often some obscure and almost latent causes, things which appear at first view of little moment, on which a very great part of its prosperity or adversity may most essentially depend. The science of government being, therefore, so practical in itself, and intended for such practical purposes, a matter which requires experience, and even more experience than any person can gain in his whole life, however sagacious and observing he may be, it is with infinite caution that any man ought to venture upon pulling down an edifice which has answered in any tolerable degree for ages the common purposes of society, or on building it up again without having models and patterns of approved utility before his eyes.

These metaphysic rights entering into common life, like rays of light which pierce into a dense medium, are, by the laws of Nature, refracted from their straight line. Indeed, in the gross and complicated mass of human passions and concerns, the primitive rights of men undergo such a variety of refractions and reflections that it becomes absurd to talk of them as if they continued in the simplicity of their original direction. The nature of man is intricate; the objects of society are of the greatest possible complexity: and therefore no simple disposition or direction of power can be suitable either to man's nature or to the quality of his affairs. When I hear the simplicity of contrivance aimed at and boasted of in any new political constitutions, I am at no loss to decide that the artificers are grossly ignorant of their trade or totally negligent of their duty. The simple governments are fundamentally defective, to say no worse of them. If you were to contemplate society in but one point of view, all these simple modes of polity are infinitely captivating. In effect each would answer its single end much more perfectly than the more complex is able to attain all its complex purposes. But it is better that the whole should be imperfectly and anomalously answered than that while some parts are provided for with great exactness, others might be totally neglected, or perhaps materially injured, by the over-care of a favorite member.

The pretended rights of these theorists are all extremes; and in proportion as they are metaphysically true, they are morally and politically false. The rights of men are in a sort of *middle,* incapable of definition, but not impossible to be discerned. The rights of men in governments are their advantages; and these are often in balances between differences of good,—in compromises sometimes between good and evil, and sometimes between evil and evil. Political reason is a computing principle: adding, subtracting, multiplying, and dividing, morally, and not metaphysically or mathematically, true moral denominations.

By these theorists the right of the people is almost always sophistically confounded with their power. The body of the community, whenever it can come to act, can meet with no effectual resistance; but till power and right are the same, the whole body of them has no right inconsistent with virtue, and the first of all virtues, prudence. Men have no right to what is not reasonable, and to what is not for their benefit.

Reflections (1790). III, 308–13.

The pretended *rights of man,* which have made this havoc, cannot be the rights of the people. For to be a people, and to have these rights, are things incompatible. The one supposes the presence, the other the absence, of a state of civil society. The very foundation of the French commonwealth is false and self-destructive; nor can its principles be adopted in any country, without the certainty of bringing it to the very same condition in which France is found. Attempts are made to introduce them into every nation in Europe. This nation, as possessing the greatest influence, they wish most to corrupt, as by that means they are assured the contagion must become general.

Appeal from the New to the Old Whigs (1791). IV, 188.

2. What Is a "People"?

Burke's conviction that a society is in some respects like an organism had as a necessary consequence that a body politic cannot be described merely in terms of economic and population statistics. He probed into what in more recent times might be called social psychology. He adopted the phrase "the discipline of Nature" for the cohesive and organizing forces which distinguish a "people" from a mere collection of persons. In the development and perpetuation of such a discipline, a natural aristocracy of leaders (not to be confused with the hereditary aristocracy of title) is indispensable. (See also Chapter V, section 2, on aristocracy and leadership.)

Mere locality does not constitute a body politic. . . . The body politic of France existed in the majesty of its throne, in the dignity of its nobility, in the honor of its gentry, in the sanctity of its clergy, in the reverence of its magistracy, in the weight and consideration due to its landed property in the several bailliages, in the respect due to its movable substance represented by the corporations of the kingdom. All these particular *moleculae* united form the great mass of what is truly the body politic in all countries. They are so many deposits and receptacles of justice; because they can only exist by justice. Nation is a moral essence, not a geographical arrangement, or a denomination of the nomenclator.

First Letter on a Regicide Peace (1796). V, 326.

In all speculations upon men and human affairs, it is of no small moment to distinguish things of accident from permanent causes, and from effects that cannot be altered. It is not every irregularity in our movement that is a total deviation from our course. I am not quite of the mind of those speculators who seem assured that necessarily, and by the constitution of things, all states have the same periods of infancy, manhood, and decrepitude that are found in the individuals who compose them. Parallels of this sort rather furnish similitudes to illustrate or to adorn than supply analogies from whence to reason. The objects which are attempted to be forced into an analogy are not found in the same classes of existence. Individuals are physical beings, subject to laws universal and invariable. The immediate cause acting in these laws may be obscure: the general results are subjects of certain calculation. But commonwealths are not physical, but moral essences. They are artificial combinations, and, in their proximate efficient cause, the arbitrary productions of the human mind. We are not yet acquainted with the laws which necessarily influence the stability of that kind of work made by that kind of agent. There is not in the physical order (with which they do not appear to hold any assignable connection) a distinct cause by which any of those fabrics must necessarily grow, flourish, or decay; nor, in my opinion, does the moral world produce anything more determinate on that subject than what may serve as an amusement (liberal, indeed, and ingenious, but still only an amusement) for speculative men. I doubt whether the history of mankind is yet complete enough, if ever it can be so, to furnish grounds for a sure theory on the internal causes which necessarily affect the fortune of a state. I am far from denying the operation of such causes: but they are infinitely uncertain, and much more obscure, and much more difficult to trace, than the foreign causes that tend to raise, to depress, and sometimes to overwhelm a community.

First Letter on a Regicide Peace (1796). V, 234–35.

The factions now so busy amongst us, in order to divest men of all love for their country, and to remove from their minds all duty with regard to the state, endeavor to propagate an opinion, that the *people,* in forming their commonwealth, have by no means parted with their power over it. This is an impregnable citadel, to which these gentlemen retreat, whenever they are pushed by the battery of laws and usages and positive conventions. Indeed, it is such, and of so great force, that all they have done in defending their outworks is so much time and labor thrown away. Discuss any of their schemes, their answer is, It is the act of the *people,* and that is sufficient. Are we to deny to a *majority* of the people the right of altering even the whole frame of their society, if such should be their pleasure? They may change it, say they, from a monarchy to a republic to-day, and to-morrow back again from a republic to a monarchy; and so backward and forward as often as they like. They are masters of the commonwealth, because in substance they are themselves the commonwealth. The French Revolution, say they, was the act of the majority of the people; and if the majority of any other people, the people of England, for instance, wish to make the same change, they have the same right.

Just the same, undoubtedly. That is, none at all. Neither the few nor the many have a right to act merely by their will, in any matter connected with duty, trust, engagement, or obligation. The Constitution of a country being once settled upon some compact, tacit or expressed, there is no power existing of force to alter it, without the breach of the covenant, or the consent of all the parties. Such is the nature of a contract. And the votes of a majority of the people, whatever their infamous flatterers may teach in order to corrupt their minds, cannot alter the moral any more than they can alter the physical essence of things. The people are not to be taught to think lightly of their engagements to their governors; else they teach governors to think lightly of their engagements towards them. In that kind of game, in the end, the people are sure to be losers. To flatter them into a contempt of faith, truth, and justice is to ruin them; for in these virtues consists their whole safety. To

flatter any man, or any part of mankind, in any description, by asserting that in engagements he or they are free, whilst any other
human creature is bound, is ultimately to vest the rule of morality
in the pleasure of those who ought to be rigidly submitted to it,—
to subject the sovereign reason of the world to the caprices of weak
and giddy men.

But, as no one of us men can dispense with public or private
faith, or with any other tie of moral obligation, so neither can any
number of us. The number engaged in crimes, instead of turning
them into laudable acts, only augments the quantity and intensity
of the guilt. I am well aware that men love to hear of their power,
but have an extreme disrelish to be told of their duty. This is of
course; because every duty is a limitation of some power. Indeed,
arbitrary power is so much to the depraved taste of the vulgar, of
the vulgar of every description, that almost all the dissensions
which lacerate the commonwealth are not concerning the manner
in which it is to be exercised, but concerning the hands in which
it is to be placed. Somewhere they are resolved to have it. Whether
they desire it to be vested in the many or the few depends with
most men upon the chance which they imagine they themselves
may have of partaking in the exercise of that arbitrary sway, in the
one mode or in the other.

It is not necessary to teach men to thirst after power. But it is
very expedient that by moral instruction they should be taught,
and by their civil constitutions they should be compelled, to put
many restrictions upon the immoderate exercise of it, and the
inordinate desire. The best method of obtaining these two great
points forms the important, but at the same time the difficult problem to the true statesman. He thinks of the place in which political
power is to be lodged with no other attention than as it may render
the more or the less practicable its salutary restraint and its prudent direction. For this reason, no legislator, at any period of the
world, has willingly placed the seat of active power in the hands
of the multitude; because there it admits of no control, no regulation, no steady direction whatsoever. The people are the natural
control on authority; but to exercise and to control together is contradictory and impossible.

As the exorbitant exercise of power cannot, under popular sway,
be effectually restrained, the other great object of political ar-

rangement, the means of abating an excessive desire of it, is in such a state still worse provided for. The democratic commonwealth is the foodful nurse of ambition. Under the other forms it meets with many restraints. Whenever, in states which have had a democratic basis, the legislators have endeavored to put restraints upon ambition, their methods were as violent as in the end they were ineffectual,—as violent, indeed, as any the most jealous despotism could invent. The ostracism could not very long save itself, and much less the state which it was meant to guard, from the attempts of ambition,—one of the natural, inbred, incurable distempers of a powerful democracy.

But to return from this short digression,—which, however, is not wholly foreign to the question of the effect of the will of the majority upon the form or the existence of their society. I cannot too often recommend it to the serious consideration of all men who think civil society to be within the province of moral jurisdiction, that, if we owe to it any duty, it is not subject to our will. Duties are not voluntary. Duty and will are even contradictory terms. Now, though civil society might be at first a voluntary act, (which in many cases it undoubtedly was,) its continuance is under a permanent standing covenant, coexisting with the society; and it attaches upon every individual of that society, without any formal act of his own. This is warranted by the general practice, arising out of the general sense of mankind. Men without their choice derive benefits from that association; without their choice they are subjected to duties in consequence of these benefits; and without their choice they enter into a virtual obligation as binding as any that is actual. Look through the whole of life and the whole system of duties. Much the strongest moral obligations are such as were never the results of our option. I allow, that, if no Supreme Ruler exists, wise to form, and potent to enforce, the moral law, there is no sanction to any contract, virtual or even actual, against the will of prevalent power. On that hypothesis, let any set of men be strong enough to set their duties at defiance, and they cease to be duties any longer. We have but this one appeal against irresistible power,—

> Si genus humanum et mortalia temnitis arma,
> At sperate Deos memores fandi atque nefandi.

["If ye contemn our human kinship and the strength of our mortal arms, yet respect the gods who remember righteous and unrighteous conduct." Virgil *Aeneid* i.543–44.]

Taking it for granted that I do not write to the disciples of the Parisian philosophy, I may assume that the awful Author of our being is the Author of our place in the order of existence,—and that, having disposed and marshalled us by a divine tactic, not according to our will, but according to His, He has in and by that disposition virtually subjected us to act the part which belongs to the place assigned us. We have obligations to mankind at large, which are not in consequence of any special voluntary pact. They arise from the relation of man to man, and the relation of man to God, which relations are not matters of choice. On the contrary, the force of all the pacts which we enter into with any particular person or number of persons amongst mankind depends upon those prior obligations. In some cases the subordinate relations are voluntary, in others they are necessary,—but the duties are all compulsive. When we marry, the choice is voluntary, but the duties are not matter of choice: they are dictated by the nature of the situation. Dark and inscrutable are the ways by which we come into the world. The instincts which give rise to this mysterious process of Nature are not of our making. But out of physical causes, unknown to us, perhaps unknowable, arise moral duties, which, as we are able perfectly to comprehend, we are bound indispensably to perform. Parents may not be consenting to their moral relation; but, consenting or not, they are bound to a long train of burdensome duties towards those with whom they have never made a convention of any sort. Children are not consenting to their relation; but their relation, without their actual consent, binds them to its duties,—or rather it implies their consent, because the presumed consent of every rational creature is in unison with the predisposed order of things. Men come in that manner into a community with the social state of their parents, endowed with all the benefits, loaded with all the duties of their situation. If the social ties and ligaments, spun out of those physical relations which are the elements of the commonwealth, in most cases begin, and always continue, independently of our will, so, without any stipulation on our own part, are we bound by that relation called our country, which comprehends (as it has been well said) "all the charities of all." [1] Nor are we left without powerful instincts to make this duty as dear and grateful to us as it is awful and coercive. Our country is not a thing of mere physical locality. It consists, in a great measure, in the ancient order into which we are born. We may have the same geographical situation, but another country; as we may have the same country in another soil. The place that determines our duty to our country is a social, civil relation. . . .

[I am] convinced that neither . . . [I], nor any man, or number of men, have a right (except what necessity, which is out of and above all rule, rather imposes than bestows) to free themselves from that primary engagement into which every man born into a community as much contracts by his being born into it as he contracts an obligation to certain parents by his having been derived from their bodies. The place of every man determines his duty. If you ask, *Quem te Deus esse jussit?* you will be answered when you resolve this other question, *Humana qua parte locatus es in re?* [2]

I admit, indeed, that in morals, as in all things else, difficulties

---

[1] "Omnes omnium charitates patria una complectitur."—CIC. [Burke] ["The love we have for our fatherland weaves into one all other loves and allegiances." Cicero *De Officiis* i.17.]

[2] A few lines in Persius contain a good summary of all the objects of moral investigation, and hint the result of our inquiry: There human will has no place.

> Quid *sumus?* et quidnam *victuri gignimur?* ordo
> Quis *datus?* et *metæ* quis mollis flexus, et unde?
> Quis modus argento? Quid *fas optare?* Quid asper
> Utile nummus habet? *Patriæ charisque propinquis*
> Quantum elargiri *debet?* Quem te Deus esse
> *Jussit?* et humana qua parte *locatus es* in re? [Burke]

> ["Learn, wretches, learn the motions of the mind,
> Why you were made, for what you were designed;
> And the great moral end of humankind.
> Study thyself, what rank or what degree
> The wise Creator has ordained for thee;
> And all the offices of that estate
> Perform, and with thy prudence guide thy fate."
> Persius *Satires* iii.67–72. Dryden's translation.]

will sometimes occur. Duties will sometimes cross one another. Then questions will arise, which of them is to be placed in subordination? which of them may be entirely superseded? These doubts give rise to that part of moral science called *casuistry,* which though necessary to be well studied by those who would become expert in that learning, who aim at becoming what I think Cicero somewhere calls *artifices officiorum,* it requires a very solid and discriminating judgment, great modesty and caution, and much sobriety of mind in the handling; else there is a danger that it may totally subvert those offices which it is its object only to methodize and reconcile. Duties, at their extreme bounds, are drawn very fine, so as to become almost evanescent. In that state some shade of doubt will always rest on these questions, when they are pursued with great subtilty. But the very habit of stating these extreme cases is not very laudable or safe; because, in general, it is not right to turn our duties into doubts. They are imposed to govern our conduct, not to exercise our ingenuity; and therefore our opinions about them ought not to be in a state of fluctuation, but steady, sure, and resolved.

Amongst these nice, and therefore dangerous points of casuistry, may be reckoned the question so much agitated in the present hour,—Whether, after the people have discharged themselves of their original power by an habitual delegation, no occasion can possibly occur which may justify the resumption of it? This question, in this latitude, is very hard to affirm or deny: but I am satisfied that no occasion can justify such a resumption, which would not equally authorize a dispensation with any other moral duty, perhaps with all of them together. However, if in general it be not easy to determine concerning the lawfulness of such devious proceedings, which must be ever on the edge of crimes, it is far from difficult to foresee the perilous consequences of the resuscitation of such a power in the people. The practical consequences of any political tenet go a great way in deciding upon its value. Political problems do not primarily concern truth or falsehood. They relate to good or evil. What in the result is likely to produce evil is politically false; that which is productive of good, politically true.

Believing it, therefore, a question at least arduous in the theory, and in the practice very critical, it would become us to ascertain as well as we can what form it is that our incantations are about to call up from darkness and the sleep of ages. When the supreme authority of the people is in question, before we attempt to extend or to confine it, we ought to fix in our minds, with some degree of distinctness, an idea of what it is we mean, when we say, the PEOPLE.

In a state of *rude* Nature there is no such thing as a people. A number of men in themselves have no collective capacity. The idea of a people is the idea of a corporation. It is wholly artificial, and made, like all other legal fictions, by common agreement. What the particular nature of that agreement was is collected from the form into which the particular society has been cast. Any other is not *their* covenant. When men, therefore, break up the original compact or agreement which gives its corporate form and capacity to a state, they are no longer a people,—they have no longer a corporate existence,—they have no longer a legal coactive force to bind within, nor a claim to be recognized abroad. They are a number of vague, loose individuals, and nothing more. With them all is to begin again. Alas! they little know how many a weary step is to be taken before they can form themselves into a mass which has a true politic personality.

We hear much, from men who have not acquired their hardiness of assertion from the profundity of their thinking, about the omnipotence of a *majority,* in such a dissolution of an ancient society as hath taken place in France. But amongst men so disbanded there can be no such thing as majority or minority, or power in any one person to bind another. The power of acting by a majority, which the gentlemen theorists seem to assume so readily, after they have violated the contract out of which it has arisen, (if at all it existed,) must be grounded on two assumptions: first, that of an incorporation produced by unanimity; and secondly, an unanimous agreement that the act of a mere majority (say of one) shall pass with them and with others as the act of the whole.

We are so little affected by things which are habitual, that we consider this idea of the decision of a *majority* as if it were a law of our original nature. But such constructive whole, residing in a part only, is one of the most violent fictions of positive law that ever has been or can be made on the principles of artificial incorporation. Out of civil society Nature knows nothing of it; nor are men, even when arranged according to civil order, otherwise than by very long training, brought at all to submit to it. The mind is brought far more easily to acquiesce in the proceedings of one man, or a few, who act under a general procuration for the state, than in the vote of a victorious majority in councils in which every man has his share in the deliberation. For there the beaten party are exasperated and soured by the previous contention, and mortified by the conclusive defeat. This mode of decision, where wills may be so nearly equal, where, according to circumstances, the smaller number may be the stronger force, and where apparent reason may be all upon one side, and on the other little else than impetuous appetite,—all this must be the result of a very particular and special convention, confirmed afterwards by long habits of obedience, by a sort of discipline in society, and by a strong hand, vested with stationary, permanent power to enforce this sort of constructive general will. What organ it is that shall declare the corporate mind is so much a matter of positive arrangement, that several states, for the validity of several of their acts, have required a proportion of voices much greater than that of a mere majority. These proportions are so entirely governed by convention that in some cases the minority decides. The laws in many countries to *condemn* require more than a mere majority; less than an equal number to *acquit*. In our judicial trials we require unanimity either to condemn or to absolve. In some incorporations one man speaks for the whole; in others, a few. Until the other day, in the Constitution of Poland unanimity was required to give validity to any act of their great national council or diet. This approaches much more nearly to rude Nature than the institutions of any other country. Such, indeed, every commonwealth must be, without a positive law to recognize in a certain number the will of the entire body.

If men dissolve their ancient incorporation in order to regenerate their community, in that state of things each man has a right, if he pleases, to remain an individual. Any number of individuals, who can agree upon it, have an undoubted right to form themselves into a state apart and wholly independent. If any of these is forced into the fellowship of another, this is conquest and not compact. On every principle which supposes society to be in virtue of a free covenant, this compulsive incorporation must be null and void.

As a people can have no right to a corporate capacity without universal consent, so neither have they a right to hold exclusively any lands in the name and title of a corporation. On the scheme of the present rulers in our neighboring country, regenerated as they are, they have no more right to the territory called France than I have. I have a right to pitch my tent in any unoccupied place I can find for it; and I may apply to my own maintenance any part of their unoccupied soil. I may purchase the house or vineyard of any individual proprietor who refuses his consent (and most proprietors have, as far as they dared, refused it) to the new incorporation. I stand in his independent place. Who are these insolent men, calling themselves the French nation, that would monopolize this fair domain of Nature? Is it because they speak a certain jargon? Is it their mode of chattering, to me unintelligible, that forms their title to my land? Who are they who claim by prescription and descent from certain gangs of banditti called Franks, and Burgundians, and Visigoths, of whom I may have never heard, and ninety-nine out of an hundred of themselves certainly never have heard, whilst at the very time they tell me that prescription and long possession form no title to property? Who are they that presume to assert that the land which I purchased of the individual, a natural person, and not a fiction of state, belongs to them, who in the very capacity in which they make their claim can exist only as an imaginary being, and in virtue of the very prescription which they reject and disown? This mode of arguing might be pushed into all the detail, so as to leave no sort of doubt, that, on their principles, and on the sort of footing on which they have thought proper to place themselves, the crowd of men, on the other side of the Channel, who have the impudence to call themselves a people, can never be the lawful, exclusive possessors of the soil. By what they call reasoning without prejudice, they leave not one stone upon another in the fabric of human society. They subvert all the authority which they hold, as well as all that which they have destroyed.

As in the abstract it is perfectly clear, that, out of a state of civil society, majority and minority are relations which can have no existence, and that, in civil society, its own specific conventions in each corporation determine what it is that constitutes the people, so as to make their act the signification of the general will,— to come to particulars, it is equally clear that neither in France nor in England has the original or any subsequent compact of the state, expressed or implied, constituted *a majority of men, told by the head,* to be the acting people of their several communities. And I see as little of policy or utility as there is of right, in laying down a principle that a majority of men told by the head are to be considered as the people, and that as such their will is to be law. What policy can there be found in arrangements made in defiance of every political principle? To enable men to act with the weight and character of a people, and to answer the ends for which they are incorporated into that capacity, we must suppose them (by means immediate or consequential) to be in that state of habitual social discipline in which the wiser, the more expert, and the more opulent conduct, and by conducting enlighten and protect, the weaker, the less knowing, and the less provided with the goods of fortune. When the multitude are not under this discipline, they can scarcely be said to be in civil society. Give once a certain constitution of things which produces a variety of conditions and circumstances in a state, and there is in Nature and reason a principle which, for their own benefit, postpones, not the interest, but the judgment, of those who are *numero plures,* to those who are *virtute et honore majores.* Numbers in a state (supposing, which is not the case in France, that a state does exist) are always of consideration,—but they are not the whole consideration. . . .

A true natural aristocracy is not a separate interest in the state, or separable from it. It is an essential integrant part of any large body rightly constituted. It is formed out of a class of legitimate presumptions, which, taken as generalities, must be admitted for actual truths. To be bred in a place of estimation; to see nothing low and sordid from one's infancy; to be taught to respect one's self; to be habituated to the censorial inspection of the public eye; to look early to public opinion; to stand upon such elevated ground as to be enabled to take a large view of the wide-spread and infinitely diversified combinations of men and affairs in a large society; to have leisure to read, to reflect, to converse; to be enabled to draw the court and attention of the wise and learned, wherever they are to be found; to be habituated in armies to command and to obey; to be taught to despise danger in the pursuit of honor and duty; to be formed to the greatest degree of vigilance, foresight, and circumspection, in a state of things in which no fault is committed with impunity and the slightest mistakes draw on the most ruinous consequences; to be led to a guarded and regulated conduct, from a sense that you are considered as an instructor of your fellow-citizens in their highest concerns, and that you act as a reconciler between God and man; to be employed as an adminis-

trator of law and justice, and to be thereby amongst the first benefactors to mankind; to be a professor of high science, or of liberal
and ingenuous art; to be amongst rich traders, who from their success are presumed to have sharp and vigorous understandings,
and to possess the virtues of diligence, order, constancy, and regularity, and to have cultivated an habitual regard to commutative
justice: these are the circumstances of men that form what I should
call a *natural* aristocracy, without which there is no nation.

The state of civil society which necessarily generates this aristocracy is a state of Nature,—and much more truly so than a savage and incoherent mode of life. For man is by nature reasonable;
and he is never perfectly in his natural state, but when he is placed
where reason may be best cultivated and most predominates. Art is
man's nature. We are as much, at least, in a state of Nature in
formed manhood as in immature and helpless infancy. Men,
qualified in the manner I have just described, form in Nature, as
she operates in the common modification of society, the leading,
guiding, and governing part. It is the soul to the body, without
which the man does not exist. To give, therefore, no more importance, in the social order, to such descriptions of men than that of
so many units is a horrible usurpation.

When great multitudes act together, under that discipline of
Nature, I recognize the PEOPLE. I acknowledge something that
perhaps equals, and ought always to guide, the sovereignty of convention. In all things the voice of this grand chorus of national harmony ought to have a mighty and decisive influence. But when you
disturb this harmony,—when you break up this beautiful order,
this array of truth and Nature, as well as of habit and prejudice,—
when you separate the common sort of men from their proper
chieftains, so as to form them into an adverse army,—I no longer
know that venerable object called the people in such a disbanded
race of deserters and vagabonds. For a while they may be terrible,
indeed,—but in such a manner as wild beasts are terrible. The
mind owes to them no sort of submission. They are, as they have
always been reputed, rebels. They may lawfully be fought with,
and brought under, whenever an advantage offers. Those who attempt by outrage and violence to deprive men of any advantage
which they hold under the laws, and to destroy the natural order
of life, proclaim war against them.

Appeal from the New to the Old Whigs (1791). IV, 162–77.

Nothing indeed can be more unnatural than the present convulsions of this country, if the above account be a true one. I confess I shall assent to it with great reluctance, and only on the compulsion of the clearest and firmest proofs; because their account resolves itself into this short, but discouraging proposition, "That we have a very good ministry, but that we are a very bad people"; that we set ourselves to bite the hand that feeds us; that with a malignant insanity, we oppose the measures, and ungratefully vilify the persons, of those whose sole object is our own peace and prosperity. If a few puny libellers, acting under a knot of factious politicians, without virtue, parts, or character, (such they are constantly represented by these gentlemen,) are sufficient to excite this disturbance, very perverse must be the disposition of that people, amongst whom such a disturbance can be excited by such means. It is besides no small aggravation of the public misfortune, that the disease, on this hypothesis, appears to be without remedy. If the wealth of the nation be the cause of its turbulence, I imagine it is not proposed to introduce poverty, as a constable to keep the peace. If our dominions abroad are the roots which feed all this rank luxuriance of sedition, it is not intended to cut them off in order to famish the fruit. If our liberty has enfeebled the executive power, there is no design, I hope, to call in the aid of despotism, to fill up the deficiencies of law. Whatever may be intended, these things are not yet professed. We seem therefore to be driven to absolute despair; for we have no other materials to work upon, but those out of which God has been pleased to form the inhabitants of this island. . . . Particular punishments are the cure for accidental distempers in the state; they inflame rather than allay those heats which arise from the settled mismanagement of the government, or from a natural indisposition in the people. It is of the utmost moment not to make mistakes in the use of strong measures; and firmness is then only a virtue when it accompanies the most perfect wisdom. In truth, inconstancy is a sort of natural corrective of folly and ignorance.

I am not one of those who think that the people are never in the wrong. They have been so, frequently and outrageously, both in other countries and in this. But I do say, that in all disputes between them and their rulers, the presumption is at least upon a par in favor of the people. Experience may perhaps justify me in going further. When popular discontents have been very prevalent, it may well be affirmed and supported, that there has been generally something found amiss in the constitution, or in the conduct of government. The people have no interest in disorder. When they do wrong, it is their error, and not their crime. But with the governing part of the state, it is far otherwise. They certainly may act ill by design, as well as by mistake. . . . If this presumption in favor of the subjects against the trustees of power be not the more probable, I am sure it is the more comfortable speculation; because it is more easy to change an administration, than to reform a people.

Upon a supposition, therefore, that, in the opening of the cause, the presumptions stand equally balanced between the parties, there seems sufficient ground to entitle any person to a fair hearing, who attempts some other scheme beside that easy one which is fashionable in some fashionable companies, to account for the present discontents. It is not to be argued that we endure no grievance, because our grievances are not of the same sort with those under which we labored formerly. . . .

It is very rare indeed for men to be wrong in their feelings concerning public misconduct; as rare to be right in their speculation upon the cause of it. I have constantly observed, that the generality of people are fifty years, at least, behindhand in their politics. There are but very few who are capable of comparing and digesting what passes before their eyes at different times and occasions, so as to form the whole into a distinct system. But in books everything is settled for them, without the exertion of any considerable diligence or sagacity. For which reason men are wise with but little reflection, and good with little self-denial, in the business of all times except their own. We are very uncorrupt and tolerably enlightened judges of the transactions of past ages; where no passions deceive, and where the whole train of circumstances, from the trifling cause to the tragical event, is set in an orderly series before us. Few are the partisans of departed tyranny; and to be a Whig on the business of an hundred years ago, is very consistent with every advantage of present servility. This retrospective wisdom, and historical patriotism, are things of wonderful convenience, and serve admirably to reconcile the old quarrel between speculation and practice. Many a stern republican, after gorging himself with a full feast of admiration of the Grecian commonwealths and of our true Saxon constitution, and discharging all the splendid bile of his virtuous indignation on King John and King James, sits down perfectly satisfied to the coarsest work and homeliest job of the day he lives in. I believe there was no professed admirer of Henry the Eighth among the instruments of the last King James; nor in the court of Henry the Eighth was there, I dare say, to be found a single advocate for the favorites of Richard the Second.

No complaisance to our court, or to our age, can make me believe nature to be so changed, but that public liberty will be among us as among our ancestors, obnoxious to some person or other; and that opportunities will be furnished for attempting, at least, some alteration to the prejudice of our constitution. These attempts will naturally vary in their mode according to times and circumstances. For ambition, though it has ever the same general views, has not at all times the same means, nor the same particular objects. A great deal of the furniture of ancient tyranny is worn to rags; the rest is entirely out of fashion. Besides, there are few statesmen so very clumsy and awkward in their business, as to fall into the identical snare which has proved fatal to their predecessors.

Thoughts on the Cause of the Present Discontents (1770). I, 439–43.

3. Liberty and Natural Rights

The theory of Natural Rights is as old as the concept of the Law of Nature, of which it is historically and logically a part. But from Locke down to the present it has been common practice to ignore the dependence of such rights upon a general law. In the revolutionary movement of the eighteenth century the sacred Rights of Nature were appealed to in attacks on the established conventions of society and government. Thus a theoretical opposition was set up between artificial society and life according to Nature. Burke questioned the validity of this distinction, and developed his own theories about Rights and Liberty in a human society.

The distinguishing part of our Constitution is its liberty. To preserve that liberty inviolate seems the particular duty and proper trust of a member of the House of Commons. But the liberty, the only liberty, I mean is a liberty connected with order: that not only exists along with order and virtue, but which cannot exist at all without them. It inheres in good and steady government, as in its substance and vital principle.

Speech at his Arrival at Bristol (1774). II, 87.

In 1778 Sir George Savile, one of Burke's friends, had pushed through the Commons a bill easing the penalties on Catholics. On June 2, 1780, a fanatical "anti-popery" mob, led by the half-crazy Lord George Gordon, invaded the halls of Parliament and rioted for six days in many parts of London. The government provided a special guard for Burke's house, which he declined. On September 6 he defended his advocacy of Catholic emancipation before his constituency at Bristol, which he had represented since 1774. But finding public opinion inflamed against him, he withdrew his candidacy for re-election.

I must fairly tell you, that so far as my principles are concerned, (principles that I hope will only depart with my last breath,) that I have no idea of a liberty unconnected with honesty and justice. Nor do I believe that any good constitutions of government, or of freedom, can find it necessary for their security to doom any part of the people to a permanent slavery. Such a constitution of freedom, if such can be, is in effect no more than another name for the tyranny of the strongest faction; and factions in republics have been, and are, full as capable as monarchs of the most cruel oppression and injustice. It is but too true, that the love, and even the very idea, of genuine liberty is extremely rare. It is but too true that there are many whose whole scheme of freedom is made up of pride, perverseness, and insolence. They feel themselves in a state of thraldom, they imagine that their souls are cooped and cabined in, unless they have some man or some body of men dependent on their mercy. This desire of having some one below them descends to those who are the very lowest of all; and a Protestant cobbler, debased by his poverty, but exalted by his share of the ruling church, feels a pride in knowing it is by his generosity alone that the peer whose footman's instep he measures is able to keep his chaplain from a jail. This disposition is the true source of the passion which many men in very humble life have taken to the American war. *Our* subjects in America; *our* colonies; *our* dependants. This lust of party power is the liberty they hunger and thirst for; and this Siren song of ambition has charmed ears that one would have thought were never organized to that sort of music.

This way of *proscribing the citizens by denominations and general descriptions,* dignified by the name of reason of state, and security for constitutions and commonwealths, is nothing better at bottom than the miserable invention of an ungenerous ambition which would fain hold the sacred trust of power, without any of the virtues or any of the energies that give a title to it,—a receipt of policy, made up of a detestable compound of malice, cowardice, and sloth. They would govern men against their will; but in that government they would be discharged from the exercise of vigilance, providence, and fortitude; and therefore, that they may sleep on their watch, they consent to take some one division of the society into partnership of the tyranny over the rest. But let government, in what form it may be, comprehend the whole in its justice, and restrain the suspicious by its vigilance,—let it keep watch and ward,—let it discover by its sagacity, and punish by its firmness, all delinquency against its power, whenever delinquency exists in the overt acts,—and then it will be as safe as ever God and Nature intended it should be. Crimes are the acts of individuals, and not of denominations: and therefore arbitrarily to class men under general descriptions, in order to proscribe and punish them in the lump for a presumed delinquency, of which perhaps but a part, perhaps none at all, are guilty, is indeed a compendious method, and saves a world of trouble about proof; but such a method, instead of being law, is an act of unnatural rebellion against the legal dominion of reason and justice; and this vice, in any constitution that entertains it, at one time or other will certainly bring on its ruin.

We are told that this is not a religious persecution; and its abettors are loud in disclaiming all severities on account of conscience. Very fine indeed! Then let it be so: they are not persecutors; they are only tyrants. With all my heart. I am perfectly indifferent concerning the pretexts upon which we torment one another,—or whether it be for the constitution of the Church of England, or for the constitution of the State of England, that people choose to make their fellow-creatures wretched. When we were sent into a place of authority, you that sent us had yourselves but one commission to give. You could give us none to wrong or oppress, or even to suffer any kind of oppression or wrong, on any grounds whatsoever: not on political, as in the affairs of America; not on commercial, as in those of Ireland; not in civil, as in the laws for debt; not in religious, as in the statutes against Protestant or Catholic dissenters. The diversified, but connected, fabric of universal justice is well cramped and bolted together in all its parts; and depend upon it, I never have employed, and I never shall employ, any engine of power which may come into my hands to wrench it asunder. All shall stand, if I can help it, and all shall stand connected. After all, to complete this work, much remains to be done: much in the East, much in the West. But, great as the work is, if our will be ready, our powers are not deficient.

Speech at Bristol Previous to the Election (1780). II, 416–19.

At that time I was connected with men of high place in the community [the Rockingham party]. They loved liberty as much as the Duke of Bedford can do; and they understood it at least as well. Perhaps their politics, as usual, took a tincture from their character, and they cultivated what they loved. The liberty they pursued was a liberty inseparable from order, from virtue, from morals, and from religion,—and was neither hypocritically nor fanatically followed. They did not wish that liberty, in itself one of the first of blessings, should in its perversion become the greatest curse which could fall upon mankind. To preserve the Constitution entire, and practically equal to all the great ends of its formation, not in one single part, but in all its parts, was to them the first object. Popularity and power they regarded alike. These were with them only different means of obtaining that object, and had no preference over each other in their minds, but as one or the other might afford a surer or a less certain prospect of arriving at that end.

Letter to a Noble Lord (1796). V, 182–83.

4. Liberty within the Social Order

Radical leaders were fond of the phrase "the chartered rights of man," the word "charter," reminiscent of the Magna Carta, being dear to any Englishman. Burke distinguished between charters which embody the principles basic to government and society from those charters which were grants to corporate bodies established by Parliament itself. Over the latter Parliament can never relinquish its control and responsibility.

I must beg leave to observe, that, if we are not able to contrive some method of governing India *well*, which will not of necessity become the means of governing Great Britain *ill*, a ground is laid for their eternal separation, but none for sacrificing the people of that country to our Constitution. I am, however, far from being persuaded that any such incompatibility of interest does at all exist. On the contrary, I am certain that every means effectual to preserve India from oppression is a guard to preserve the British Constitution from its worst corruption. To show this, I will consider the objections . . .

1st, That the bill is an attack on the chartered rights of men. . . . I must observe that the phrase of "the chartered rights *of men*" is full of affectation, and very unusual in the discussion of privileges conferred by charters of the present description. But it is not difficult to discover what end that ambiguous mode of expression, so often reiterated, is meant to answer.

The rights of *men*—that is to say, the natural rights of mankind —are indeed sacred things; and if any public measure is proved mischievously to affect them, the objection ought to be fatal to that measure, even if no charter at all could be set up against it. If these natural rights are further affirmed and declared by express covenants, if they are clearly defined and secured against chicane, against power and authority, by written instruments and positive engagements, they are in a still better condition: they partake not only of the sanctity of the object so secured, but of that solemn public faith itself which secures an object of such importance. Indeed, this formal recognition, by the sovereign power, of an original right in the subject, can never be subverted, but by rooting up the holding radical principles of government, and even of society itself. The charters which we call by distinction *great* are public instruments of this nature: I mean the charters of King John and King Henry the Third. The things secured by these instruments may, without any deceitful ambiguity, be very fitly called *the chartered rights of men.*

These charters have made the very name of a charter dear to the heart of every Englishman. But, Sir, there may be, and there are, charters, not only different in nature, but formed on principles *the very reverse* of those of the Great Charter. Of this kind is the charter of the East India Company. *Magna Charta* is a charter to restrain power and to destroy monopoly. The East India charter is a charter to establish monopoly and to create power. Political power and commercial monopoly are *not* the rights of men; and the rights to them derived from charters it is fallacious and sophistical to call "the chartered rights of men." These chartered rights (to speak of such charters and of their effects in terms of the greatest possible moderation) do at least suspend the natural rights of mankind at large, and in their very frame and constitution are liable to fall into a direct violation of them.

It is a charter of this latter description (that is to say, a charter of power and monopoly) which is affected by the bill before you. The bill, Sir, does without question affect it: it does affect it essentially and substantially. But, having stated to you of what description the chartered rights are which this bill touches, I feel no difficulty at all in acknowledging the existence of those chartered rights in their fullest extent. They belong to the Company in the surest manner, and they are secured to that body by every sort of public sanction. They are stamped by the faith of the king; they are stamped by the faith of Parliament: they have been bought for money, for money honestly and fairly paid; they have been bought for valuable consideration, over and over again.

I therefore freely admit to the East India Company their claim to exclude their fellow-subjects from the commerce of half the globe. I admit their claim to administer an annual territorial revenue of seven millions sterling, to command an army of sixty thousand men, and to dispose (under the control of a sovereign, imperial discretion, and with the due observance of the natural and local law) of the lives and fortunes of thirty millions of their fellow-creatures. All this they possess by charter, and by Acts of Parliament, (in my opinion,) without a shadow of controversy.

Those who carry the rights and claims of the Company the furthest do not contend for more than this; and all this I freely grant. But, granting all this, they must grant to me, in my turn, that all political power which is set over men, and that all privilege claimed or exercised in exclusion of them, being wholly artificial, and for so much a derogation from the natural equality of mankind at large, ought to be some way or other exercised ultimately for their benefit.

If this is true with regard to every species of political dominion and every description of commercial privilege, none of which can be original, self-derived rights, or grants for the mere private benefit of the holders, then such rights, or privileges, or whatever else you choose to call them, are all in the strictest sense *a trust:* and it is of the very essence of every trust to be rendered *account-able,*—and even totally to *cease,* when it substantially varies from the purposes for which alone it could have a lawful existence.

This I conceive, Sir, to be true of trusts of power vested in the highest hands, and of such as seem to hold of no human creature. But about the application of this principle to subordinate *deriva-tive* trusts I do not see how a controversy can be maintained. To whom, then, would I make the East India Company accountable? Why, to Parliament, to be sure,—to Parliament, from whom their trust was derived,—to Parliament, which alone is capable of com-prehending the magnitude of its object, and its abuse, and alone capable of an effectual legislative remedy. The very charter, which is held out to exclude Parliament from correcting malversation with regard to the high trust vested in the Company, is the very thing which at once gives a title and imposes a duty on us to inter-fere with effect, wherever power and authority originating from ourselves are perverted from their purposes, and become instru-ments of wrong and violence.

If Parliament, Sir, had nothing to do with this charter, we might have some sort of Epicurean excuse to stand aloof, indifferent spec-tators of what passes in the Company's name in India and in Lon-don. But if we are the very cause of the evil, we are in a special manner engaged to the redress; and for us passively to bear with oppressions committed under the sanction of our own authority is in truth and reason for this House to be an active accomplice in the abuse.

That the power, notoriously grossly abused, has been bought from us is very certain. But this circumstance, which is urged against the bill, becomes an additional motive for our interfer-ence, lest we should be thought to have sold the blood of millions of men for the base consideration of money. We sold, I admit, all that we had to sell,—that is, our authority, not our control. We had not a right to make a market of our duties.

Speech on Mr. Fox's East India Bill (1783). II, 436–40.

You hope, sir, that I think the French deserving of liberty. I cer-tainly do. I certainly think that all men who desire it, deserve it. It is not the reward of our merit, or the acquisition of our industry. It is our inheritance. It is the birthright of our species. We cannot forfeit our right to it, but by what forfeits our title to the privileges of our kind. I mean the abuse, or oblivion, of our rational faculties, and a ferocious indocility which makes us prompt to wrong and violence, destroys our social nature, and transforms us into something little better than the description of wild beasts. To men so degraded, a state of strong constraint is a sort of necessary substitute for freedom; since, bad as it is, it may deliver them in some measure from the worst of all slavery,—that is, the despotism of their own blind and brutal passions.

You have kindly said that you began to love freedom from your intercourse with me. Permit me then to continue our conversation, and to tell you what the freedom is that I love, and that to which I think all men entitled. This is the more necessary, because, of all the loose terms in the world, liberty is the most indefinite. It is not solitary, unconnected, individual, selfish liberty, as if every man was to regulate the whole of his conduct by his own will. The liberty I mean is *social* freedom. It is that state of things in which liberty is secured by the equality of restraint. A constitution of things in which the liberty of no one man, and no body of men, and no number of men, can find means to trespass on the liberty of any person, or any description of persons, in the society. This kind of liberty is, indeed, but another name for justice; ascertained by wise laws, and secured by well-constructed institutions. I am sure that liberty, so incorporated, and in a manner identified with justice, must be infinitely dear to everyone who is capable of conceiving what it is. But whenever a separation is made between liberty and justice, neither is, in my opinion, safe. I do not believe that men ever did submit, certain I am that they never ought to have submitted, to the arbitrary pleasure of one man; but, under circumstances in which the arbitrary pleasure of many persons in the community pressed with an intolerable hardship upon the just and equal rights of their fellows, such a choice might be made, as among evils. The moment *will* is set above reason and justice, in any community, a great question may arise in sober minds, in what part or portion of the community that dangerous dominion of *will* may be the least mischievously placed.

Letter to Mons. Dupont, October, 1789.
Correspondence. III, 105–7.

I flatter myself that I love a manly, moral, regulated liberty as well as any gentleman of that society, be he who he will; and perhaps I have given as good proofs of my attachment to that cause, in the whole course of my public conduct. I think I envy liberty as little as they do to any other nation. But I cannot stand forward, and give praise or blame to anything which relates to human actions and human concerns on a simple view of the object, as it stands stripped of every relation, in all the nakedness and solitude of metaphysical abstraction. Circumstances (which with some gentlemen pass for nothing) give in reality to every political principle its distinguishing color and discriminating effect. The circumstances are what render every civil and political scheme beneficial or noxious to mankind. Abstractedly speaking, government, as well as liberty, is good; yet could I, in common sense, ten years ago, have felicitated France on her enjoyment of a government, (for she then had a government,) without inquiry what the nature of that government was, or how it was administered? Can I now congratulate the same nation upon its freedom? Is it because liberty in the abstract may be classed amongst the blessings of mankind, that I am seriously to felicitate a madman who has escaped from the protecting restraint and wholesome darkness of his cell on his restoration to the enjoyment of light and liberty? Am I to congratulate a highwayman and murderer who has broke prison upon the recovery of his natural rights? This would be to act over again the scene of the criminals condemned to the galleys, and their heroic deliverer, the metaphysic Knight of the Sorrowful Countenance.

When I see the spirit of liberty in action, I see a strong principle at work; and this, for a while, is all I can possibly know of it. The wild gas, the fixed air, is plainly broke loose: but we ought to suspend our judgment until the first effervescence is a little subsided, till the liquor is cleared, and until we see something deeper than the agitation of a troubled and frothy surface. I must be tolerably sure, before I venture publicly to congratulate men upon a blessing, that they have really received one. Flattery corrupts both the receiver and the giver; and adulation is not of more service to the people than to kings. I should therefore suspend my congratulations on the new liberty of France, until I was informed how it had been combined with government, with public force, with the discipline and obedience of armies, with the collection of an effective and well-distributed revenue, with morality and religion, with solidity and property, with peace and order, with civil and social manners. All these (in their way) are good things, too; and without them, liberty is not a benefit whilst it lasts, and is not likely to continue long. The effect of liberty to individuals is, that they may do what they please: we ought to see what it will please them to do, before we risk congratulations, which may be soon turned into complaints. Prudence would dictate this in the case of separate, insulated, private men. But liberty, when men act in bodies, is *power*. Considerate people, before they declare themselves, will observe the use which is made of *power*,—and particularly of so trying a thing as *new* power in *new* persons, of whose principles, tempers, and dispositions they have little or no experience, and in situations where those who appear the most stirring in the scene may possibly not be the real movers.

Reflections (1790). III, 240–42.

The effects of the incapacity shown by the popular leaders [of the French Revolution] in all the great members of the commonwealth are to be covered with the "all-atoning name" of Liberty. In some people I see great liberty, indeed; in many, if not in the most, an oppressive, degrading servitude. But what is liberty without wisdom and without virtue? It is the greatest of all possible evils; for it is folly, vice, and madness, without tuition or restraint. Those who know what virtuous liberty is cannot bear to see it disgraced by incapable heads, on account of their having high-sounding words in their mouths. Grand, swelling sentiments of liberty I am sure I do not despise. They warm the heart; they enlarge and liberalize our minds; they animate our courage in a time of conflict. Old as I am, I read the fine raptures of Lucan and Corneille with pleasure. Neither do I wholly condemn the little arts and devices of popularity. They facilitate the carrying of many points of moment; they keep the people together; they refresh the mind in its exertions; and they diffuse occasional gayety over the severe brow of moral freedom. Every politician ought to sacrifice to the Graces, and to join compliance with reason. But in such an undertaking as that in France all these subsidiary sentiments and artifices are of little avail. To make a government requires no great prudence. Settle the seat of power, teach obedience, and the work is done. To give freedom is still more easy. It is not necessary to guide; it only requires to let go the rein. But to form a *free government*, that is, to temper together these opposite elements of liberty and restraint in one consistent work, requires much thought, deep reflection, a sagacious, powerful, and combining mind. This I do not find in those who take the lead in the National Assembly. Perhaps they are not so miserably deficient as they appear. I rather believe it. It would put them below the common level of human understanding. But when the leaders choose to make themselves bidders at an auction of popularity, their talents, in the construction of the state, will be of no service. They will become flatterers instead of legislators,—the instruments, not the guides of the people. If any of them should happen to propose a scheme of liberty soberly limited, and defined with proper qualifications, he will be immediately outbid by his competitors, who will produce something more splendidly popular. Suspicions will be raised of his fidelity to his cause. Moderation will be stigmatized as the virtue of cowards, and compromise as the prudence of traitors,—until, in hopes of preserving the credit which may enable him to temper and moderate on some occasions, the popular leader is obliged to become active in propagating doctrines and establishing powers that will afterwards defeat any sober purpose at which he ultimately might have aimed.

But am I so unreasonable as to see nothing at all that deserves commendation in the indefatigable labors of this Assembly? I do not deny, that, among an infinite number of acts of violence and folly, some good may have been done. They who destroy everything certainly will remove some grievance. They who make everything new have a chance that they may establish something beneficial. To give them credit for what they have done in virtue of the authority they have usurped, or to excuse them in the crimes by which that authority has been acquired, it must appear that the same things could not have been accomplished without producing such a revolution. Most assuredly they might; because almost every one of the regulations made by them, which is not very equivocal, was either in the cession of the king, voluntarily made at the meeting of the States, or in the concurrent instructions to the orders. Some usages have been abolished on just grounds; but they were such, that, if they had stood as they were to all eternity, they would little detract from the happiness and prosperity of any state. The improvements of the National Assembly are superficial, their errors fundamental.

Whatever they are, I wish my countrymen rather to recommend to our neighbors the example of the British Constitution than to take models from them for the improvement of our own. In the former they have got an invaluable treasure. They are not, I think, without some causes of apprehension and complaint; but these they do not owe to their Constitution, but to their own conduct. I think our happy situation owing to our Constitution,—but owing to the whole of it, and not to any part singly,—owing in a great measure to what we have left standing in our several reviews and reformations, as well as to what we have altered or superadded. Our people will find employment enough for a truly patriotic, free, and independent spirit, in guarding what they possess from violation. I would not exclude alteration neither; but even when I changed, it should be to preserve. I should be led to my remedy by a great grievance. In what I did, I should follow the example of our ancestors. I would make the reparation as nearly as possible in the style of the building. A politic caution, a guarded circumspection, a moral rather than a complexional timidity, were among the ruling principles of our forefathers in their most decided conduct. Not being illuminated with the light of which the gentlemen of France tell us they have got so abundant a share, they acted under a strong impression of the ignorance and fallibility of mankind. He that had made them thus fallible rewarded them for having in their conduct attended to their nature. Let us imitate their caution, if we wish to deserve their fortune or to retain their bequests. Let us add, if we please, but let us preserve what they have left; and standing on the firm ground of the British Constitution, let us be satisfied to admire, rather than attempt to follow in their desperate flights, the aëronauts of France.

I have told you candidly my sentiments. I think they are not likely to alter yours. I do not know that they ought. You are young; you cannot guide, but must follow, the fortune of your country. But hereafter they may be of some use to you, in some future form which your commonwealth may take. In the present it can hardly remain; but before its final settlement, it may be obliged to pass, as one of our poets says, "through great varieties of untried being," and in all its transmigrations to be purified by fire and blood.

Reflections (1790). III, 559–62.

Burke believed in the Church Establishment as a corporate body created by law. But he also insisted on toleration of Catholics and Dissenters, and fought for the repeal of penal laws under which they suffered. In March 1773, when a bill for the relief of Protestant Dissenters was before the House, a curious petition was presented from some Methodists from Chatham objecting to the bill because they feared other Dissenters might receive too much liberty. Burke treated this support of the Church with irony, and declared his support of the Bill.

I assure you, Sir, that the honorable gentleman who spoke last but one need not be in the least fear that I should make a war of particles upon his opinion, whether the Church of England *should*, *would*, or *ought* to be alarmed. I am very clear that this House has no one reason in the world to think she is alarmed by the bill brought before you. It is something extraordinary that the only symptom of alarm in the Church of England should appear in the petition of some Dissenters, with whom, I believe, very few in this House are yet acquainted, and of whom you know no more than that you are assured by the honorable gentleman that they are not Mahometans. Of the Church we know they are not, by the name that they assume. They are, then, Dissenters. The first symptom of an alarm comes from some Dissenters assembled round the lines of Chatham: these lines become the security of the Church of England! The honorable gentleman, in speaking of the lines of Chatham, tells us that they serve not only for the security of the wooden walls of England, but for the defence of the Church of England. I suspect the wooden walls of England secure the lines of Chatham, rather than the lines of Chatham secure the wooden walls of England.

Sir, the Church of England, if only defended by this miserable petition upon your table, must, I am afraid, upon the principles of true fortification, be soon destroyed. But, fortunately, her walls, bulwarks, and bastions are constructed of other materials than of stubble and straw,—are built up with the strong and stable matter of the gospel of liberty, and founded on a true, constitutional, legal establishment. But, Sir, she has other securities: she has the security of her own doctrines; she has the security of the piety, the sanctity, of her own professors,—their learning is a bulwark to defend her; she has the security of the two universities, not shook in any single battlement, in any single pinnacle.

But the honorable gentleman has mentioned, indeed, principles which astonish me rather more than ever. The honorable gentleman thinks that the Dissenters enjoy a large share of liberty under a connivance; and he thinks that the establishing toleration by law is an attack upon Christianity.

The first of these is a contradiction in terms. Liberty under a connivance! Connivance is a relaxation from slavery, not a definition of liberty. What is connivance, but a state under which all slaves live? If I was to describe slavery, I would say, with those who *hate* it, it is living under will, not under law; if as it is stated by its advocates, I would say, that, like earthquakes, like thunder, or other wars the elements make upon mankind, it happens rarely, it occasionally comes now and then upon people, who, upon ordinary occasions, enjoy the same legal government of liberty. Take it under the description of those who would soften those features, the state of slavery and connivance is the same thing. If the liberty enjoyed be a liberty not of toleration, but of connivance, the only question is, whether establishing such by law is an attack upon Christianity. Toleration an attack upon Christianity! What, then! are we come to this pass, to suppose that nothing can support Christianity but the principles of persecution? Is that, then, the idea of establishment? Is it, then, the idea of Christianity itself, that it ought to have establishments, that it ought to have laws against Dissenters, but the breach of which laws is to be connived at? What a picture of toleration! what a picture of laws, of establishments! what a picture of religious and civil liberty! I am persuaded the honorable gentleman does not see it in this light. But these very terms become the strongest reasons for my support of the bill: for I am persuaded that toleration, so far from being an attack upon Christianity, becomes the best and surest support that possibly can be given to it. The Christian religion itself arose without establishment,—it arose even without toleration; and whilst its own principles were not tolerated, it conquered all the powers of darkness, it conquered all the powers of the world. The moment it began to depart from these principles, it converted the establishment into tyranny; it subverted its foundations from that very hour. Zealous as I am for the principle of an establishment, so just an abhorrence do I conceive against whatever may shake it. I know nothing but the supposed necessity of persecution that can make an establishment disgusting. I would have toleration a part of establishment, as a principle favorable to Christianity, and as a part of Christianity.

Speech on Relief of Protestant Dissenters (1773). VII, 23–25.

It is certain that I have, to the best of my power, supported the establishment of the church, upon grounds and principles which I am happy to find countenanced by your approbation. This you have been told; but you have not heard that I supported also the petition of the dissenters, for a larger toleration than they enjoy at present under the letter of the act of King William. In fact, my opinion in favor of toleration goes far beyond the limits of that act, which was no more than a provision for certain sets of men, under certain circumstances, and by no means what is commonly called "an act of toleration." I am greatly deceived, if my opinions on this subject are not consistent with the strictest and the best supported church establishment. I cannot consider our dissenters, of almost any kind, as schismatics; whatever some of their leaders might originally have been in the eye of Him, who alone knows whether they acted under the direction of such a conscience as they had, or at the instigation of pride and passion. There are many things amongst most of them, which I rather *dislike* than dare to *condemn*. My ideas of toleration go far beyond even theirs. I would give full civil protection, in which I include an immunity from all disturbance of their public religious worship, and a power of teaching in schools as well as temples, to Jews, Mahometans, and even Pagans; especially if they are already possessed of those advantages by long and prescriptive usage, which are as sacred in this exercise of rights, as in any other. Much more am I inclined to tolerate those whom I look upon as our brethren. I mean all those who profess our common hope, extending to all the reformed and unreformed churches, both at home and abroad; in none of whom I find any thing capitally amiss, but their mutual hatred of each other. I can never think any man a heretic, or schismatic, by *education*. It must be, as I conceive, by an act, in which his *own choice* (influenced by blameable passions) is more concerned than it can be by his early prejudices, and his being aggregated to bodies, for whom men naturally form a great degree of reverence and affection. This is my opinion, and my conduct has been conformable to it. Another age will see it more general; and I think that this general affection to religion will never introduce indifference, but will rather increase real zeal, Christian fervor, and pious emulation; that it will make common cause against Epicureanism, and everything that corrupts the mind and renders it unworthy of the family [of its origin]. But toleration does not exclude national preference, either as to mode or opinions, and all the lawful and honest means which may be used for the support of that preference.

Letter to William Burgh, February 9, 1775.
Correspondence. II, 17–19.

Then, Sir, from these six capital sources, of descent, of form of government, of religion in the northern provinces, of manners in the southern, of education, of the remoteness of situation from the first mover of government,—from all these causes a fierce spirit of liberty has grown up. It has grown with the growth of the people in your colonies, and increased with the increase of their wealth: a spirit, that, unhappily meeting with an exercise of power in England, which, however lawful, is not reconcilable to any ideas of liberty, much less with theirs, has kindled this flame that is ready to consume us.

I do not mean to commend either the spirit in this excess, or the moral causes which produce it. Perhaps a more smooth and accommodating spirit of freedom in them would be more acceptable to us. Perhaps ideas of liberty might be desired more reconcilable with an arbitrary and boundless authority. Perhaps we might wish the colonists to be persuaded that their liberty is more secure when held in trust for them by us (as their guardians during a perpetual minority) than with any part of in their own hands. But the question is not, whether their spirit deserves praise or blame,—what, in the name of God, shall we do with it? You have before you the object, such as it is,—with all its glories, with all its imperfections on its head. You see the magnitude, the importance, the temper, the habits, the disorders. By all these considerations we are strongly urged to determine something concerning it. We are called upon to fix some rule and line for our future conduct, which may give a little stability to our politics, and prevent the return of such unhappy deliberations as the present. Every such return will bring the matter before us in a still more untractable form. For what astonishing and incredible things have we not seen already! What monsters have not been generated from this unnatural contention! Whilst every principle of authority and resistance has been pushed, upon both sides, as far as it would go, there is nothing so solid and certain, either in reasoning or in practice, that has not been shaken. Until very lately, all authority in America seemed to be nothing but an emanation from yours. Even the popular part of the colony constitution derived all its activity, and its first vital movement, from the pleasure of the crown. We thought, Sir, that the utmost which the discontented colonists could do was to disturb authority; we never dreamt they could of themselves supply it, knowing in general what an operose business it is to establish a government absolutely new. But having, for our purposes in this contention, resolved that none but an obedient assembly should sit, the humors of the people there, finding all passage through the legal channel stopped, with great violence broke out another way. Some provinces have tried their experiment, as we have tried ours; and theirs has succeeded. They have formed a government sufficient for its purposes, without the bustle of a revolution, or the troublesome formality of an election. Evident necessity and tacit consent have done the business in an instant. So well they have done it, that Lord Dunmore (the account is among the fragments on your table) tells you that the new institution is infinitely better obeyed than the ancient government ever was in its most fortunate periods. Obedience is what makes government, and not the names by which it is called: not the name of Governor, as formerly, or Committee, as at present. This new government has originated directly from the people, and was not transmitted through any of the ordinary artificial media of a positive constitution. It was not a manufacture ready formed, and transmitted to them in that condition from England. The evil arising from hence is this: that the colonists having once found the possibility of enjoying the advantages of order in the midst of a struggle for liberty, such struggles will not henceforward seem so terrible to the settled and sober part of mankind as they had appeared before the trial.

Pursuing the same plan of punishing by the denial of the exercise of government to still greater lengths, we wholly abrogated the ancient government of Massachusetts. We were confident that the first feeling, if not the very prospect of anarchy, would instantly enforce a complete submission. The experiment was tried. A new, strange, unexpected face of things appeared. Anarchy is found tolerable. A vast province has now subsisted, and subsisted in a considerable degree of health and vigor, for near a twelvemonth, without governor, without public council, without judges, without executive magistrates. How long it will continue in this state, or what may arise out of this unheard-of situation, how can the wisest of us conjecture? Our late experience has taught us that many of those fundamental principles formerly believed infallible are either not of the importance they were imagined to be, or that we have not at all adverted to some other far more important and far more powerful principles which entirely overrule those we had considered as omnipotent. I am much against any further experiments which tend to put to the proof any more of these allowed opinions which contribute so much to the public tranquillity. In effect, we suffer as much at home by this loosening of all ties, and this concussion of all established opinions, as we do abroad. For, in order to prove that the Americans have no right to their liberties, we are every day endeavoring to subvert the maxims which preserve the whole spirit of our own. To prove that the Americans ought not to be free, we are obliged to depreciate the value of freedom itself; and we never seem to gain a paltry advantage over them in debate, without attacking some of those principles, or deriding some of those feelings, for which our ancestors have shed their blood.

Speech on Conciliation with America (1775). II, 126–30.

CHAPTER IV

Government and Human Nature

Already in 1769, in one of his earliest pamphlets, Burke laid down the proposition that "politics ought to be adjusted, not to human reasonings, but to human nature; of which reason is but a part, and by no means the greatest part." Both by temperament and by conviction Burke was bound to oppose the avowedly rationalistic and geometrical manner of reasoning about politics which was practiced by revolutionary philosophers in both England and France. His conception of Prudence as a political virtue has been presented in Chapter II. In this chapter his mode of political thinking is illustrated from his discussion of the policies toward the American Colonies, and his explanation of the importance of religion and manners among the practical forces of a society and state.

1. On Conciliation with the American Colonies

The Stamp Act of 1765, by which the British government expected to raise about £100,000 by taxes in America, aroused resistance and serious disorders in the Colonies. It was repealed in 1766 at the instance of the new Rockingham ministry. Burke, new in Parliament, allied himself with the party of the Marquis of Rockingham and supported the repeal. But in July 1766, the King dismissed Rockingham, a new ministry was formed, and a new set of American import duties was imposed. From this time on the mutual irritation between the Colonies and England continually worsened until it resulted in open rebelllion and war. Throughout this period Burke urged conciliation with the Colonies, but without success. Of his speeches and pamphlets on American policy John Morley said that "they compose the most perfect manual in our literature, or in any literature, for one who approaches the study of public affairs, whether for knowledge or for practice."

Nations are not primarily ruled by laws: less by violence. Whatever original energy may be supposed either in force or regulation, the operation of both is, in truth, merely instrumental. Nations are governed by the same methods, and on the same principles, by which an individual without authority is often able to govern those who are his equals or his superiors; by a knowledge of their temper, and by a judicious management of it; I mean,—when public affairs are steadily and quietly conducted; not when government is nothing but a continued scuffle between the magistrate and the multitude; in which sometimes the one and sometimes the other is uppermost; in which they alternately yield and prevail, in a series of contemptible victories, and scandalous submissions. The temper of the people amongst whom he presides ought therefore to be the first study of a statesman. And the knowledge of this temper it is by no means impossible for him to attain, if he has not an interest in being ignorant of what it is his duty to learn.

Thoughts on the Cause of the Present Discontents (1770). I, 436.

Taxes for the purpose of raising revenue had hitherto been sparingly attempted in America. Without ever doubting the extent of its lawful power, Parliament always doubted the propriety of such impositions. And the Americans on their part never thought of contesting a right by which they were so little affected. Their assemblies in the main answered all the purposes necessary to the internal economy of a free people, and provided for all the exigencies of government which arose amongst themselves. In the midst of that happy enjoyment, they never thought of critically settling the exact limits of a power, which was necessary to their union, their safety, their equality, and even their liberty. Thus the two very difficult points, superiority in the presiding state, and freedom in the subordinate, were on the whole sufficiently, that is, practically, reconciled; without agitating those vexatious questions, which in truth rather belong to metaphysics than politics, and which can never be moved without shaking the foundations of the best governments that have ever been constituted by human wisdom. By this measure was let loose that dangerous spirit of disquisition, not in the coolness of philosophical inquiry, but inflamed with all the passions of a haughty, resentful people, who thought themselves deeply injured, and that they were contending for everything that was valuable in the world.

Observations on a Late Publication on the Present State of the Nation (1769). I, 385–86.

Whoever goes about to reason on any part of the policy of this country with regard to America, upon the mere abstract principles of government, or even upon those of our own ancient constitution, will be often misled. Those who resort for arguments to the most respectable authorities, ancient or modern, or rest upon the clearest maxims, drawn from the experience of other states and empires, will be liable to the greatest errors imaginable. The object is wholly new in the world. It is singular; it is grown up to this magnitude and importance within the memory of man; nothing in history is parallel to it. All the reasonings about it, that are likely to be at all solid, must be drawn from its actual circumstances. In this new system a principle of commerce, of artificial commerce, must predominate. This commerce must be secured by a multitude of restraints very alien from the spirit of liberty; and a powerful authority must reside in the principal state, in order to enforce them. But the people who are to be the subjects of these restraints are descendants of Englishmen; and of a high and free spirit. To hold over them a government made up of nothing but restraints and penalties, and taxes in the granting of which they can have no share, will neither be wise nor long practicable. People must be governed in a manner agreeable to their temper and disposition; and men of free character and spirit must be ruled with, at least, some condescension to this spirit and this character. The British colonist must see something which will distinguish him from the colonists of other nations.

Those reasonings, which infer from the many restraints under which we have already laid America, to our right to lay it under still more, and indeed under all manner of restraints, are conclusive; conclusive as to right; but the very reverse as to policy and practice. We ought rather to infer from our having laid the colonies under many restraints, that it is reasonable to compensate them by every indulgence that can by any means be reconciled to our interest. We have a great empire to rule, composed of a vast mass of heterogeneous governments, all more or less free and popular in their forms, all to be kept in peace, and kept out of conspiracy, with one another, all to be held in subordination to this country; while the spirit of an extensive and intricate and trading interest pervades the whole, always qualifying, and often controlling, every general idea of constitution and government. It is a great and difficult object; and I wish we may possess wisdom and temper enough to manage it as we ought. Its importance is infinite. . . . This colony intercourse is a new world of commerce in a manner created; it stands upon principles of its own; principles hardly worth endangering for any little consideration of extorted revenue.

The reader sees, that I do not enter so fully into this matter as obviously I might. I have already been led into greater lengths than I intended. It is enough to say, that before the ministers of 1765 had determined to propose the repeal of the Stamp Act in Parliament, they had the whole of the American constitution and commerce very fully before them. They considered maturely; they decided with wisdom: let me add, with firmness. For they resolved, as a preliminary to that repeal, to assert in the fullest and least equivocal terms the unlimited legislative right of this country over its colonies; and, having done this, to propose the repeal, on principles, not of constitutional right, but on those of expediency, of equity, of lenity, and of the true interests present and future of that great object for which alone the colonies were founded, navigation and commerce. This plan I say, required an uncommon degree of firmness, when we consider that some of those persons who might be of the greatest use in promoting the repeal, violently withstood the declaratory act; and they who agreed with administration in the principles of that law, equally made, as well the reasons on which the declaratory act itself stood, as those on which it was opposed, grounds for an opposition to the repeal.

If the then ministry resolved first to declare the right, it was not from any opinion they entertained of its future use in regular taxation. Their opinions were full and declared against the ordinary use of such a power. But it was plain, that the general reasonings which were employed against that power went directly to our whole legislative right; and one part of it could not be yielded to such arguments, without a virtual surrender of all the rest. Besides, if that very specific power of levying money in the colonies were not retained as a sacred trust in the hands of Great Britain (to be used, not in the first instance for supply, but in the last exigence for control), it is obvious, that the presiding authority of Great Britain, as the head, the arbiter, and director of the whole empire, would vanish into an empty name, without operation or energy. With the habitual exercise of such a power in the ordinary course of supply, no trace of freedom could remain to America.[1] If Great Britain were stripped of this right, every principle of unity and subordination in the empire was gone forever. Whether all this can be reconciled in legal speculation, is a matter of no consequence. It is reconciled in policy: and politics ought to be adjusted, not to human reasonings, but to human nature; of which the reason is but a part, and by no means the greatest part.

Founding the repeal on this basis, it was judged proper to lay before Parliament the whole detail of the American affairs, as fully as it had been laid before the ministry themselves. Ignorance of those affairs had misled Parliament. Knowledge alone could bring it into the right road. Every paper of office was laid upon the table of the two Houses; every denomination of men, either of America, or connected with it by office, by residence, by commerce, by interest, even by injury; men of civil and military capacity, officers of the revenue, merchants, manufacturers of every species, and from every town in England, attended at the bar. Such evidence never [before] was laid before Parliament. If an emulation arose among the ministers and members of Parliament, . . . for the repeal of this act, as well as for the other regulations, it was not on the confident assertions, the airy speculations, or the vain promises of ministers, that it arose. It was the sense of Parliament on the evidence before them. No one so much as suspects that ministerial allurements or terrors had any share in it. . . .

Upon these principles was the act repealed, and it produced all the good effect which was expected from it: quiet was restored; trade generally returned to its ancient channels; time and means were furnished for the better strengthening of government there, as well as for recovering, by judicious measures, the affections of

---

[1] I do not here enter into the unsatisfactory disquisition concerning representation real or presumed. I only say, that a great people who have their property, without any reserve, in all cases, disposed of by another people, at an immense distance from them, will not think themselves in the enjoyment of freedom. It will be hard to show to those who are in such a state, which of the usual parts of the definition or description of a free people are applicable to them; and it is neither pleasant nor wise to attempt to prove that they have no right to be comprehended in such a description. [Burke]

the people, had that ministry continued, or had a ministry succeeded with dispositions to improve that opportunity.

Such an administration did not succeed. Instead of profiting of that season of tranquillity, in the very next year they chose to return to measures of the very same nature with those which had been so solemnly condemned; though upon a smaller scale. The effects have been correspondent. America is again in disorder; not indeed in the same degree as formerly, nor anything like it. Such good effects have attended the repeal of the Stamp Act, that the colonies have actually paid the taxes; and they have sought their redress (upon however improper principles) not in their own violence, as formerly; but in the experienced benignity of Parliament. . . . Whether the return to the system of 1764, for raising a revenue in America, the discontents which have ensued in consequence of it, the general suspension of the assemblies in consequence of these discontents, the use of the military power, and the new and dangerous commissions which now hang over them, will produce equally good effects, is greatly to be doubted. Never, I fear, will this nation and the colonies fall back upon their true centre of gravity, and natural point of repose, until the ideas of 1766 are resumed, and steadily pursued.

Observations on a Late Publication on the Present State of the Nation (1769). I, 395–403.

Again, and again, revert to your old principles, seek peace and ensue it,—leave America, if she has taxable matter in her, to tax herself. I am not here going into the distinctions of rights, nor attempting to mark their boundaries. I do not enter into these metaphysical distinctions; I hate the very sound of them. Leave the Americans as they anciently stood, and these distinctions, born of our unhappy contest, will die along with it. They and we, and their and our ancestors, have been happy under that system. Let the memory of all actions in contradiction to that good old mode, on both sides, be extinguished forever. Be content to bind America by laws of trade: you have always done it. Let this be your reason for binding their trade. Do not burden them by taxes: you were not used to do so from the beginning. Let this be your reason for not taxing. These are the arguments of states and kingdoms. Leave the rest to the schools; for there only they may be discussed with safety. But if, intemperately, unwisely, fatally, you sophisticate and poison the very source of government, by urging subtle deductions, and consequences odious to those you govern, from the unlimited and illimitable nature of supreme sovereignty, you will teach them by these means to call that sovereignty itself in question. When you drive him hard, the boar will surely turn upon the hunters. If that sovereignty and their freedom cannot be reconciled, which will they take? They will cast your sovereignty in your face. Nobody will be argued into slavery.

Speech on American Taxation (1774). II, 72–73.

. . . the people of the colonies are descendants of Englishmen. England, Sir, is a nation which still, I hope, respects, and formerly adored, her freedom. The colonists emigrated from you when this part of your character was most predominant; and they took this bias and direction the moment they parted from your hands. They are therefore not only devoted to liberty, but to liberty according to English ideas and on English principles. Abstract liberty, like other mere abstractions, is not to be found. Liberty inheres in some sensible object; and every nation has formed to itself some favorite point, which by way of eminence becomes the criterion of their happiness. It happened, you know, Sir, that the great contests for freedom in this country were from the earliest times chiefly upon the question of taxing. Most of the contests in the ancient commonwealths turned primarily on the right of election of magistrates, or on the balance among the several orders of the state. The question of money was not with them so immediate. But in England it was otherwise. On this point of taxes the ablest pens and most eloquent tongues have been exercised, the greatest spirits have acted and suffered. In order to give the fullest satisfaction concerning the importance of this point, it was not only necessary for those who in argument defended the excellence of the English Constitution to insist on this privilege of granting money as a dry point of fact, and to prove that the right had been acknowledged in ancient parchments and blind usages to reside in a certain body called an House of Commons: they went much further: they attempted to prove, and they succeeded, that in theory it ought to be so, from the particular nature of a House of Commons, as an immediate representative of the people, whether the old records had delivered this oracle or not. They took infinite pains to inculcate, as a fundamental principle, that in all monarchies the people must in effect themselves, mediately or immediately, possess the power of granting their own money, or no shadow of liberty could subsist. The colonies draw from you, as with their life-blood, these ideas and principles. Their love of liberty, as with you, fixed and attached on this specific point of taxing. Liberty might be safe or might be endangered in twenty other particulars without their being much pleased or alarmed. Here they felt its pulse; and as they found that beat, they thought themselves sick or sound. I do not say whether they were right or wrong in applying your general arguments to their own case. It is not easy, indeed, to make a monopoly of theorems and corollaries. The fact is, that they did thus apply those general arguments; and your mode of governing them, whether through lenity or indolence, through wisdom or mistake, confirmed them in the imagination, that they, as well as you, had an interest in these common principles.

Speech on Conciliation with America (1775). II, 120–22.

The capital leading questions on which you must this day decide are these two: First, whether you ought to concede; and secondly, what your concession ought to be. On the first of these questions we have gained (as I have just taken the liberty of observing to you) some ground. But I am sensible that a good deal more is still to be done. Indeed, Sir, to enable us to determine both on the one and the other of these great questions with a firm and precise judgment, I think it may be necessary to consider distinctly the true nature and the peculiar circumstances of the object which we have before us: because, after all our struggle, whether we will or not, we must govern America according to that nature and to those circumstances, and not according to our own imaginations, not according to abstract ideas of right, by no means according to mere general theories of government, the resort to which appears to me, in our present situation, no better than arrant trifling.

Speech on Conciliation with America (1775). II, 108–9.

Sir, I think you must perceive that I am resolved this day to have nothing at all to do with the question of the right of taxation. Some gentlemen startle,—but it is true: I put it totally out of the question. It is less than nothing in my consideration. I do not indeed wonder, nor will you, Sir, that gentlemen of profound learning are fond of displaying it on this profound subject. But my consideration is narrow, confined, and wholly limited to the policy of the question. I do not examine whether the giving away a man's money be a power excepted and reserved out of the general trust of government, and how far all mankind, in all forms of polity, are entitled to an exercise of that right by the charter of Nature,—or whether, on the contrary, a right of taxation is necessarily involved in the general principle of legislation, and inseparable from the ordinary supreme power. These are deep questions, where great names militate against each other, where reason is perplexed, and an appeal to authorities only thickens the confusion: for high and reverend authorities lift up their heads on both sides, and there is no sure footing in the middle. This point is the *great Serbonian bog, betwixt Damiata and Mount Casius old, where armies whole have sunk.* I do not intend to be overwhelmed in that bog, though in such respectable company. The question with me is, not whether you have a right to render your people miserable, but whether it is not your interest to make them happy. It is not what a lawyer tells me I *may* do, but what humanity, reason, and justice tell me I ought to do. Is a politic act the worse for being a generous one? Is no concession proper, but that which is made from your want of right to keep what you grant? Or does it lessen the grace or dignity of relaxing in the exercise of an odious claim, because you have your evidence-room full of titles, and your magazines stuffed with arms to enforce them? What signify all those titles and all those arms? Of what avail are they, when the reason of the thing tells me that the assertion of my title is the loss of my suit, and that I could do nothing but wound myself by the use of my own weapons?

Such is steadfastly my opinion of the absolute necessity of keeping up the concord of this empire by a unity of spirit, though in a diversity of operations, that, if I were sure the colonists had, at their leaving this country, sealed a regular compact of servitude, that they had solemnly abjured all the rights of citizens, that they had made a vow to renounce all ideas of liberty for them and their posterity to all generations, yet I should hold myself obliged to conform to the temper I found universally prevalent in my own day, and to govern two million of men, impatient of servitude, on the principles of freedom. I am not determining a point of law; I am restoring tranquillity; and the general character and situation of a people must determine what sort of government is fitted for them. That point nothing else can or ought to determine.

Speech on Conciliation with America (1775). II, 140–41.

But to clear up my ideas on this subject,—a revenue from America transmitted hither. Do not delude yourselves: you can never receive it,—no, not a shilling. We have experience that from remote countries it is not to be expected. If, when you attempted to extract revenue from Bengal, you were obliged to return in loan what you had taken in imposition, what can you expect from North America? For, certainly, if ever there was a country qualified to produce wealth, it is India; or an institution fit for the transmission, it is the East India Company. America has none of these aptitudes. If America gives you taxable objects on which you lay your duties here, and gives you at the same time a surplus by a foreign sale of her commodities to pay the duties on these objects which you tax at home, she has performed her part to the British revenue. But with regard to her own internal establishments, she may, I doubt not she will, contribute in moderation. I say in moderation; for she ought not to be permitted to exhaust herself. She ought to be reserved to a war; the weight of which, with the enemies that we are most likely to have, must be considerable in her quarter of the globe. There she may serve you, and serve you essentially.

For that service, for all service, whether of revenue, trade, or empire, my trust is in her interest in the British Constitution. My hold of the colonies is in the close affection which grows from common names, from kindred blood, from similar privileges, and equal protection. These are ties which, though light as air, are as strong as links of iron. Let the colonies always keep the idea of their civil rights associated with your government,—they will cling and grapple to you, and no force under heaven will be of power to tear them from their allegiance. But let it be once understood that your government may be one thing and their privileges another, that these two things may exist without any mutual relation,—the cement is gone, the cohesion is loosened, and everything hastens to decay and dissolution. As long as you have the wisdom to keep the sovereign authority of this country as the sanctuary of liberty, the sacred temple consecrated to our common faith, wherever the chosen race and sons of England worship freedom, they will turn their faces towards you. The more they multiply, the more friends you will have; the more ardently they love liberty, the more perfect will be their obedience. Slavery they can have anywhere. It is a weed that grows in every soil. They may have it from Spain, they may have it from Prussia. But, until you become lost to all feeling of your true interest and your natural dignity, freedom they can have from none but you. This is the commodity of price, of which you have the monopoly. This is the true Act of Navigation, which binds to you the commerce of the colonies, and through them secures to you the wealth of the world. Deny them this participation of freedom, and you break that sole bond which originally made, and must still preserve, the unity of the empire. Do not entertain so weak an imagination as that your registers and your bonds, your affidavits and your sufferances, your cockets and your clearances, are what form the great securities of your commerce. Do not dream that your letters of office, and your instructions, and your suspending clauses are the things that hold together the great contexture of this mysterious whole. These things do not make your government. Dead instruments, passive tools as they are, it is the spirit of the English communion that gives all their life and efficacy to them. It is the spirit of the English Constitution, which, infused through the mighty mass, pervades, feeds, unites, invigorates, vivifies every part of the empire, even down to the minutest member.

Is it not the same virtue which does everything for us here in England? Do you imagine, then, that it is the Land-Tax Act which raises your revenue? that it is the annual vote in the Committee of Supply which gives you your army? or that it is the Mutiny Bill which inspires it with bravery and discipline? No! surely, no! It is the love of the people; it is their attachment to their government, from the sense of the deep stake they have in such a glorious institution, which gives you your army and your navy, and infuses into both that liberal obedience without which your army would be a base rabble and your navy nothing but rotten timber.

All this, I know well enough, will sound wild and chimerical to the profane herd of those vulgar and mechanical politicians who have no place among us: a sort of people who think that nothing exists but what is gross and material,—and who, therefore, far from being qualified to be directors of the great movement of empire, are not fit to turn a wheel in the machine. But to men truly initiated and rightly taught, these ruling and master principles, which in the opinion of such men as I have mentioned have no substantial existence, are in truth everything, and all in all. Magnanimity in politics is not seldom the truest wisdom; and a great empire and little minds go ill together. If we are conscious of our situation, and glow with zeal to fill our place as becomes our station and ourselves, we ought to auspicate all our public proceedings on America with the old warning of the Church, *Sursum corda!* [Lift up your hearts!] We ought to elevate our minds to the greatness of that trust to which the order of Providence has called us. By adverting to the dignity of this high calling our ancestors have turned a savage wilderness into a glorious empire, and have made the most extensive and the only honorable conquests, not by destroying, but by promoting the wealth, the number, the happiness of the human race. Let us get an American revenue as we have got an American empire. English privileges have made it all that it is; English privileges alone will make it all it can be.

Speech on Conciliation with America (1775). II, 178–82.

In 1777, when Burke was representing Bristol in the House of Commons, he published a pamphlet, in form a letter to the Sheriffs of Bristol, explaining to his constituents and to the nation his stand on some public questions, especially on the policy toward America. It contains one of his most vigorous vindications of political prudence against the extremes of abstract political theory.

I have always wished, that as the dispute had its apparent origin from things done in Parliament, and as the acts passed there had provoked the war, that the foundations of peace should be laid in Parliament also. I have been astonished to find that those whose zeal for the dignity of our body was so hot as to light up the flames of civil war should even publicly declare that these delicate points ought to be wholly left to the crown. Poorly as I may be thought affected to the authority of Parliament, I shall never admit that our constitutional rights can ever become a matter of ministerial negotiation.

I am charged with being an American. If warm affection towards those over whom I claim any share of authority be a crime, I am guilty of this charge. But I do assure you, (and they who know me publicly and privately will bear witness to me,) that, if ever one man lived more zealous than another for the supremacy of Parliament and the rights of this imperial crown, it was myself. Many others, indeed, might be more knowing in the extent of the foundation of these rights. I do not pretend to be an antiquary, a lawyer, or qualified for the chair of professor in metaphysics. I never ventured to put your solid interests upon speculative

grounds. My having constantly declined to do so has been attributed to my incapacity for such disquisitions; and I am inclined to
believe it is partly the cause. I never shall be ashamed to confess,
that, where I am ignorant, I am diffident. I am, indeed, not very
solicitous to clear myself of this imputed incapacity; because men
even less conversant than I am in this kind of subtleties, and placed
in stations to which I ought not to aspire, have, by the mere force
of civil discretion, often conducted the affairs of great nations with
distinguished felicity and glory.

When I first came into a public trust, I found your Parliament in
possession of an unlimited legislative power over the colonies. I
could not open the statute-book without seeing the actual exercise
of it, more or less, in all cases whatsoever. This possession passed
with me for a title. It does so in all human affairs. No man examines
into the defects of his title to his paternal estate or to his established government. Indeed, common sense taught me that a legislative authority not actually limited by the express terms of its
foundation, or by its own subsequent acts, cannot have its powers
parcelled out by argumentative distinctions, so as to enable us to
say that here they can and there they cannot bind. Nobody was so
obliging as to produce to me any record of such distinctions, by
compact or otherwise, either at the successive formation of the
several colonies or during the existence of any of them. If any gentlemen were able to see how one power could be given up (merely
on abstract reasoning) without giving up the rest, I can only say
that they saw further than I could. Nor did I ever presume to condemn any one for being clear-sighted when I was blind. I praise
their penetration and learning, and hope that their practice has
been correspondent to their theory.

I had, indeed, very earnest wishes to keep the whole body of
this authority perfect and entire as I found it,—and to keep it so,
not for our advantage solely, but principally for the sake of those
on whose account all just authority exists: I mean the people to
be governed. For I thought I saw that many cases might well happen in which the exercise of every power comprehended in the
broadest idea of legislature might become, in its time and circumstances, not a little expedient for the peace and union of the colonies amongst themselves, as well as for their perfect harmony with
Great Britain. Thinking so, (perhaps erroneously, but being honestly of that opinion,) I was at the same time very sure that the

authority of which I was so jealous could not, under the actual circumstances of our plantations, be at all preserved in any of its members, but by the greatest reserve in its application, particularly in those delicate points in which the feelings of mankind are the most irritable. They who thought otherwise have found a few more difficulties in their work than (I hope) they were thoroughly aware of, when they undertook the present business. I must beg leave to observe, that it is not only the invidious branch of taxation that will be resisted, but that no other given part of legislative rights can be exercised, without regard to the general opinion of those who are to be governed. That general opinion is the vehicle and organ of legislative omnipotence. Without this, it may be a theory to entertain the mind, but it is nothing in the direction of affairs. The completeness of the legislative authority of Parliament *over this kingdom* is not questioned; and yet many things indubitably included in the abstract idea of that power, and which carry no absolute injustice in themselves, yet being contrary to the opinions and feelings of the people, can as little be exercised as if Parliament in that case had been possessed of no right at all. I see no abstract reason, which can be given, why the same power which made and repealed the High Commission Court and the Star-Chamber might not revive them again; and these courts, warned by their former fate, might possibly exercise their powers with some degree of justice. But the madness would be as unquestionable as the competence of that Parliament which should attempt such things. If anything can be supposed out of the power of human legislature, it is religion; I admit, however, that the established religion of this country has been three or four times altered by act of Parliament, and therefore that a statute binds even in that case. But we may very safely affirm, that, notwithstanding this apparent omnipotence, it would be now found as impossible for King and Parliament to alter the established religion of this country as it was to King James alone, when he attempted to make such an alteration without a Parliament. In effect, to follow, not to force, the public inclination,—to give a direction, a form, a technical dress, and a specific sanction, to the general sense of the community, is the true end of legislature.

It is so with regard to the exercise of all the powers which our Constitution knows in any of its parts, and indeed to the substantial existence of any of the parts themselves. The king's negative to bills is one of the most indisputed of the royal prerogatives; and it extends to all cases whatsoever. I am far from certain, that if several laws, which I know, had fallen under the stroke of that sceptre, that the public would have had a very heavy loss. But it is not the *propriety* of the exercise which is in question. The exercise itself is wisely forborne. Its repose may be the preservation of its existence; and its existence may be the means of saving the Constitution itself, on an occasion worthy of bringing it forth.

As the disputants whose accurate and logical reasonings have brought us into our present condition think it absurd that powers or members of any constitution should exist, rarely, if ever, to be exercised, I hope I shall be excused in mentioning another instance that is material. We know that the Convocation of the Clergy had formerly been called, and sat with nearly as much regularity to business as Parliament itself. It is now called for form only. It sits for the purpose of making some polite ecclesiastical compliments to the king, and, when that grace is said, retires and is heard of no more. It is, however, *a part of the Constitution,* and may be called out into act and energy, whenever there is occasion, and whenever those who conjure up that spirit will choose to abide the consequences. It is wise to permit its legal existence: it is much wiser to continue it a legal existence only. So truly has prudence (constituted as the god of this lower world) the entire dominion over every exercise of power committed into its hands! And yet I have lived to see prudence and conformity to circumstances wholly set at nought in our late controversies, and treated as if they were the most contemptible and irrational of all things. I have heard it an hundred times very gravely alleged, that, in order to keep power in wind, it was necessary, by preference, to exert it in those very points in which it was most likely to be resisted and the least likely to be productive of any advantage.

These were the considerations, Gentlemen, which led me early to think, that, in the comprehensive dominion which the Divine Providence had put into our hands, instead of troubling our understandings with speculations concerning the unity of empire and the identity or distinction of legislative powers, and inflaming our passions with the heat and pride of controversy, it was our duty, in all soberness, to conform our government to the character and circumstances of the several people who composed this mighty and strangely diversified mass. I never was wild enough to conceive that one method would serve for the whole, that the natives of Hindostan and those of Virginia could be ordered in the same manner, or that the Cutchery court and the grand jury of Salem could be regulated on a similar plan. I was persuaded that government was a practical thing, made for the happiness of mankind, and not to furnish out a spectacle of uniformity to gratify the schemes of visionary politicians. Our business was to rule, not to wrangle; and it would have been a poor compensation that we had triumphed in a dispute, whilst we lost an empire.

If there be one fact in the world perfectly clear, it is this,—"that the disposition of the people of America is wholly averse to any other than a free government"; and this is indication enough to any honest statesman how he ought to adapt whatever power he finds in his hands to their case. If any ask me what a free government is, I answer, that, for any practical purpose, it is what the people think so,—and that they, and not I, are the natural, lawful, and competent judges of this matter. If they practically allow me a greater degree of authority over them than is consistent with any correct ideas of perfect freedom, I ought to thank them for so great a trust, and not to endeavor to prove from thence that they have reasoned amiss, and that, having gone so far, by analogy they must hereafter have no enjoyment but by my pleasure.

If we had seen this done by any others, we should have concluded them far gone in madness. It is melancholy, as well as ridiculous, to observe the kind of reasoning with which the public has been amused, in order to divert our minds from the common sense of our American policy. There are people who have split and anatomized the doctrine of free government, as if it were an abstract question concerning metaphysical liberty and necessity, and not a matter of moral prudence and natural feeling. They have disputed whether liberty be a positive or a negative idea; whether it does not consist in being governed by laws, without considering what are the laws, or who are the makers; whether man has any rights by Nature; and whether all the property he enjoys be not the alms of his government, and his life itself their favor and indulgence. Others, corrupting religion as these have perverted philosophy, contend that Christians are redeemed into captivity, and the blood of the Saviour of mankind has been shed to make them the slaves of a few proud and insolent sinners. These shocking extremes provoking to extremes of another kind, speculations are

let loose as destructive to all authority as the former are to all freedom; and every government is called tyranny and usurpation
which is not formed on their fancies. In this manner the stirrers-up
of this contention, not satisfied with distracting our dependencies
and filling them with blood and slaughter, are corrupting our understandings: they are endeavoring to tear up, along with practical
liberty, all the foundations of human society, all equity and justice,
religion and order.

Civil freedom, Gentlemen, is not, as many have endeavored to
persuade you, a thing that lies hid in the depth of abstruse science.
It is a blessing and a benefit, not an abstract speculation; and all
the just reasoning that can be upon it is of so coarse a texture as
perfectly to suit the ordinary capacities of those who are to enjoy,
and of those who are to defend it. Far from any resemblance to
those propositions in geometry and metaphysics which admit no
medium, but must be true or false in all their latitude, social and
civil freedom, like all other things in common life, are variously
mixed and modified, enjoyed in very different degrees, and shaped
into an infinite diversity of forms, according to the temper and circumstances of every community. The *extreme* of liberty (which is
its abstract perfection, but its real fault) obtains nowhere, nor
ought to obtain anywhere; because extremes, as we all know, in
every point which relates either to our duties or satisfactions in
life, are destructive both to virtue and enjoyment. Liberty, too,
must be limited in order to be possessed. The degree of restraint
it is impossible in any case to settle precisely. But it ought to be
the constant aim of every wise public counsel to find out by cautious experiments, and rational, cool endeavors, with how little,
not how much, of this restraint the community can subsist: for
liberty is a good to be improved, and not an evil to be lessened. It
is not only a private blessing of the first order, but the vital spring
and energy of the state itself, which has just so much life and
vigor as there is liberty in it. But whether liberty be advantageous
or not, (for I know it is a fashion to decry the very principle,)
none will dispute that peace is a blessing; and peace must, in the
course of human affairs, be frequently bought by some indulgence
and toleration at least to liberty: for, as the Sabbath (though of
divine institution) was made for man, not man for the Sabbath,
government, which can claim no higher origin or authority, in its
exercise at least, ought to conform to the exigencies of the time,

and the temper and character of the people with whom it is concerned, and not always to attempt violently to bend the people to their theories of subjection. The bulk of mankind, on their part, are not excessively curious concerning any theories whilst they are really happy; and one sure symptom of an ill-conducted state is the propensity of the people to resort to them.

But when subjects, by a long course of such ill conduct, are once thoroughly inflamed, and the state itself violently distempered, the people must have some satisfaction to their feelings more solid than a sophistical speculation on law and government. Such was our situation: and such a satisfaction was necessary to prevent recourse to arms; it was necessary towards laying them down; it will be necessary to prevent the taking them up again and again. Of what nature this satisfaction ought to be I wish it had been the disposition of Parliament seriously to consider. It was certainly a deliberation that called for the exertion of all their wisdom.

I am, and ever have been, deeply sensible of the difficulty of reconciling the strong presiding power, that is so useful towards the conservation of a vast, disconnected, infinitely diversified empire, with that liberty and safety of the provinces which they must enjoy, (in opinion and practice at least,) or they will not be provinces at all. I know, and have long felt, the difficulty of reconciling the unwieldy haughtiness of a great ruling nation, habituated to command, pampered by enormous wealth, and confident from a long course of prosperity and victory, to the high spirit of free dependencies, animated with the first glow and activity of juvenile heat, and assuming to themselves, as their birthright, some part of that very pride which oppresses them. They who perceive no difficulty in reconciling these tempers (which, however, to make peace, must some way or other be reconciled) are much above my capacity, or much below the magnitude of the business. Of one thing I am perfectly clear: that it is not by deciding the suit, but by compromising the difference, that peace can be restored or kept. They who would put an end to such quarrels by declaring roundly in favor of the whole demands of either party have mistaken, in my humble opinion, the office of a mediator. . . .

At the first fatal opening of this contest, the wisest course seemed to be to put an end as soon as possible to the immediate causes of the dispute, and to quiet a discussion, not easily settled upon clear principles, and arising from claims which pride would permit neither party to abandon, by resorting as nearly as possible to the old, successful course. A mere repeal of the obnoxious tax, with a declaration of the legislative authority of this kingdom, was then fully sufficient to procure peace to *both sides*. Man is a creature of habit, and, the first breach being of very short continuance, the colonies fell back exactly into their ancient state. The Congress has used an expression with regard to this pacification which appears to me truly significant. After the repeal of the Stamp Act, "the colonies fell," says this assembly, "into their ancient state of *unsuspecting confidence in the mother country*." This unsuspecting confidence is the true centre of gravity amongst mankind, about which all the parts are at rest. It is this *unsuspecting confidence* that removes all difficulties, and reconciles all the contradictions which occur in the complexity of all ancient puzzled political establishments. Happy are the rulers which have the secret of preserving it!

The whole empire has reason to remember with eternal gratitude the wisdom and temper of that man [the Marquis of Rockingham] and his excellent associates, who, to recover this confidence, formed a plan of pacification in 1766. That plan, being built upon the nature of man, and the circumstances and habits of the two countries, and not on any visionary speculations, perfectly answered its end, as long as it was thought proper to adhere to it. Without giving a rude shock to the dignity (well or ill understood) of this Parliament, they gave perfect content to our dependencies. Had it not been for the mediatorial spirit and talents of that great man between such clashing pretensions and passions, we should then have rushed headlong (I know what I say) into the calamities of that civil war in which, by departing from his system, we are at length involved; and we should have been precipitated into that war at a time when circumstances both at home and abroad were far, very far, more unfavorable unto us than they were at the breaking out of the present troubles.

I had the happiness of giving my first votes in Parliament for that pacification. I was one of those almost unanimous members who, in the necessary concessions of Parliament, would as much as possible have preserved its authority and respected its honor. I could not at once tear from my heart prejudices which were dear to me, and which bore a resemblance to virtue. I had then, and I have still, my partialities. What Parliament gave up I wished to be given as of grace and favor and affection, and not as a restitution of stolen goods. High dignity relented as it was soothed; and a benignity from old acknowledged greatness had its full effect on our dependencies. Our unlimited declaration of legislative authority produced not a single murmur. If this undefined power has become odious since that time, and full of horror to the colonies, it is because the *unsuspicious confidence* is lost, and the parental affection, in the bosom of whose boundless authority they reposed their privileges, is become estranged and hostile.

It will be asked, if such was then my opinion of the mode of pacification, how I came to be the very person who moved, not only for a repeal of all the late coercive statutes, but for mutilating, by a positive law, the entireness of the legislative power of Parliament, and cutting off from it the whole right of taxation. I answer, Because a different state of things requires a different conduct. When the dispute had gone to these last extremities, (which no man labored more to prevent than I did,) the concessions which had satisfied in the beginning could satisfy no longer; because the violation of tacit faith required explicit security. The same cause which has introduced all formal compacts and covenants among men made it necessary: I mean habits of soreness, jealousy, and distrust. I parted with it as with a limb, but as a limb to save the body: and I would have parted with more, if more had been necessary; anything rather than a fruitless, hopeless, unnatural civil war. This mode of yielding would, it is said, give way to independency without a war. I am persuaded, from the nature of things, and from every information, that it would have had a directly contrary effect. But if it had this effect, I confess that I should prefer independency without war to independency with it; and I have so much trust in the inclinations and prejudices of mankind, and so little in anything else, that I should expect ten times more benefit to this kingdom from the affection of America, though under a separate establishment, than from her perfect submission to the crown and Parliament, accompanied with her terror, disgust, and abhorrence. Bodies tied together by so unnatural a bond of union as mutual hatred are only connected to their ruin.

Letter to the Sheriffs of Bristol (1777). II, 222–36.

It were better to forget, once for all, the *encyclopédie* and the whole body of [French] economists, and to revert to those old rules and principles which have hitherto made princes great, and nations happy. . . . A wise prince, as I hope the emperor is, will study the genius of his people. He will indulge them in their humors, he will preserve them in their privileges, he will act upon the circumstances of his states as he finds them, and whilst thus acting upon the practical principles of a practical policy, he is the happy prince of a happy people. He will not care what the Condorcet and the Raynal, and the whole flight of the magpies and jays of philosophy, may fancy and chatter concerning his conduct and character.

Letter to the Chevalier de Rivarol, June 1, 1791.
Correspondence. III, 210–11.

The operation of dangerous and delusive first principles obliges us to have recourse to the true ones. In the intercourse between nations, we are apt to rely too much on the instrumental part. We lay too much weight upon the formality of treaties and compacts. We do not act much more wisely, when we trust to the interests of men as guaranties of their engagements. The interests frequently tear to pieces the engagements, and the passions trample upon both. Entirely to trust to either is to disregard our own safety, or not to know mankind. Men are not tied to one another by papers and seals. They are led to associate by resemblances, by conformities, by sympathies. It is with nations as with individuals. Nothing is so strong a tie of amity between nation and nation as correspondence in laws, customs, manners, and habits of life. They have more than the force of treaties in themselves. They are obligations written in the heart. They approximate men to men without their knowledge, and sometimes against their intentions. The secret, unseen, but irrefragable bond of habitual intercourse holds them together, even when their perverse and litigious nature sets them to equivocate, scuffle, and fight about the terms of their written obligations.

As to war, if it be the means of wrong and violence, it is the sole means of justice among nations. Nothing can banish it from the world. They who say otherwise, intending to impose upon us, do not impose upon themselves. But it is one of the greatest objects of human wisdom to mitigate those evils which we are unable to remove. The conformity and analogy of which I speak, incapable, like everything else, of preserving perfect trust and tranquillity among men, has a strong tendency to facilitate accommodation, and to produce a generous oblivion of the rancor of their quarrels. With this similitude, peace is more of peace, and war is less of war. I will go further. There have been periods of time in which communities apparently in peace with each other have been more perfectly separated than in later times many nations in Europe have been in the course of long and bloody wars. The cause must be sought in the similitude throughout Europe of religion, laws, and manners. At bottom, these are all the same. The writers on public law have often called this *aggregate* of nations a commonwealth. They had reason. It is virtually one great state, having the same basis of general law, with some diversity of provincial customs and local establishments. The nations of Europe have had the very same Christian religion, agreeing in the fundamental parts, varying a little in the ceremonies and in the subordinate doctrines. The whole of the polity and economy of every country in Europe has been derived from the same sources. It was drawn from the old Germanic or Gothic Customary,—from the feudal institutions, which must be considered as an emanation from that Customary; and the whole has been improved and digested into system and discipline by the Roman law. From hence arose the several orders, with or without a monarch, (which are called States) in every European country; the strong traces of which, where monarchy predominated, were never wholly extinguished or merged in despotism. In the few places where monarchy was cast off, the spirit of European monarchy was still left. Those countries still continued countries of States,—that is, of classes, orders, and distinctions, such as had before subsisted, or nearly so. Indeed, the force and form of the institution called States continued in greater perfection in those republican communities than under monarchies. From all these sources arose a system of manners and of education which was nearly similar in all this quarter of the globe,—and which softened, blended, and harmonized the colors of the whole. There was little difference in the form of the universities for the education of their youth, whether with regard to faculties, to sciences, or to the more liberal and elegant kinds of erudition. From this resemblance in the modes of intercourse, and in the whole form and fashion of life, no citizen of Europe could be altogether an exile in any part of it. There was nothing more than a pleasing variety to recreate and instruct the mind, to enrich the imagination, and to meliorate the heart. When a man travelled or resided, for health, pleasure, business, or necessity, from his own country, he never felt himself quite abroad.

First Letter on a Regicide Peace (1796). V, 317–20.

2. Religion and the State

Among the reforms of the French Revolution were the abolition of the State Church and the heavy confiscation of church property. Burke objected to confiscation as a tyrannical and disrupting sin against economic and social stability (see Chapter VII, section 2). But he was also moved to protest against the antireligious philosophy of the prophets and leaders of the French Revolution. Such professed atheists and materialists as Helvetius, d'Holbach, and Diderot, had prepared the way for hostility, not only toward the Roman Catholic Church, but toward any religion. Burke had been familiar with their books and teachings ever since his visit to Paris in 1774. In his criticism of the French Revolution he undertook to defend religion as a constituent element of human nature and society. He was happy to point to the important place of the Church Establishment in the national life of England.

We know, and, what is better, we feel inwardly, that religion is the basis of civil society, and the source of all good, and of all comfort.[2] In England we are so convinced of this, that there is no

[2] Sit igitur hoc ab initio persuasum civibus, dominos esse omnium rerum ac moderatores deos; eaque, quæ gerantur, eorum geri vi, ditione, ac numine; eosdemque optime de genere hominum mereri; et qualis quisque sit, quid agat, quid in se admittat, qua mente, qua pietate colat religiones intueri: piorum et impiorum habere rationem. His enim rebus imbutæ mentes haud sane abhorrebunt ab utili et a vera sententia.—Cic. de Legibus, l. 2. [Burke]

["Therefore we must persuade our citizens that it is a basic truth that the gods are lords and rulers over all things, and that all that is done is by their judgment and command, that they are the benefactors of man, and that they observe the character of every person, what he does, how he indulges himself in wrong-doing, whether he performs his religious duties with piety, taking note of the pious and the impious. Minds imbued with such conceptions we may be sure will not shrink from true and useful opinions."]

rust of superstition, with which the accumulated absurdity of the human mind might have crusted it over in the course of ages, that ninety-nine in a hundred of the people of England would not prefer to impiety. We shall never be such fools as to call in an enemy to the substance of any system to remove its corruptions, to supply its defects, or to perfect its construction. If our religious tenets should ever want a further elucidation, we shall not call on Atheism to explain them. We shall not light up our temple from that unhallowed fire. It will be illuminated with other lights. It will be perfumed with other incense than the infectious stuff which is imported by the smugglers of adulterated metaphysics. If our ecclesiastical establishment should want a revision, it is not avarice or rapacity, public or private, that we shall employ for the audit or receipt or application of its consecrated revenue. Violently condemning neither the Greek nor the Armenian, nor, since heats are subsided, the Roman system of religion, we prefer the Protestant: not because we think it has less of the Christian religion in it, but because, in our judgment, it has more. We are Protestants, not from indifference, but from zeal.

We know, and it is our pride to know, that man is by his constitution a religious animal; that atheism is against, not only our reason, but our instincts; and that it cannot prevail long. But if, in the moment of riot, and in a drunken delirium from the hot spirit drawn out of the alembic of hell, which in France is now so furiously boiling, we should uncover our nakedness, by throwing off that Christian religion which has hitherto been our boast and comfort, and one great source of civilization amongst us, and among many other nations, we are apprehensive (being well aware that the mind will not endure a void) that some uncouth, pernicious, and degrading superstition might take place of it.

For that reason, before we take from our establishment the natural, human means of estimation, and give it up to contempt, as you have done, and in doing it have incurred the penalties you well deserve to suffer, we desire that some other may be presented to us in the place of it. We shall then form our judgment.

On these ideas, instead of quarrelling with establishments, as some do, who have made a philosophy and a religion of their hostility to such institutions, we cleave closely to them. We are resolved to keep an established church, an established monarchy, an established aristocracy, and an established democracy, each in the degree it exists, and in no greater. I shall show you presently how much of each of these we possess.

It has been the misfortune (not, as these gentlemen think it, the glory) of this age, that everything is to be discussed, as if the Constitution of our country were to be always a subject rather of altercation than enjoyment. For this reason, as well as for the satisfaction of those among you (if any such you have among you) who may wish to profit of examples, I venture to trouble you with a few thoughts upon each of these establishments. I do not think they were unwise in ancient Rome, who, when they wished to new-model their laws, sent commissioners to examine the best-constituted republics within their reach.

First I beg leave to speak of our Church Establishment, which is the first of our prejudices,—not a prejudice destitute of reason, but involving in it profound and extensive wisdom. I speak of it first. It is first, and last, and midst in our minds. For, taking ground on that religious system of which we are now in possession, we continue to act on the early received and uniformly continued sense of mankind. That sense not only, like a wise architect, hath built up the august fabric of states, but, like a provident proprietor, to preserve the structure from profanation and ruin, as a sacred temple, purged from all the impurities of fraud and violence and injustice and tyranny, hath solemnly and forever consecrated the commonwealth, and all that officiate in it. This consecration is made, that all who administer in the government of men, in which they stand in the person of God Himself, should have high and worthy notions of their function and destination; that their hope should be full of immortality; that they should not look to the paltry pelf of the moment, nor to the temporary and transient praise of the vulgar, but to a solid, permanent existence, in the permanent part of their nature, and to a permanent fame and glory, in the example they leave as a rich inheritance to the world.

Such sublime principles ought to be infused into persons of exalted situations, and religious establishments provided that may continually revive and enforce them. Every sort of moral, every sort of civil, every sort of politic institution, aiding the rational and natural ties that connect the human understanding and affections to the divine, are not more than necessary, in order to build up that wonderful structure, Man,—whose prerogative it is, to be in a great degree a creature of his own making, and who, when made as he ought to be made, is destined to hold no trivial place in the creation. But whenever man is put over men, as the better nature ought ever to preside, in that case more particularly he should as nearly as possible be approximated to his perfection.

The consecration of the state by a state religious establishment is necessary also to operate with a wholesome awe upon free citizens; because, in order to secure their freedom, they must enjoy some determinate portion of power. To them, therefore, a religion connected with the state, and with their duty towards it, becomes even more necessary than in such societies where the people, by the terms of their subjection, are confined to private sentiments, and the management of their own family concerns. All persons possessing any portion of power ought to be strongly and awfully impressed with an idea that they act in trust, and that they are to account for their conduct in that trust to the one great Master, Author, and Founder of society.

This principle ought even to be more strongly impressed upon the minds of those who compose the collective sovereignty than upon those of single princes. Without instruments, these princes can do nothing. Whoever uses instruments, in finding helps, finds also impediments. Their power is therefore by no means complete; nor are they safe in extreme abuse. Such persons, however elevated by flattery, arrogance, and self-opinion, must be sensible, that, whether covered or not by positive law, in some way or other they are accountable even here for the abuse of their trust. If they are not cut off by a rebellion of their people, they may be strangled by the very janissaries kept for their security against all other rebellion. Thus we have seen the king of France sold by his soldiers for an increase of pay. But where popular authority is absolute and unrestrained, the people have an infinitely greater, because a far better founded, confidence in their own power. They are themselves in a great measure their own instruments. They are nearer to their objects. Besides, they are less under responsibility to one of the greatest controlling powers on earth, the sense of fame and estimation. The share of infamy that is likely to fall to the lot of each individual in public acts is small indeed: the operation of opinion being in the inverse ratio to the numbers of those who abuse power. Their own approbation of their own acts has to them the appearance of a public judgment in their favor. A perfect democracy is therefore the most shameless thing in the world. As it is the most shameless, it is also the most fearless. No man apprehends in his person that he can be made subject to punishment. Certainly the people at large never ought: for, as all punishments are for example towards the conservation of the people at large, the people at large can never become the subject of punishment by any human hand.[3] It is therefore of infinite importance that they should not be suffered to imagine that their will, any more than that of kings, is the standard of right and wrong. They ought to be persuaded that they are full as little entitled, and far less qualified, with safety to themselves, to use any arbitrary power whatsoever; that therefore they are not, under a false show of liberty, but in truth to exercise an unnatural, inverted domination, tyrannically to exact from those who officiate in the state, not an entire devotion to their interest, which is their right, but an abject submission to their occasional will: extinguishing thereby, in all those who serve them, all moral principle, all sense of dignity, all use of judgment, and all consistency of character; whilst by the very same process they give themselves up a proper, a suitable, but a most contemptible prey to the servile ambition of popular sycophants or courtly flatterers.

When the people have emptied themselves of all the lust of selfish will, which without religion it is utterly impossible they ever should,—when they are conscious that they exercise, and exercise perhaps in a higher link of the order of delegation, the power which to be legitimate must be according to that eternal, immutable law in which will and reason are the same,—they will be more careful how they place power in base and incapable hands. In their nomination to office, they will not appoint to the exercise of authority as to a pitiful job, but as to a holy function; not according to their sordid, selfish interest, nor to their wanton caprice, nor to their arbitrary will; but they will confer that power (which any man may well tremble to give or to receive) on those only in whom they may discern that predominant pro-

---

[3] Quicquid multis peccatur inultum. [Burke] ["When whole multitudes join (in mutiny) the guilt goes unpunished." Lucan *Pharsalia* v.260.]

portion of active virtue and wisdom, taken together and fitted to the charge, such as in the great and inevitable mixed mass of human imperfections and infirmities is to be found.

When they are habitually convinced that no evil can be acceptable, either in the act or the permission, to Him whose essence is good, they will be better able to extirpate out of the minds of all magistrates, civil, ecclesiastical, or military, anything that bears the least resemblance to a proud and lawless domination.

But one of the first and most leading principles on which the commonwealth and the laws are consecrated is lest the temporary possessors and life-renters in it, unmindful of what they have received from their ancestors, or of what is due to their posterity, should act as if they were the entire masters; that they should not think it amongst their rights to cut off the entail or commit waste on the inheritance, by destroying at their pleasure the whole original fabric of their society: hazarding to leave to those who come after them a ruin instead of an habitation,—and teaching these successors as little to respect their contrivances as they had themselves respected the institutions of their forefathers. By this unprincipled facility of changing the state as often and as much and in as many ways as there are floating fancies or fashions, the whole chain and continuity of the commonwealth would be broken; no one generation could link with the other; men would become little better than the flies of a summer.

And first of all, the science of jurisprudence, the pride of the human intellect, which, with all its defects, redundancies, and errors, is the collected reason of ages, combining the principles of original justice with the infinite variety of human concerns, as a heap of old exploded errors, would be no longer studied. Personal self-sufficiency and arrogance (the certain attendants upon all those who have never experienced a wisdom greater than their own) would usurp the tribunal. Of course no certain laws, establishing invariable grounds of hope and fear, would keep the actions of men in a certain course, or direct them to a certain end. Nothing stable in the modes of holding property or exercising function could form a solid ground on which any parent could speculate in the education of his offspring, or in a choice for their future establishment in the world. No principles would be early worked into the habits. As soon as the most able instructor had completed his laborious course of institution, instead of sending forth his pupil accomplished in a virtuous discipline fitted to procure him attention and respect in his place in society, he would find everything altered, and that he had turned out a poor creature to the contempt and derision of the world, ignorant of the true grounds of estimation. Who would insure a tender and delicate sense of honor to beat almost with the first pulses of the heart, when no man could know what would be the test of honor in a nation continually varying the standard of its coin? No part of life would retain its acquisitions. Barbarism with regard to science and literature, unskilfulness with regard to arts and manufactures, would infallibly succeed to the want of a steady education and settled principle; and thus the commonwealth itself would in a few generations crumble away, be disconnected into the dust and powder of individuality, and at length dispersed to all the winds of heaven.

To avoid, therefore, the evils of inconstancy and versatility, ten thousand times worse than those of obstinacy and the blindest prejudice, we have consecrated the state, that no man should approach to look into its defects or corruptions but with due caution; that he should never dream of beginning its reformation by its subversion; that he should approach to the faults of the state as to the wounds of a father, with pious awe and trembling solicitude. By this wise prejudice we are taught to look with horror on those children of their country who are prompt rashly to hack that aged parent in pieces and put him into the kettle of magicians, in hopes that by their poisonous weeds and wild incantations they may regenerate the paternal constitution and renovate their father's life.

Society is, indeed, a contract. Subordinate contracts for objects of mere occasional interest may be dissolved at pleasure; but the state ought not to be considered as nothing better than a partnership agreement in a trade of pepper and coffee, calico or tobacco, or some other such low concern, to be taken up for a little temporary interest, and to be dissolved by the fancy of the parties. It is to be looked on with other reverence; because it is not a partnership in things subservient only to the gross animal existence of a temporary and perishable nature. It is a partnership in all science, a partnership in all art, a partnership in every virtue and in all perfection. As the ends of such a partnership cannot be obtained in many generations, it becomes a partnership not only between those who are living, but between those who are living, those who are dead, and those who are to be born. Each contract of each particular state is but a clause in the great primeval contract of eternal society, linking the lower with the higher natures, connecting the visible and invisible world, according to a fixed compact sanctioned by the inviolable oath which holds all physical and all moral natures each in their appointed place. This law is not subject to the will of those who, by an obligation above them, and infinitely superior, are bound to submit their will to that law. The municipal corporations of that universal kingdom are not morally at liberty, at their pleasure, and on their speculations of a contingent improvement, wholly to separate and tear asunder the bands of their subordinate community, and to dissolve it into an unsocial, uncivil, unconnected chaos of elementary principles. It is the first and supreme necessity only, a necessity that is not chosen, but chooses, a necessity paramount to deliberation, that admits no discussion and demands no evidence, which alone can justify a resort to anarchy. This necessity is no exception to the rule; because this necessity itself is a part, too, of that moral and physical disposition of things to which man must be obedient by consent or force: but if that which is only submission to necessity should be made the object of choice, the law is broken, Nature is disobeyed, and the rebellious are outlawed, cast forth, and exiled, from this world of reason, and order, and peace, and virtue, and fruitful penitence, into the antagonist world of madness, discord, vice, confusion, and unavailing sorrow.

These, my dear Sir, are, were, and, I think, long will be, the sentiments of not the least learned and reflecting part of this kingdom. They who are included in this description form their opinions on such grounds as such persons ought to form them. The less inquiring receive them from an authority which those whom Providence dooms to live on trust need not be ashamed to rely on. These two sorts of men move in the same direction, though in a different place. They both move with the order of the universe. They all know or feel this great ancient truth:—

"*Quod illi principi et præpotenti Deo quiomnem hunc mundum regit nihil eorum quæ quidem fiant in terris acceptius quam concilia et cœtus hominum jure sociati quæ civitates appellantur.*"

["For nothing done on earth is more pleasing to that supreme
God who rules the whole universe than the assemblies and
gatherings of men associated in justice which are called governments." Cicero *De Republica* vi.13.] They take this tenet of the
head and heart, not from the great name which it immediately
bears, nor from the greater from whence it is derived, but from
that which alone can give true weight and sanction to any learned
opinion, the common nature and common relation of men. Persuaded that all things ought to be done with reference, and
referring all to the point of reference to which all should be
directed, they think themselves bound, not only as individuals in
the sanctuary of the heart, or as congregated in that personal
capacity, to renew the memory of their high origin and cast,
but also in their corporate character to perform their national
homage to the Institutor and Author and Protector of civil society, without which civil society man could not by any possibility arrive at the perfection of which his nature is capable,
nor even make a remote and faint approach to it. They conceive that He who gave our nature to be perfected by our virtue
willed also the necessary means of its perfection: He willed,
therefore, the state: He willed its connection with the source
and original archetype of all perfection. They who are convinced
of this His will, which is the law of laws and the sovereign of
sovereigns, cannot think it reprehensible that this our corporate
fealty and homage, that this our recognition of a signiory paramount, I had almost said this oblation of the state itself, as a
worthy offering on the high altar of universal praise, should be
performed, as all public, solemn acts are performed, in buildings, in music, in decoration, in speech, in the dignity of persons,
according to the customs of mankind, taught by their nature,—
that is, with modest splendor, with unassuming state, with mild
majesty and sober pomp. For those purposes they think some
part of the wealth of the country is as usefully employed as it
can be in fomenting the luxury of individuals. It is the public
ornament. It is the public consolation. It nourishes the public
hope. The poorest man finds his own importance and dignity in
it, whilst the wealth and pride of individuals at every moment
makes the man of humble rank and fortune sensible of his in-
feriority, and degrades and vilifies his condition. It is for the man
in humble life, and to raise his nature, and to put him in mind

of a state in which the privileges of opulence will cease, when he will be equal by nature, and may be more than equal by virtue, that this portion of the general wealth of his country is employed and sanctified.

I assure you I do not aim at singularity. I give you opinions which have been accepted amongst us, from very early times to this moment, with a continued and general approbation, and which, indeed, are so worked into my mind that I am unable to distinguish what I have learned from others from the results of my own meditation.

It is on some such principles that the majority of the people of England, far from thinking a religious national establishment unlawful, hardly think it lawful to be without one. In France you are wholly mistaken, if you do not believe us above all other things attached to it, and beyond all other nations; and when this people has acted unwisely and unjustifiably in its favor, (as in some instances they have done, most certainly,) in their very errors you will at least discover their zeal.

This principle runs through the whole system of their polity. They do not consider their Church establishment as convenient, but as essential to their state: not as a thing heterogeneous and separable,—something added for accommodation,—what they may either keep up or lay aside, according to their temporary ideas of convenience. They consider it as the foundation of their whole Constitution, with which, and with every part of which, it holds an indissoluble union. Church and State are ideas inseparable in their minds, and scarcely is the one ever mentioned without mentioning the other.

Our education is so formed as to confirm and fix this impression. Our education is in a manner wholly in the hands of ecclesiastics, and in all stages from infancy to manhood. Even when our youth, leaving schools and universities, enter that most important period of life which begins to link experience and study together, and when with that view they visit other countries, instead of old domestics whom we have seen as governors to principal men from other parts, three fourths of those who go abroad with our young nobility and gentlemen are ecclesiastics: not as austere masters, nor as mere followers: but as friends and companions of a graver character, and not seldom persons as well born as themselves. With them, as relations, they most commonly keep up a close connection through life. By this connection we conceive that we attach our gentlemen to the Church; and we liberalize the Church by an intercourse with the leading characters of the country.

So tenacious are we of the old ecclesiastical modes and fashions of institution, that very little alteration has been made in them since the fourteenth or fifteenth century: adhering in this particular, as in all things else, to our old settled maxim, never entirely nor at once to depart from antiquity. We found these old institutions, on the whole, favorable to morality and discipline; and we thought they were susceptible of amendment, without altering the ground. We thought that they were capable of receiving and meliorating, and above all of preserving, the accessions of science and literature, as the order of Providence should successively produce them. And after all, with this Gothic and monkish education, (for such it is in the groundwork,) we may put in our claim to as ample and as early a share in all the improvements in science, in arts, and in literature, which have illuminated and adorned the modern world, as any other nation in Europe: we think one main cause of this improvement was our not despising the patrimony of knowledge which was left us by our forefathers.

It is from our attachment to a Church establishment, that the English nation did not think it wise to intrust that great fundamental interest of the whole to what they trust no part of their civil or military public service,—that is, to the unsteady and precarious contribution of individuals. They go further. They certainly never have suffered, and never will suffer, the fixed estate of the Church to be converted into a pension, to depend on the Treasury, and to be delayed, withheld, or perhaps to be extinguished by fiscal difficulties: which difficulties may sometimes be pretended for political purposes, and are in fact often brought on by the extravagance, negligence, and rapacity of politicians. The people of England think that they have constitutional motives, as well as religious, against any project of turning their independent clergy into ecclesiastical pensioners of state. They tremble for their liberty, from the influence of a clergy dependent on the crown; they tremble for the public tranquillity, from the disorders of a factious clergy, if it were made to depend upon any other than the crown. They therefore made their Church, like their king and their nobility, independent.

From the united considerations of religion and constitutional policy, from their opinion of a duty to make a sure provision for the consolation of the feeble and the instruction of the ignorant, they have incorporated and identified the estate of the Church with the mass of *private property*, of which the state is not the proprietor, either for use or dominion, but the guardian only and the regulator. They have ordained that the provision of this establishment might be as stable as the earth on which it stands, and should not fluctuate with the Euripus of funds and actions.

The men of England, the men, I mean, of light and leading in England, whose wisdom (if they have any) is open and direct, would be ashamed, as of a silly, deceitful trick, to profess any religion in name, which by their proceedings they appear to contemn. If by their conduct (the only language that rarely lies) they seemed to regard the great ruling principle of the moral and the natural world as a mere invention to keep the vulgar in obedience, they apprehend that by such a conduct they would defeat the politic purpose they have in view. They would find it difficult to make others believe in a system to which they manifestly gave no credit themselves. The Christian statesmen of this land would, indeed, first provide for the *multitude*, because it is the *multitude*, and is therefore, as such, the first object in the ecclesiastical institution, and in all institutions. They have been taught that the circumstance of the Gospel's being preached to the poor was one of the great tests of its true mission. They think, therefore, that those do not believe it who do not take care it should be preached to the poor. But as they know that charity is not confined to any one description, but ought to apply itself to all men who have wants, they are not deprived of a due and anxious sensation of pity to the distresses of the miserable great. They are not repelled, through a fastidious delicacy, at the stench of their arrogance and presumption, from a medicinal attention to their mental blotches and running sores. They are sensible that religious instruction is of more consequence to them than to any others: from the greatness of the temptation to which they are exposed; from the important consequences that attend their faults; from the contagion of their ill example; from the necessity of bowing down the stubborn neck of their pride and ambition to the yoke of moderation and virtue; from a consideration of the fat stupidity and gross ignorance concerning what imports men most to know, which prevails at courts, and at the head of armies, and in senates, as much as at the loom and in the field.

The English people are satisfied, that to the great the consolations of religion are as necessary as its instructions. They, too, are among the unhappy. They feel personal pain and domestic sorrow. In these they have no privilege, but are subject to pay their full contingent to the contributions levied on mortality. They want this sovereign balm under their gnawing cares and anxieties, which, being less conversant about the limited wants of animal life, range without limit, and are diversified by infinite combinations in the wild and unbounded regions of imagination. Some charitable dole is wanting to these, our often very unhappy brethren, to fill the gloomy void that reigns in minds which have nothing on earth to hope or fear; something to relieve in the killing languor and over-labored lassitude of those who have nothing to do; something to excite an appetite to existence in the palled satiety which attends on all pleasures which may be bought, where Nature is not left to her own process, where even desire is anticipated, and therefore fruition defeated by meditated schemes and contrivances of delight, and no interval, no obstacle, is interposed between the wish and the accomplishment.

The people of England know how little influence the teachers of religion are likely to have with the wealthy and powerful of long standing, and how much less with the newly fortunate, if they appear in a manner no way assorted to those with whom they must associate, and over whom they must even exercise, in some cases, something like an authority. What must they think of that body of teachers, if they see it in no part above the establishment of their domestic servants? If the poverty were voluntary, there might be some difference. Strong instances of self-denial operate powerfully on our minds; and a man who has no wants has obtained great freedom and firmness, and even dignity. But as the mass of any description of men are but men, and their poverty cannot be voluntary, that disrespect which attends upon all lay poverty will not depart from the ecclesiastical. Our provident Constitution has therefore taken care that those who are to instruct presumptuous ignorance, those who are to be censors over insolent vice, should neither incur their contempt nor live upon their alms; nor will it tempt the rich to a neglect of the true medicine of their minds. For these reasons, whilst we provide first for the poor, and with a parental solicitude, we have not relegated religion (like something we were ashamed to show) to obscure municipalities or rustic villages. No! we will have her to exalt her mitred front in courts and parliaments. We will have her mixed throughout the whole mass of life, and blended with all the classes of society. The people of England will show to the haughty potentates of the world, and to their talking sophisters, that a free, a generous, an informed nation honors the high magistrates of its Church; that it will not suffer the insolence of wealth and titles, or any other species of proud pretension, to look down with scorn upon what they look up to with reverence, nor presume to trample on that acquired personal nobility which they intend always to be, and which often is, the fruit, not the reward, (for what can be the reward?) of learning, piety, and virtue. They can see, without pain or grudging, an archbishop precede a duke. They can see a bishop of Durham or a bishop of Winchester in possession of ten thousand pounds a year, and cannot conceive why it is in worse hands than estates to the like amount in the hands of this earl or that squire; although it may be true that so many dogs and horses are not kept by the former, and fed with the victuals which ought to nourish the children of the people. It is true, the whole Church revenue is not always employed, and to every shilling, in charity; nor perhaps ought it; but something is generally so employed. It is better to cherish virtue and humanity, by leaving much to free will, even with some loss to the object, than to attempt to make men mere machines and instruments of a political benevolence. The world on the whole will gain by a liberty without which virtue cannot exist.

When once the commonwealth has established the estates of the Church as property, it can consistently hear nothing of the more or the less. Too much and too little are treason against property. What evil can arise from the quantity in any hand, whilst the supreme authority has the full, sovereign superintendence over this, as over any property, to prevent every species of abuse,—and whenever it notably deviates, to give to it a direction agreeable to the purposes of its institution?

                                                    Reflections (1790). III, 350–69.

In 1772 some clergymen of the Church of England presented a petition to be relieved from subscription to the Thirty-Nine Articles as required by the Act of Uniformity of 1662. On this occasion Burke made a speech in opposition to the petition, presenting his views on the legal and moral situation created by a Church Establishment.

If ever there was anything to which, from reason, nature, habit, and principle, I am totally averse, it is persecution for conscientious difference in opinion. If these gentlemen complained justly of any compulsion upon them on that article, I would hardly wait for their petitions; as soon as I knew the evil, I would haste to the cure; I would even run before their complaints.

I will not enter into the abstract merits of our Articles and Liturgy. Perhaps there are some things in them which one would wish had not been there. They are not without the marks and characters of human frailty.

But it is not human frailty and imperfection, and even a considerable degree of them, that becomes a ground for your alteration; for by no alteration will you get rid of those errors, however you may delight yourselves in varying to infinity the fashion of them. But the ground for a legislative alteration of a legal establishment is this, and this only,—that you find the inclinations of the majority of the people, concurring with your own sense of the intolerable nature of the abuse, are in favor of a change.

If this be the case in the present instance, certainly you ought to make the alteration that is proposed, to satisfy your own consciences, and to give content to your people. But if you have no evidence of this nature, it ill becomes your gravity, on the petition of a few gentlemen, to listen to anything that tends to shake one of the capital pillars of the state, and alarm the body of your people upon that one ground, in which every hope and fear, every interest, passion, prejudice, everything which can affect the human breast, are all involved together. If you make this a season for religious alterations, depend upon it, you will soon find it a season of religious tumults and religious wars.

These gentlemen complain of hardship. No considerable number shows discontent; but, in order to give satisfaction to any number of respectable men, who come in so decent and constitutional a mode before us, let us examine a little what that hardship is. They want to be preferred clergymen in the Church of England as by law established; but their consciences will not suffer them to conform to the doctrines and practices of that Church: that is, they want to be teachers in a church to which they do not belong; and it is an odd sort of hardship. They want to receive the emoluments appropriated for teaching one set of doctrines, whilst they are teaching another. A church, in any legal sense, is only a certain system of religious doctrines and practices fixed and ascertained by some law,—by the difference of which laws different churches (as different commonwealths) are made in various parts of the world; and the establishment is a tax laid by the same sovereign authority for payment of those who so teach and so practise: for no legislature was ever so absurd as to tax its people to support men for teaching and acting as they please, but by some prescribed rule.

The hardship amounts to this,—that the people of England are not taxed two shillings in the pound to pay them for teaching, as divine truths, their own particular fancies. For the state has so taxed the people; and by way of relieving these gentlemen, it would be a cruel hardship on the people to be compelled to pay, from the sweat of their brow, the most heavy of all taxes to men, to condemn as heretical the doctrines which they repute to be orthodox, and to reprobate as superstitious the practices which they use as pious and holy. If a man leaves by will an establishment for preaching, such as Boyle's Lectures, or for charity sermons, or funeral sermons, shall any one complain of an hardship, because he has an excellent sermon upon matrimony, or on the martyrdom of King Charles, or on the Restoration, which I, the trustee of the establishment, will not pay him for preaching? . . . Such is the hardship which they complain of under the present Church establishment, that they have not the power of taxing the people of England for the maintenance of their private opinions.

The laws of toleration provide for every real grievance that these gentlemen can rationally complain of. Are they hindered from professing their belief of what they think to be truth? If they do not like the Establishment, there are an hundred different modes of Dissent in which they may teach. But even if they are so unfortunately circumstanced that of all that variety none will please them, they have free liberty to assemble a congregation of their own; and if any persons think their fancies (they may be brilliant imaginations) worth paying for, they are at liberty to maintain them as their clergy: nothing hinders it. But if they cannot get an hundred people together who will pay for their reading a liturgy after their form, with what face can they insist upon the nation's conforming to their ideas, for no other visible purpose than the enabling them to receive with a good conscience the tenth part of the produce of your lands?

Therefore, beforehand, the Constitution has thought proper to take a security that the tax raised on the people shall be applied only to those who profess such doctrines and follow such a mode of worship as the legislature, representing the people, has thought most agreeable to their general sense,—binding, as usual, the minority, not to an assent to the doctrines, but to a payment of the tax.

But how do you ease and relieve? How do you know, that, in making a new door into the Church for these gentlemen, you do not drive ten times their number out of it? Supposing the contents and not-contents strictly equal in numbers and consequence, the possession, to avoid disturbance, ought to carry it. You displease all the clergy of England now actually in office, for the chance of obliging a score or two, perhaps, of gentlemen, who are, or want to be, beneficed clergymen: and do you oblige? Alter your Liturgy,—will it please all even of those who wish an alteration? will they agree in what ought to be altered? And after it is altered to the mind of every one, you are no further advanced than if you had not taken a single step; because a large body of men will then say you ought to have no liturgy at all: and then these men, who now complain so bitterly that they are shut out, will themselves bar the door against thousands of others. Dissent, not satisfied with toleration, is not conscience, but ambition.

You altered the Liturgy for the Directory. This was settled by a set of most learned divines and learned laymen: Selden sat amongst them. Did this please? It was considered upon both sides as a most unchristian imposition. Well, at the Restoration they rejected the Directory, and reformed the Common Prayer, —which, by the way, had been three times reformed before. Were they then contented? Two thousand (or some great number) of clergy resigned their livings in one day rather than read it: and truly, rather than raise that second idol, I should have adhered to the Directory, as I now adhere to the Common Prayer. Nor can you content other men's conscience, real or pretended, by any concessions: follow your own; seek peace and ensue it. You have no symptoms of discontent in the people to their Establishment. The churches are too small for their congregations. The livings are too few for their candidates. The spirit of religious controversy has slackened by the nature of things: by act you may revive it. I will not enter into the question, how much truth is preferable to peace. Perhaps truth may be far better. But as we have scarcely ever the same certainty in the one that we have in the other, I would, unless the truth were evident indeed, hold fast to peace, which has in her company charity, the highest of the virtues.

The business appears in two points of view: 1st, Whether it is a matter of grievance; 2nd, Whether it is within our province to redress it with propriety and prudence. Whether it comes properly before us on a petition upon matter of grievance I would not inquire too curiously. I know, technically speaking, that nothing agreeable to law can be considered as a grievance. But an over-attention to the rules of any act does sometimes defeat the ends of it; and I think it does so in this Parliamentary act, as much at least as in any other. I know many gentlemen think that the very essence of liberty consists in being governed according to law, as if grievances had nothing real and intrinsic; but I cannot be of that opinion. Grievances may subsist by law. Nay, I do not know whether any grievance can be considered as intolerable, until it is established and sanctified by law. If the Act of Toleration were not perfect, if there were a complaint of it, I would gladly consent to amend it. But when I heard a complaint of a pressure on religious liberty, to my astonishment I find that there was no complaint whatsoever of the insufficiency of the act of King William, nor any attempt to make it more sufficient. The matter, therefore, does not concern toleration, but establishment; and it is not the rights of private conscience that are in question, but the propriety of the terms which are proposed by law as a title to public emoluments: so that the complaint is not, that there is not toleration of diversity in opinion, but that diversity in opinion is not rewarded by bishoprics, rectories, and collegiate stalls. When gentlemen complain of the subscription as matter of grievance, the complaint arises from confounding private judgment, whose rights are anterior to law, and the qualifications which the law creates for its own magistracies, whether civil or religious. To take away from men their lives, their liberty, or their property, those things for the protection of which society was introduced, is great hardship and intolerable tyranny; but to annex any condition you please to benefits artificially created is the most just, natural, and proper thing in the world. When *e novo* you form an arbitrary benefit, an advantage, preëminence, or emolument, not by Nature, but institution, you order and modify it with all the power of a creator over his creature. Such benefits of institution are royalty, nobility, priesthood, all of which you may limit to birth: you might prescribe even shape and stature. The Jewish priesthood was hereditary. Founders' kinsmen have a preference in the election of fellows in many colleges of our universities: the qualifications at All Souls are, that they should be *optime nati, bene vestiti, mediocriter docti* [of excellent birth, well dressed, and moderately learned].

By contending for liberty in the candidate for orders, you take away the liberty of the elector, which is the people, that is, the state. If they can choose, they may assign a reason for their choice; if they can assign a reason, they may do it in writing, and prescribe it as a condition; they may transfer their authority to their representatives, and enable them to exercise the same. In all human institutions, a great part, almost all regulations, are made from the mere necessity of the case, let the theoretical merits of the question be what they will. For nothing happened at the Reformation but what will happen in all such revolutions. When tyranny is extreme, and abuses of government intolerable, men resort to the rights of Nature to shake it off. When they have done so, the very same principle of necessity of human affairs to establish some other authority, which shall preserve the order of this new institution, must be obeyed, until they grow intolerable; and you shall not be suffered to plead original liberty against such an institution. . . .

If you will have religion publicly practised and publicly taught, you must have a power to say what that religion will be which you will protect and encourage, and to distinguish it by such marks and characteristics as you in your wisdom shall think fit. As I said before, your determination may be unwise in this as in other matters; but it cannot be unjust, hard, or oppressive, or contrary to the liberty of any man, or in the least degree exceeding your province. It is, therefore, as a grievance, fairly none at all,—nothing but what is essential, not only to the order, but to the liberty, of the whole community.

The petitioners are so sensible of the force of these arguments, that they do admit of one subscription,—that is, to the Scripture. I shall not consider how forcibly this argument militates with their whole principle against subscription as an usurpation on the rights of Providence: I content myself with submitting to the consideration of the House, that, if that rule were once established, it must have some authority to enforce the obedience; because, you well know, a law without a sanction will be ridiculous. Somebody must sit in judgment on his conformity; he must judge on the charge; if he judges, he must ordain execution. These things are necessary consequences one of the other; and then this judgment is an equal and a superior violation of private judgment; the right of private judgment is violated in a much greater degree than it can be by any previous subscription. You come round again to subscription, as the best and easiest method; men must judge of his doctrine, and judge definitively: so that either his test is nugatory, or men must first or last prescribe his public interpretation of it.

If the Church be, as Mr. Locke defines it, *a voluntary society,* &c., then it is essential to this voluntary society to exclude from her voluntary society any member she thinks fit, or to oppose the entrance of any upon such conditions as she thinks proper. For, otherwise, it would be a voluntary society acting contrary to her will, which is a contradiction in terms. And this is Mr. Locke's opinion, the advocate for the largest scheme of ecclesiastical and civil toleration to Protestants (for to Papists he allows no toleration at all).

They dispute only the extent of the subscription; they therefore tacitly admit the equity of the principle itself. Here they do not resort to the original rights of Nature, because it is manifest that those rights give as large a power of controverting every part of Scripture, or even the authority of the whole, as they do to the controverting any articles whatsoever. When a man requires you to sign an assent to Scripture, he requires you to assent to a doctrine as contrary to your natural understanding, and to your rights of free inquiry, as those who require your conformity to any one article whatsoever.

The subscription to Scripture is the most astonishing idea I ever heard, and will amount to just nothing at all. Gentlemen so acute have not, that I have heard, ever thought of answering a plain, obvious question: What is that Scripture to which they are content to subscribe? They do not think that a book becomes of divine authority because it is bound in blue morocco, and is printed by John Baskett and his assigns. The Bible is a vast collection of different treatises: a man who holds the divine authority of one may consider the other as merely human. What is his Canon? The Jewish? St. Jerome's? that of the Thirty-Nine Articles? Luther's? There are some who reject the Canticles; others, six of the Epistles; the Apocalypse has been suspected even as heretical, and was doubted of for many ages, and by many great men. As these narrow the Canon, others have enlarged it by admitting St. Barnabas's Epistles, the Apostolic Constitutions, to say nothing of many other Gospels. Therefore, to ascertain Scripture, you must have one article more; and you must define what that Scripture is which you mean to teach. There are, I believe, very few who, when Scripture is so ascertained, do not see the absolute necessity of knowing what general doctrine a man draws from it, before he is sent down authorized by the state to teach it as pure doctrine, and receive a tenth of the produce of our lands.

The Scripture is no one summary of doctrines regularly digested, in which a man could not mistake his way. It is a most venerable, but most multifarious, collection of the records of the divine economy: a collection of an infinite variety,—of cosmogony, theology, history, prophecy, psalmody, morality, apologue, allegory, legislation, ethics, carried through different books, by different authors, at different ages, for different ends and purposes. It is necessary to sort out what is intended for example, what only as narrative,—what to be understood literally, what figuratively,—where one precept is to be controlled and modified by another,—what is used directly, and what only as an argument *ad hominem*,—what is temporary, and what of perpetual obligation,—what appropriated to one state and to one set of men, and what the general duty of all Christians. If we do not get some security for this, we not only permit, but we actually pay for, all the dangerous fanaticism which can be produced to corrupt our people, and to derange the public worship of the country. We owe the best we can (not infallibility, but prudence) to the subject,—first sound doctrine, then ability to use it.

Speech on the Acts of Uniformity (1772). VII, 5–19.

3. Manners

It is characteristic of Burke's comprehensive view of society and the state, and of his insight into the complexities of human nature, that he should attribute such great importance to manners. But by *manners* he meant, of course, not mere etiquette, but a large social heritage, a way of life, including not only modes of behavior but also feelings, opinions, and values.

It is now sixteen or seventeen years since I saw the queen of France, then the Dauphiness, at Versailles; and surely never lighted on this orb, which she hardly seemed to touch, a more delightful vision. I saw her just above the horizon, decorating and cheering the elevated sphere she just began to move in,— glittering like the morning-star, full of life and splendor and joy. Oh! what a revolution! and what an heart must I have, to contemplate without emotion that elevation and that fall! Little did I dream, when she added titles of veneration to those of enthusiastic, distant, respectful love, that she should ever be obliged to carry the sharp antidote against disgrace concealed in that bosom! little did I dream that I should have lived to see such disasters fallen upon her in a nation of gallant men, in a nation of men of honor, and of cavaliers! I thought ten thousand swords must have leaped from their scabbards to avenge even a look that threatened her with insult. But the age of chivalry is gone. That of sophisters, economists, and calculators has succeeded; and the glory of Europe is extinguished forever. Never, never more, shall we behold that generous loyalty to rank and sex, that proud submission, that dignified obedience, that subordination of the heart, which kept alive, even in servitude itself, the spirit of an exalted freedom! The unbought grace of life, the cheap defence of nations, the nurse of manly sentiment and heroic enterprise, is gone! It is gone, that sensibility of principle, that chastity of honor, which felt a stain like a wound, which inspired courage whilst it mitigated ferocity, which ennobled whatever it touched, and under which vice itself lost half its evil by losing all its grossness!

This mixed system of opinion and sentiment had its origin in the ancient chivalry; and the principle, though varied in its appearance by the varying state of human affairs, subsisted and influenced through a long succession of generations, even to the time we live in. If it should ever be totally extinguished, the loss, I fear, will be great. It is this which has given its character to modern Europe. It is this which has distinguished it under all its forms of government, and distinguished it to its advantage, from the states of Asia, and possibly from those states which flourished in the most brilliant periods of the antique world. It was this, which, without confounding ranks, had produced a noble equality, and handed it down through all the gradations of social life. It was this opinion which mitigated kings into companions, and raised private men to be fellows with kings. Without force or opposition, it subdued the fierceness of pride and power; it obliged sovereigns to submit to the soft collar of social esteem, compelled stern authority to submit to elegance, and gave a domination, vanquisher of laws, to be subdued by manners.

But now all is to be changed. All the pleasing illusions which made power gentle and obedience liberal, which harmonized the different shades of life, and which by a bland assimilation incorporated into politics the sentiments which beautify and soften private society, are to be dissolved by this new conquering empire of light and reason. All the decent drapery of life is to be rudely torn off. All the superadded ideas, furnished from the wardrobe of a moral imagination, which the heart owns and the understanding ratifies, as necessary to cover the defects of our naked, shivering nature, and to raise it to dignity in our own estimation, are to be exploded, as a ridiculous, absurd, and antiquated fashion.

On this scheme of things, a king is but a man, a queen is but a woman, a woman is but an animal,—and an animal not of the highest order. All homage paid to the sex in general as such, and without distinct views, is to be regarded as romance and folly. Regicide, and parricide, and sacrilege, are but fictions of superstition, corrupting jurisprudence by destroying its simplicity. The murder of a king, or a queen, or a bishop, or a father, are only common homicide,—and if the people are by any chance or in any way gainers by it, a sort of homicide much the most pardonable, and into which we ought not to make too severe a scrutiny.

On the scheme of this barbarous philosophy, which is the offspring of cold hearts and muddy understandings, and which is as void of solid wisdom as it is destitute of all taste and elegance, laws are to be supported only by their own terrors, and by the concern which each individual may find in them from his own private speculations, or can spare to them from his own private interests. In the groves of *their* academy, at the end of every visto, you see nothing but the gallows. Nothing is left which engages the affections on the part of the commonwealth. On the principles of this mechanic philosophy, our institutions can never be embodied, if I may use the expression, in persons,—so as to create in us love, veneration, admiration, or attachment. But that sort of reason which banishes the affections is incapable of filling their place. These public affections, combined with manners, are required sometimes as supplements, sometimes as correctives, always as aids to law. The precept given by a wise man, as well as a great critic, for the construction of poems, is equally true as to states:—*"Non satis est pulchra esse poemata, dulcia sunto."* There ought to be a system of manners in every nation which a well-formed mind would be disposed to relish. To make us love our country, our country ought to be lovely.

But power, of some kind or other, will survive the shock in which manners and opinions perish; and it will find other and worse means for its support. The usurpation, which, in order to subvert ancient institutions, has destroyed ancient principles, will hold power by arts similar to those by which it has acquired it. When the old feudal and chivalrous spirit of *fealty*, which, by freeing kings from fear, freed both kings and subjects from the precautions of tyranny, shall be extinct in the minds of men, plots and assassinations will be anticipated by preventive murder and preventive confiscation, and that long roll of grim and bloody maxims which form the political code of all power not standing on its own honor and the honor of those who are to obey it. Kings will be tyrants from policy, when subjects are rebels from principle.

When ancient opinions and rules of life are taken away, the loss cannot possibly be estimated. From that moment we have no compass to govern us, nor can we know distinctly to what port we steer. Europe, undoubtedly, taken in a mass, was in a flourishing condition the day on which your Revolution was completed. How much of that prosperous state was owing to the spirit of our old manners and opinions is not easy to say; but as such causes cannot be indifferent in their operation, we must presume, that, on the whole, their operation was beneficial.

We are but too apt to consider things in the state in which we find them, without sufficiently adverting to the causes by which they have been produced, and possibly may be upheld. Nothing is more certain than that our manners, our civilization, and all the good things which are connected with manners and with civilization, have, in this European world of ours, depended for ages upon two principles, and were, indeed, the result of both combined: I mean the spirit of a gentleman, and the spirit of religion. The nobility and the clergy, the one by profession, and the other by patronage, kept learning in existence, even in the midst of arms and confusions, and whilst governments were rather in their causes than formed. Learning paid back what it received to nobility and to priesthood, and paid it with usury, by enlarging their ideas, and by furnishing their minds. Happy, if they had all continued to know their indissoluble union, and their proper place! Happy, if learning, not debauched by ambition, had been satisfied to continue the instructor, and not aspired to be the master! Along with its natural protectors and guardians, learning will be cast into the mire and trodden down under the hoofs of a swinish multitude.

If, as I suspect, modern letters owe more than they are always willing to own to ancient manners, so do other interests which we value as much as they are worth. Even commerce, and trade, and manufacture, the gods of our economical politicians, are themselves perhaps but creatures, are themselves but effects, which, as first causes, we choose to worship. They certainly grew under the same shade in which learning flourished. They, too, may decay with their natural protecting principles. With you, for the present at least, they all threaten to disappear together. Where trade and manufactures are wanting to a people, and the spirit of nobility and religion remains, sentiment supplies, and not always ill supplies, their place; but if commerce and the arts should be lost in an experiment to try how well a state may stand without these old fundamental principles, what sort of a thing must be a nation of gross, stupid, ferocious, and at the same time poor and sordid barbarians, destitute of religion, honor, or manly pride, possessing nothing at present, and hoping for nothing hereafter?

I wish you may not be going fast, and by the shortest cut, to that horrible and disgustful situation. Already there appears a poverty of conception, a coarseness and vulgarity, in all the proceedings of the Assembly and of all their instructors. Their liberty is not liberal. Their science is presumptuous ignorance. Their humanity is savage and brutal.

It is not clear whether in England we learned those grand and decorous principles and manners, of which considerable traces yet remain, from you, or whether you took them from us. But to you, I think, we trace them best. You seem to me to be *gentis incunabula nostræ* [the cradle of our race]. France has always more or less influenced manners in England; and when your fountain is choked up and polluted, the stream will not run long or not run clear with us, or perhaps with any nation. This gives all Europe, in my opinion, but too close and connected a concern in what is done in France. Excuse me, therefore, if I have dwelt too long on the atrocious spectacle of the sixth of October, 1789, or have given too much scope to the reflections which have arisen in my mind on occasion of the most important of all revolutions, which may be dated from that day: I mean a revolution in sentiments, manners, and moral opinions. As things now stand, with everything respectable destroyed without us, and an attempt to destroy within us every principle of respect, one is almost forced to apologize for harboring the common feelings of men.

Reflections (1790). III, 331–37.

The act of which I speak is among the fruits of the American war,—a war in my humble opinion productive of many mischiefs, of a kind which distinguishes it from all others. Not only our policy is deranged, and our empire distracted, but our laws and our legislative spirit appear to have been totally perverted by it. We have made war on our colonies, not by arms only, but by laws. As hostility and law are not very concordant ideas, every step we have taken in this business has been made by trampling on some maxim of justice or some capital principle of wise government. What precedents were established, and what principles overturned, (I will not say of English privilege, but of general justice,) in the Boston Port, the Massachusetts Charter, the Military Bill, and all that long array of hostile acts of Parliament by which the war with America has been begun and supported! Had the principles of any of these acts been first exerted on English ground, they would probably have expired as soon as they touched it. But by being removed from our persons, they have rooted in our laws, and the latest posterity will taste the fruits of them.

Nor is it the worst effect of this unnatural contention, that our *laws* are corrupted. Whilst *manners* remain entire, they will correct the vices of law, and soften it at length to their own temper. But we have to lament that in most of the late proceedings we see very few traces of that generosity, humanity, and dignity of mind, which formerly characterized this nation. War suspends the rules of moral obligation, and what is long suspended is in danger of being totally abrogated. Civil wars strike deepest of all into the manners of the people. They vitiate their politics; they corrupt their morals; they pervert even the natural taste and relish of equity and justice. By teaching us to consider our fellow-citizens in an hostile light, the whole body of our nation becomes gradually less dear to us. The very names of affection and kindred, which were the bond of charity whilst we agreed, become new incentives to hatred and rage when the communion of our country is dissolved. We may flatter ourselves that we shall not fall into this misfortune. But we have no charter of exemption, that I know of, from the ordinary frailties of our nature.

What but that blindness of heart which arises from the frenzy of civil contention could have made any persons conceive the present situation of the British affairs as an object of triumph to themselves or of congratulation to their sovereign? Nothing surely could be more lamentable to those who remember the flourishing days of this kingdom than to see the insane joy of several unhappy people, amidst the sad spectacle which our affairs and conduct exhibit to the scorn of Europe. We behold (and it seems some people rejoice in beholding) our native land, which used to sit the envied arbiter of all her neighbors, reduced to a servile dependence on their mercy,—acquiescing in assurances of friendship which she does not trust,—complaining of hostilities which she dares not resent,—deficient to her allies, lofty to her subjects, and submissive to her enemies,—whilst the liberal government of this free nation is supported by the hireling sword of German boors and vassals, and three millions of the subjects of Great Britian are seeking for protection to English privileges in the arms of France!

Letter to the Sheriffs of Bristol (1777). II, 202–4.

CHAPTER V

Practical Politics

1. Political Parties

The Whig and Tory parties originated in 1679 and party organization was henceforth a regular feature of English politics. But parties were considered an evil, each party insisting that it was the voice of the nation and that the other was a "faction." Burke was one of the first to understand that parties are indispensable in a democracy, and he was always avowedly and proudly a party man.

We know that parties must ever exist in a free country.
Speech on Conciliation with America (1775). II, 177–78.

I have said all I mean to say in vindication of my having gloried in my political connections, and in the part I have taken along with them. My principles, indeed the principles of common sense, lead me to act in *corps*. Accident first threw me into this party. When I was again at liberty, knowledge and reflection induced me to re-enter it; principle and experience have confirmed me in it. Your lordship will find it difficult to show where a man, who wished to act systematically in public business, could have arranged himself more reputably. By arranging myself with them, I trust I have given some sort of security to the public for my good behaviour. That versatility, those sudden evolutions, which have derogated something from the credit of all public professions, are things not so easy in large bodies, as when men act alone, or in light squadrons. A man's virtue is best secured by shame, and best improved by emulation in the society of virtuous men.
Draft of Letter to the Bishop of Chester, 1771.
Correspondence. I, 296.

The press, in reality, has made every government, in its spirit, almost democratic.

Second Letter on a Regicide Peace (1796–97). V, 380.

I am satisfied that there is so much good in mankind at large, that one of the main causes of the mutual hatred in parties, is our mutual ignorance of each other. Let us take care, on our part, that our speaking so ill of our adversaries does not give them occasion to conceive ill of ourselves.

Letter to Patrick Bowie, March 30, 1779.
Correspondence. II, 258.

The idea of short parliaments is, I confess, plausible enough; so is the idea of an election by ballot; but I believe neither will stand their ground when entered into minutely, and with a reference to actually existing circumstances. If no remedy can be found in the dispositions of capital people, in the temper, spirit, (and docility too) of the lower, and in the thorough union of both, nothing can be done by any alteration in forms.

Letter to Richard Shackleton, August 15, 1770.
Correspondence. I, 231.

Party divisions, whether on the whole operating for good or evil, are things inseparable from free government. This is a truth which, I believe, admits little dispute, having been established by the uniform experience of all ages. The part a good citizen ought to take in these divisions has been a matter of much deeper controversy. But God forbid that any controversy relating to our essential morals should admit of no decision. It appears to me, that this question, like most of the others which regard our duties in life, is to be determined by our station in it. Private men may be wholly neutral, and entirely innocent: but they who are legally invested with public trust, or stand on the high ground of rank and dignity, which is trust implied, can hardly in any case remain indifferent, without the certainty of sinking into insignificance; and thereby in effect deserting that post in which, with the fullest authority, and for the wisest purposes, the laws and institutions of their country have fixed them. However, if it be the office of those who are thus circumstanced, to take a decided part, it is no less their duty that it should be a sober one. It ought to be circumscribed by the same laws of decorum, and balanced by the same temper, which bound and regulate all the virtues. In a word, we ought to act in party with all the moderation which does not absolutely enervate that vigor, and quench that fervency of spirit, without which the best wishes for the public good must evaporate in empty speculation.

Thoughts on the Present State of the Nation (1770). I, 271–72.

Party is a body of men united for promoting by their joint endeavors the national interest upon some particular principle in which they are all agreed. For my part, I find it impossible to conceive, that any one believes in his own politics, or thinks them to be of any weight, who refuses to adopt the means of having them reduced into practice. It is the business of the speculative philosopher to mark the proper ends of government. It is the business of the politician, who is the philosopher in action, to find out proper means toward those ends, and to employ them with effect. Therefore every honorable connection will avow it is their first purpose, to pursue every just method to put the men who hold their opinions into such a condition as may enable them to carry their common plans into execution, with all the power and authority of the state. As this power is attached to certain situations, it is their duty to contend for these situations. Without a proscription of others, they are bound to give to their own party the preference in all things; and by no means, for private considerations, to accept any offers of power in which the whole body is not included; nor to suffer themselves to be led, or to be controlled, or to be overbalanced, in office or in council, by those who contradict the very fundamental principles on which their party is formed, and even those upon which every fair connection must stand. Such a generous contention for power, on such manly and honorable maxims, will easily be distinguished from the mean and interested struggle for place and emolument. The very style of such persons will serve to discriminate them from those numberless impostors, who have deluded the ignorant with professions incompatible with human practice, and have afterwards incensed them by practices below the level of vulgar rectitude.

It is an advantage to all narrow wisdom and narrow morals, that their maxims have a plausible air: and, on a cursory view, appear equal to first principles. They are light and portable. They are as current as copper coin; and about as valuable. They serve equally the first capacities and the lowest; and they are, at least, as useful to the worst men as to the best. Of this stamp is the cant of *Not men, but measures;* a sort of charm by which many people get loose from every honorable engagement. When I see a man acting this desultory and disconnected part, with as much detriment to his own fortune as prejudice to the cause of any party, I am not persuaded that he is right; but I am ready to believe he is in earnest. I respect virtue in all its situations; even when it is found in the unsuitable company of weakness. I lament to see qualities, rare and valuable, squandered away without any public utility. But when a gentleman with great visible emoluments abandons the party in which he has long acted, and tells you, it is because he proceeds upon his own judgment; that he acts on the merits of the several measures as they arise; and that he is obliged to follow his own conscience, and not that of others; he gives reasons which it is impossible to controvert, and discovers a character which it is impossible to mistake. What shall we think of him who never differed from a certain set of men until the moment they lost their power, and who never agreed with them in a single instance afterwards? Would not such a coincidence of interest and opinion be rather fortunate? Would it not be an extraordinary cast upon the dice, that a man's connections should degenerate into faction, precisely at the critical moment when they lose their power, or he accepts a place? When people desert their connections, the desertion is a manifest *fact,* upon which a direct simple issue lies, triable by plain men. Whether a *measure* of government be right or wrong, is *no matter of fact,* but a mere affair of opinion, on which men may, as they do, dispute and wrangle without end. But whether the individual *thinks* the measure right or wrong, is a point at still a greater distance from the reach of all human decision. It is therefore very convenient to politicians, not to put the judgment of their conduct on overt acts, cognizable in any ordinary court, but upon such matter as can be triable only in that secret tribunal, where they are sure of being heard with favor, or where at worst the sentence will be only private whipping.

I believe the reader would wish to find no substance in a doctrine which has a tendency to destroy all test of character as deduced from conduct. He will therefore excuse my adding something more, towards the further clearing up a point, which the great convenience of obscurity to dishonesty has been able to cover with some degree of darkness and doubt.

In order to throw an odium on political connection, these politicians suppose it a necessary incident to it, that you are blindly to follow the opinions of your party, when in direct opposition to your own clear ideas; a degree of servitude that no worthy man could bear the thought of submitting to; and such as, I believe, no connections (except some court factions) ever could be so senselessly tyrannical as to impose. Men thinking freely, will, in particular instances, think differently. But still as the greater part of the measures which arise in the course of public business are related to, or dependent on, some great, *leading, general principles in government,* a man must be peculiarly unfortunate in the choice of his political company, if he does not agree with them at least nine times in ten. If he does not concur in these general principles upon which the party is founded, and which necessarily draw on a concurrence in their application, he ought from the beginning to have chosen some other, more conformable to his opinions. When the question is in its nature doubtful, or not very material, the modesty which becomes an individual, and, (in spite of our court moralists) that partiality which becomes a well-chosen friendship, will frequently bring on an acquiescence in the general sentiment. Thus the disagreement will naturally be rare; it will be only enough to indulge freedom, without violating concord, or disturbing arrangement. And this is all that ever was required for a character of the greatest uniformity and steadiness in connection. How men can proceed without any connection at all, is to me utterly incomprehensible. Of what sort of materials must that man be made, how must he be tempered and put together, who can sit whole years in Parliament, with five hundred and fifty of his fellow-citizens, amidst the storm of such tempestuous passions, in the sharp conflict of so many wits, and tempers, and characters, in the agitation of such mighty questions, in the discussion of such vast and ponderous interests, without seeing any one sort of men, whose character, conduct, or disposition, would lead him to associate himself with them, to aid and be aided, in any one system of public utility?

I remember an old scholastic aphorism, which says, "that the man who lives wholly detached from others, must be either an angel or a devil." [1] When I see in any of these detached gentlemen of our times the angelic purity, power, and beneficence, I shall admit them to be angels. In the mean time we are born only to be men. We shall do enough if we form ourselves to be good ones. It is therefore our business carefully to cultivate in our minds, to rear to the most perfect vigor and maturity, every sort of generous and honest feeling, that belongs to our nature. To bring the dispositions that are lovely in private life into the service and conduct of the commonwealth; so to be patriots, as not to forget we are gentlemen. To cultivate friendships, and to incur enmities. To have both strong, but both selected: in the one, to be placable; in the other immovable. To model our principles to our duties and our situation. To be fully persuaded, that all virtue which is impracticable is spurious; and rather to run the risk of falling into faults in a course which leads us to act with effect and energy, than to loiter out our days without blame, and without use. Public life is a situation of power and energy; he trespasses against his duty who sleeps upon his watch, as well as he that goes over to the enemy.

There is, however, a time for all things. It is not every conjuncture which calls with equal force upon the activity of honest men; but critical exigencies now and then arise; and I am mistaken, if this be not one of them. Men will see the necessity of honest combination; but they may see it when it is too late. They may embody, when it will be ruinous to themselves, and of no advantage to the country; when, for want of such a timely union as may enable them to oppose in favor of the laws, with the laws on their side, they may at length find themselves under the necessity of conspiring, instead of consulting. The law, for which they stand, may become a weapon in the hands of its bitterest enemies; and they will be cast, at length, into that miserable

[1] This saying originated with Aristotle *Politics* 1253a, 28–30.

alternative between slavery and civil confusion, which no good man can look upon without horror; an alternative in which it is impossible he should take either part, with a conscience perfectly at repose. To keep that situation of guilt and remorse at the utmost distance is, therefore, our first obligation. Early activity may prevent late and fruitless violence. As yet we work in the light. The scheme of the enemies of public tranquillity has disarranged, it has not destroyed us.

If the reader believes that there really exists such a faction as I have described; a faction ruling by the private inclinations of a court, against the general sense of the people; and that this faction, whilst it pursues a scheme for undermining all the foundations of our freedom, weakens (for the present at least) all the powers of executory government, rendering us abroad contemptible, and at home distracted; he will believe also, that nothing but a firm combination of public men against this body, and that, too, supported by the hearty concurrence of the people at large, can possibly get the better of it. The people will see the necessity of restoring public men to an attention to the public opinion, and of restoring the constitution to its original principles. Above all, they will endeavor to keep the House of Commons from assuming a character which does not belong to it. They will endeavor to keep that House, for its existence, for its powers, and its privileges, as independent of every other, and as dependent upon themselves, as possible. This servitude is to a House of Commons (like obedience to the Divine law) "perfect freedom." For if they once quit this natural, rational, and liberal obedience, having deserted the only proper foundation of their power, they must seek a support in an abject and unnatural dependence somewhere else. When, through the medium of this just connection with their constituents, the genuine dignity of the House of Commons is restored, it will begin to think of casting from it, with scorn, as badges of servility, all the false ornaments of illegal power, with which it has been, for some time, disgraced. It will begin to think of its old office of CONTROL. It will not suffer that last of evils to predominate in the country: men without popular confidence, public opinion, natural connection, or mutual trust, invested with all the powers of government.

Thoughts on the Cause of the Present Discontents (1770). I, 530–36.

2. Aristocracy and Leadership

Aristocracy and leadership are essential to Burke's conception of society and a people (see Chapter III, section 2). The aristocracy he thought society needs he called a "natural aristocracy," and its members might be either noblemen or commoners. But Burke admonished his titled friends to remember the responsibilities into which they were born.

I am accused, I am told abroad, of being a man of aristocratic principles. If by aristocracy they mean the peers, I have no vulgar admiration, nor any vulgar antipathy towards them; I hold their order in cold and decent respect. I hold them to be of an absolute necessity in the Constitution; but I think they are only good when kept within their proper bounds. I trust, whenever there has been a dispute between these Houses, the part I have taken has not been equivocal. If by the aristocracy (which, indeed, comes nearer to the point) they mean an adherence to the rich and powerful against the poor and weak, this would, indeed, be a very extraordinary part. I have incurred the odium of gentlemen in this House for not paying sufficient regard to men of ample property. When, indeed, the smallest rights of the poorest people in the kingdom are in question, I would set my face against any act of pride and power countenanced by the highest that are in it; and if it should come to the last extremity, and to a contest of blood,—God forbid! God forbid!—my part is taken: I would take my fate with the poor and low and feeble. But if these people came to turn their liberty into a cloak for maliciousness, and to seek a privilege of exemption, not from power, but from the rules of morality and virtuous discipline, then I would join my hand to make them feel the force which a few united in a good cause have over a multitude of the profligate and ferocious.

Speech on Repeal of the Marriage Act (1781). VII, 133–34.

In 1770, when the English Constitution was menaced by the attempts of George III to increase the prerogatives of the Crown by means of servile ministers and the corruption of the Commons, the opposition was led by men of noble rank. The Court party raised a cry of a danger to the Constitution from an oligarchical influence. Burke insisted that the real danger was from the excessive Crown influence.

It is true, that the peers have a great influence in the kingdom, and in every part of the public concerns. While they are men of property, it is impossible to prevent it, except by such means as must prevent all property from its natural operation: an event not easily to be compassed, while property is power; nor by any means to be wished, while the least notion exists of the method by which the spirit of liberty acts, and of the means by which it is preserved. If any particular peers, by their uniform, upright, constitutional conduct, by their public and their private virtues, have acquired an influence in the country; the people, on whose favor that influence depends, and from whom it arose, will never be duped into an opinion, that such greatness in a peer is the despotism of an aristocracy, when they know and feel it to be the effect and pledge of their own importance.

I am no friend to aristocracy, in the sense at least in which that word is usually understood. If it were not a bad habit to moot cases on the supposed ruin of the constitution, I should be free to declare, that if it must perish, I would rather by far see it resolved into any other form, than lost in that austere and insolent domination. But, whatever my dislikes may be, my fears are not upon that quarter. The question, on the influence of a court, and of a peerage, is not, which of the two dangers is the more eligible, but which is the more imminent. He is but a poor observer, who has not seen, that the generality of peers, far from supporting themselves in a state of independent greatness, are but too apt to fall into an oblivion of their proper dignity, and to run headlong into an abject servitude. Would to God it were true, that the fault of our peers were too much spirit. It is worthy of some observation that these gentlemen, so jealous of aristocracy, make no complaints of the power of those peers (neither few nor inconsiderable) who are always in the train of a court, and whose whole weight must be considered as a portion of the settled influence of the crown. This is all safe and right; but if some peers (I am very sorry they are not as many as they ought to be) set themselves, in the great concern of peers and commons, against a back-stairs influence and clandestine government, then the alarm begins; then the constitution is in danger of being forced into an aristocracy.

I rest a little the longer on this court topic, because it was much insisted upon at the time of the great change, and has been since frequently revived by many of the agents of that party; for, whilst they are terrifying the great and opulent with the horrors of mob-government, they are by other managers attempting (though hitherto with little success) to alarm the people with a phantom of tyranny in the nobles. All this is done upon their favorite principle of disunion, of sowing jealousies amongst the different orders of the state, and of disjointing the natural strength of the kingdom; that it may be rendered incapable of resisting the sinister designs of wicked men, who have engrossed the royal power.

Thus much of the topics chosen by the courtiers to recommend their system; it will be necessary to open a little more at large the nature of that party which was formed for its support. Without this, the whole would have been no better than a visionary amusement, like the scheme of Harrington's political club, and not a business in which the nation had a real concern. As a powerful party, and a party constructed on a new principle, it is a very inviting object of curiosity.

Thoughts on the Cause of the Present Discontents (1770). I, 458–59.

It may be expected, Sir, that, when I am giving my reasons why I limit myself in the reduction of employments, or of their profits, I should say something of those which seem of eminent inutility in the state: I mean the number of officers who, by their places, are attendant on the person of the king. Considering the commonwealth merely as such, and considering those officers only as relative to the direct purposes of the state, I admit that they are of no use at all. But there are many things in the constitution of establishments, which appear of little value on the first view, which in a secondary and oblique manner produce very material advantages. It was on full consideration that I determined not to lessen any of the offices of honor about the crown, in their number or their emoluments. These emoluments, except in one or two cases, do not much more than answer the charge of attendance. Men of condition naturally love to be about a court; and women of condition love it much more. But there is in all regular attendance so much of constraint, that, if it were a mere charge, without any compensation, you would soon have the court deserted by all the nobility of the kingdom.

Sir, the most serious mischiefs would follow from such a desertion. Kings are naturally lovers of low company. They are so elevated above all the rest of mankind that they must look upon all their subjects as on a level. They are rather apt to hate than to love their nobility, on account of the occasional resistance to their will which will be made by their virtue, their petulance, or their pride. It must, indeed, be admitted that many of the nobility are as perfectly willing to act the part of flatterers, tale-bearers, parasites, pimps, and buffoons, as any of the lowest and vilest of mankind can possibly be. But they are not properly qualified for this object of their ambition. The want of a regular education, and early habits, and some lurking remains of their dignity, will never permit them to become a match for an Italian eunuch, a mountebank, a fiddler, a player, or any regular practitioner of that tribe. The Roman emperors, almost from the beginning, threw themselves into such hands; and the mischief increased every day till the decline and final ruin of the empire. It is therefore of very great importance (provided the thing is not over-done) to contrive such an establishment as must, almost whether a prince will or not, bring into daily and hourly offices about his person a great number of his first nobility; and it is rather an useful prejudice that gives them a pride in such a servitude. Though they are not much the better for a court, a court will be much the better for them. I have therefore not attempted to reform any of the offices of honor about the king's person.

Speech on the Plan for Economical Reform (1780). II, 336–38.

Whoever seriously considers the excellent argument of Lord Somers, in the Bankers' Case, will see he bottoms himself upon the very same maxim which I do; and one of his principal grounds of doctrine for the alienability of the domain in England,[2] contrary to the maxim of the law in France, he lays in the constitutional policy of furnishing a permanent reward to public service, of making that reward the origin of families, and the foundation of wealth as well as of honors. It is, indeed, the only genuine, unadulterated origin of nobility. It is a great principle in government, a principle at the very foundation of the whole

---

[2] Before the statute of Queen Anne, which limited the alienation of land. [Burke]

structure. The other judges who held the same doctrine went beyond Lord Somers with regard to the remedy which they thought was given by law against the crown upon the grant of pensions. Indeed, no man knows, when he cuts off the incitements to a virtuous ambition, and the just rewards of public service, what infinite mischief he may do his country through all generations. Such saving to the public may prove the worst mode of robbing it.

Speech on the Plan for Economical Reform (1780). II, 330–31.

The legislators who framed the ancient republics knew that their business was too arduous to be accomplished with no better apparatus than the metaphysics of an undergraduate and the mathematics and arithmetic of an exciseman. They had to do with men, and they were obliged to study human nature. They had to do with citizens, and they were obliged to study the effects of those habits which are communicated by the circumstances of civil life. They were sensible that the operation of this second nature on the first produced a new calculation,—and thence arose many diversities amongst men, according to their birth, their education, their professions, the periods of their lives, their residence in towns or in the country, their several ways of acquiring and of fixing property, and according to the quality of the property itself, all of which rendered them, as it were, so many different species of animals. From hence they thought themselves obliged to dispose their citizens into such classes, and to place them in such situations in the state, as their peculiar habits might qualify them to fill, and to allot to them such appropriated privileges as might secure to them what their specific occasions required, and which might furnish to each description such force as might protect it in the conflict caused by the diversity of interests that must exist, and must contend, in all complex society . . . It is for this reason that Montesquieu observed, very justly, that, in their classification of the citizens, the great legislators of antiquity made the greatest display of their powers.

Reflections (1790). III, 476–77.

As to the good people of England, they seem to partake every day, more and more, of the character of that administration [of Lord North, servile to the king] which they have been induced to tolerate. I am satisfied that within a few years there has been a great change in the national character. We seem no longer that eager, inquisitive, jealous, fiery people which we have been formerly, and which we have been a very short time ago. The people look back, without pleasure or indignation; and forward, without hope or fear. No man commends the measures which have been pursued, or expects any good from those which are in preparation; but it is a cold, languid opinion, like what men discover in affairs that do not concern them. It excites to no passion; it prompts to no action. . . . I do not think that weeks, or even months or years, will bring the monarch, the ministers, or the people, to feeling. To bring the people to a feeling, such a feeling, I mean, as tends to amendment or alteration of system, there must be plan and management. All direction of public humor and opinion must originate in a few. Perhaps a good deal of that humor and opinion must be owing to such direction. Events supply materials; times furnish dispositions; but conduct alone can bring them to bear to any useful purpose. I never yet knew an instance of any general temper in the nation, that might not have been tolerably well traced to some particular persons. If things are left to themselves, it is my clear opinion that a nation may slide down fair and softly from the highest point of grandeur and prosperity to the lowest state of imbecility and meanness, without any one's marking a particular period in this declension, without asking a question about it, or in the least speculating on any of the innumerable acts which have stolen in this silent and insensible revolution. Every event so prepares the subsequent, that, when it arrives, it produces no surprise, nor any extraordinary alarm.

Letter to the Marquis of Rockingham, August 23, 1775.
Correspondence. II, 47–49.

Persons in your station of life ought to have long views. You people of great families and hereditary trusts and fortunes, are not like such as I am, who, whatever we may be, by the rapidity of our growth, and even by the fruit we bear, and flatter ourselves that, while we creep on the ground, we belly into melons that are exquisite for size and flavor, yet still are but annual plants, that perish with our season, and leave no sort of traces behind us. You, if you are what you ought to be, are in my eye the great oaks that shade a country, and perpetuate your benefits from generation to generation. The immediate power of a Duke of Richmond, or a Marquis of Rockingham, is not so much of moment; but if their conduct and example hand down their principles to their successors, then their houses become the public repositories and offices of record for the constitution; not like the Tower, or the Rollschapel, where it is searched for and sometimes in vain, in rotten parchments under dripping and perishing walls, but in full vigor, and acting with vital energy and power, in the character of the leading men and natural interests of the country. It has been remarked that there were two eminent families at Rome, that for several ages were distinguished uniformly by opposite characters and principles, the Claudian and Valerian. The former were high and haughty, but public-spirited, firm, and active, and attached to the aristocracy. The latter were popular in their tempers, manners, and principles. So far the remark:—but I add that any one who looks attentively to their history, will see that the balance of that famous constitution was kept up for some ages, by the personal characters, dispositions, and traditionary politics of certain families, as much as by anything in the laws and orders of the state.

Letter to the Duke of Richmond, November 17, 1772.
Correspondence. I, 381–82.

I confess I do not entirely enter into the idea of waiting until the public discontents grow riper. They never did, do, or will ripen, to any purpose, unless they are matured by proper means. To be useful, they must have direction given to them; and hope must be held out somewhere.

Letter to the Marquis of Rockingham, December 20, 1774.
Correspondence. I, 518.

Is it that the people are changed, that the commonwealth cannot be protected by its laws? I hardly think so. On the contrary, I conceive that these things happen because men are not changed, but remain always what they always were; they remain what the bulk of us ever must be, when abandoned to our vulgar propensities, without guide, leader, or control: that is, made to be full of a blind elevation in prosperity; to despise untried dangers; to be overpowered with unexpected reverses; to find no clew in a labyrinth of difficulties; to get out of a present inconvenience with any risk of future ruin; to follow and to bow to fortune; to admire successful, though wicked enterprise, and to imitate what we admire; to contemn the government which announces danger from sacrilege and regicide whilst they are only in their infancy and their struggle, but which finds nothing that can alarm in their adult state, and in the power and triumph of those destructive principles. In a mass we can not be left to ourselves. We must have leaders. If none will undertake to lead us right, we shall find guides who will contrive to conduct us to shame and ruin.

First Letter on a Regicide Peace (1796). V, 249–50.

3. The Duties of Popular Representatives

Burke held a rather low opinion of the capacity of the multitude of voters to understand the complexities of government problems and to determine policy. The people, he often said, were surely the best judges as to whether they were governed well or badly. But their elected representatives must assume the responsibility for the practical solution of problems. A member of the House of Commons must be more than a hired agent of his constituents; he must be a free and intelligent member of a deliberative body. Burke once remarked that he had never seen any bill or proposal that had not been improved by debate or discussion.

As well may we fancy that of itself the sea will swell, and that without winds the billows will insult the adverse shore, as that the gross mass of the people will be moved, and elevated, and continue by a steady and permanent direction to bear upon one point, without the influence of superior authority or superior mind.

First Letter on a Regicide Peace (1796). V, 302.

Never was there a jar or discord between genuine sentiment and sound policy. Never, no, never, did Nature say one thing and Wisdom say another. Nor are sentiments of elevation in themselves turgid and unnatural. Nature is never more truly herself than in her grandest forms. The Apollo of Belvedere (if the universal robber has yet left him at Belvedere) is as much in Nature as any figure from the pencil of Rembrandt or any clown in the rustic revels of Téniers. Indeed, it is when a great nation is in great difficulties that minds must exalt themselves to the occasion, or all is lost.

Third Letter on a Regicide Peace (1796–97). V, 407.

When leaders choose to make themselves bidders at an auction of popularity, their talents, in the construction of the state, will be of no service. They will become flatterers instead of legislators,—the instruments, not the guides of the people. If any of them should happen to propose a scheme of liberty soberly limited, and defined with proper qualifications, he will be immediately outbid by his competitors, who will produce something more splendidly popular. Suspicions will be raised of his fidelity to his cause. Moderation will be stigmatized as the virtue of cowards, and compromise as the prudence of traitors,—until, in hopes of preserving the credit which may enable him to temper and moderate on some occasions, the popular leader is obliged to become active in propagating doctrines and establishing powers that will afterwards defeat any sober purpose at which he ultimately might have aimed.

Reflections (1790). III, 560.

To deliver an opinion is the right of all men; that of constituents is a weighty and respectable opinion, which a representative ought always to rejoice to hear, and which he ought always most seriously to consider. But *authoritative* instructions, *mandates* issued, which the member is bound blindly and implicitly to obey, to vote, and to argue for, though contrary to the clearest conviction of his judgment and conscience,—these are things utterly unknown to the laws of this land, and which arise from a fundamental mistake of the whole order and tenor of our Constitution.

Parliament is not a *congress* of ambassadors from different and hostile interests, which interests each must maintain, as an agent and advocate, against other agents and advocates; but Parliament is a *deliberative* assembly of *one* nation, with *one* interest, that of the whole—where not local purposes, not local prejudices, ought to guide, but the general good, resulting from the general reason of the whole. You choose a member, indeed; but when you have chosen him, he is not member of Bristol, but he is a member of *Parliament*. If the local constituent should have an interest or should form an hasty opinion evidently opposite to the real good of the rest of the community, the member for that place ought to be as far as any other from any endeavor to give it effect.

Speech to Electors of Bristol (1774). II, 96.

We [the members of the House of Commons] are like other men, who all want to be moved by praise or shame; by reward and punishment. We must be encouraged by our constituents, and we must be kept in awe of them, or we never shall do our duty as we ought. Believe me, it is a great truth, that there never was, for any long time, a corrupt representative of a virtuous people; or a mean, sluggish, careless people that ever had a good government of any form. If it be true in any degree, that the governors form the people, I am certain it is as true that the people in their turn impart their characters to their rulers. Such as you are, sooner or later, must parliament be. I therefore wish that you, at least, would not suffer yourselves to be amused by the style, now grown so common, of railing at the corruption of members of parliament. This kind of general invective has no kind of effect, that I know of, but to make you think ill of that very institution, which, do what you will, you must religiously preserve, or you must give over all thoughts of being a free people. An opinion of the indiscriminate corruption of the House of Commons will, at length, induce a disgust of parliaments. They are the corrupters themselves, who circulate this general charge of corruption. It is they that have an interest in confounding all distinctions, and involving the whole in one general charge. They hope to corrupt private life by the example of the public; and having produced a despair, from a supposed general failure of principles, they hope that they may persuade you, that since it is impossible to do any good, you may as well have your share in the profits of doing ill.

Letter to a Member of the Bell-Club, Bristol, October 31, 1777.
Correspondence. II, 194–95.

I hope there are none of you corrupted with the doctrine taught by wicked men for the worst purposes, and received by the malignant credulity of envy and ignorance, which is, that the men who act upon the public stage are all alike, all equally corrupt, all influenced by no other views than the sordid lure of salary and pension. The thing I know by experience to be false. Never expecting to find perfection in men, and not looking for divine attributes in created beings, in my commerce with my contemporaries I have found much human virtue. I have seen not a little public spirit, a real subordination of interest to duty, and a decent and regulated sensibility to honest fame and reputation. The age unquestionably produces (whether in a greater or less number than former times I know not) daring profligates and insidious hypocrites. What then? Am I not to avail myself of whatever good is to be found in the world, because of the mixture of evil that will always be in it? The smallness of the quantity in currency only heightens the value. They who raise suspicions on the good on account of the behavior of ill men are of the party of the latter. The common cant is no justification for taking this party. I have been deceived, say they, by *Titius* and *Mævius;* I have been the dupe of this pretender or of that mountebank; and I can trust appearances no longer. But my credulity and want of discernment cannot, as I conceive, amount to a fair presumption against any man's integrity. A conscientious person would rather doubt his own judgment than condemn his species. He would say, "I have observed without attention, or judged upon erroneous maxims; I trusted to profession, when I ought to have attended to conduct." Such a man will grow wise, not malignant, by his acquaintance with the world. But he that accuses all mankind of corruption ought to remember that he is sure to convict only one. In truth, I should much rather admit those whom at any time I have disrelished the most to be patterns of perfection than seek a consolation to my own unworthiness in a general communion of depravity with all about me.

That this ill-natured doctrine should be preached by the missionaries of a court I do not wonder. It answers their purpose. But that it should be heard among those who pretend to be strong assertors of liberty is not only surprising, but hardly natural. This moral levelling is a *servile principle*. It leads to practical passive obedience far better than all the doctrines which the pliant accommodation of theology to power has ever produced. It cuts up by the roots, not only all idea of forcible resistance, but even of civil opposition. It disposes men to an abject submission, not by opinion, which may be shaken by argument or altered by passion, but by the strong ties of public and private interest. For, if all men who act in a public situation are equally selfish, corrupt, and venal, what reason can be given for desiring any sort of change, which, besides the evils which must attend all changes, can be productive of no possible advantage? The active men in the state are true samples of the mass. If they are universally depraved, the commonwealth itself is not sound. We may amuse ourselves with talking as much as we please of the virtue of middle or humble life; that is, we may place our confidence in the virtue of those who have never been tried. But if the persons who are continually emerging out of that sphere be no better than those whom birth has placed above it, what hopes are there in the remainder of the body which is to furnish the perpetual succession of the state? All who have ever written on government are unanimous, that among a people generally corrupt liberty cannot long exist. And, indeed, how is it possible, when those who are to make the laws, to guard, to enforce, or to obey them, are, by a tacit confederacy of manners, indisposed to the spirit of all generous and noble institutions?

Letter to the Sheriffs of Bristol (1777). II, 240–42.

4. Elections and Parliamentary Reform

There was strong agitation in Burke's time for extending the suffrage and reducing the limit to the life of Parliament from seven years to three. Under the political circumstances of the time, Burke feared that these changes might only strengthen the control of the King's servile ministry over the Commons, especially in view of the heavy expense incurred by any candidate standing for election. But he was in general less sanguine than some of his friends who advocated these reforms that the results would be up to expectations.

It is always to be lamented, when men are driven to search into the foundations of the commonwealth. It is certainly necessary to resort to the theory of your government, whenever you propose any alteration in the frame of it,—whether that alteration means the revival of some former antiquated and forsaken constitution of state, or the introduction of some new improvement in the commonwealth. The object of our deliberation is, to promote the good purposes for which elections have been instituted, and to prevent their inconveniences. If we thought frequent elections attended with no inconvenience, or with but a trifling inconvenience, the strong overruling principle of the Constitution would sweep us like a torrent towards them. But your remedy is to be suited to your disease, your present disease, and to your whole disease. That man thinks much too highly, and therefore he thinks weakly and delusively, of any contrivance of human wisdom, who believes that it can make any sort of approach to perfection. There is not, there never was, a principle of government under heaven, that does not, in the very pursuit of the good it proposes, naturally and inevitably lead into some inconvenience which makes it absolutely necessary to counterwork and weaken the application of that first principle itself, and to abandon something of the extent of the advantage you proposed by it, in order to prevent also the inconveniences which have arisen from the instrument of all the good you had in view.

To govern according to the sense and agreeably to the interests of the people is a great and glorious object of government. This object cannot be obtained but through the medium of popular election; and popular election is a mighty evil. It is such and so great an evil, that, though there are few nations whose monarchs were not originally elective, very few are now elected. They are the distempers of elections that have destroyed all free states. To cure these distempers is difficult, if not impossible; the only thing, therefore, left to save the commonwealth is, to prevent their return too frequently. The objects in view are, to have Parliaments as frequent as they can be without distracting them in the prosecution of public business: on one hand, to secure their dependence upon the people; on the other, to give them that quiet in their minds and that ease in their fortunes as to enable them to perform the most arduous and most painful duty in the world with spirit, with efficiency, with independency, and with experience, as real public counsellors, not as the canvassers at a perpetual election. It is wise to compass as many good ends as possibly you can, and, seeing there are inconveniences on both sides, with benefits on both, to give up a part of the benefit to soften the inconvenience. The perfect cure is impracticable; because the disorder is dear to those from whom alone the cure can possibly be derived. The utmost to be done is to palliate, to mitigate, to respite, to put off the evil day of the Constitution to its latest possible hour,—and may it be a very late one! . . .

All are agreed that Parliaments should not be perpetual; the only question is, What is the most convenient time for their duration?—on which there are three opinions. We are agreed, too, that the term ought not to be chosen most likely in its operation to spread corruption, and to augment the already overgrown influence of the crown. On these principles I mean to debate the question. It is easy to pretend a zeal for liberty. Those who think themselves not likely to be incumbered with the performance of their promises, either from their known inability or total indifference about the performance, never fail to entertain the most lofty ideas. They are certainly the most specious; and they cost them neither reflection to frame, nor pains to modify, nor management to support. The task is of another nature to those who mean to promise nothing that it is not in their intention, or may possibly be in their power to perform,—to those who are bound and principled no more to delude the understandings than to violate the liberty of their fellow-subjects. Faithful watchmen we ought to be over the rights and privileges of the people. But our duty, if we are qualified for it as we ought, is to give them information, and not to receive it from them: we are not to go to school to them, to learn the principles of law and government. In doing so, we should not dutifully serve, but we should basely and scandalously betray the people, who are not capable of this service by nature, nor in any instance called to it by the Constitution. I reverentially look up to the opinion of the people, and with an awe that is almost superstitious. I should be ashamed to show my face before them, if I changed my ground as they cried up or cried down men or things or opinions,—if I wavered and shifted about with every change, and joined in it or opposed as best answered any low interest or passion,—if I held them up hopes which I knew I never intended, or promised what I well knew I could not perform. Of all these things they are perfect sovereign judges without appeal; but as to the detail of particular measures, or to any general schemes of policy, they have neither enough of speculation in the closet nor of experience in business to decide upon it. They can well see whether we are tools of a court or their honest servants. Of that they can well judge,—and I wish that they always exercised their judgment; but of the particular merits of a measure I have other standards. . . .

Theory, I know, would suppose that every general election is to the representative a day of judgment, in which he appears before his constituents to account for the use of the talent with which they intrusted him, and for the improvement he has made of it for the public advantage. It would be so, if every corruptible representative were to find an enlightened and incorruptible constituent. But the practice and knowledge of the world will not suffer us to be ignorant that the Constitution on paper is one thing, and in fact and experience is another. We must know that the candidate, instead of trusting at his election to the testimony of his behavior in Parliament, must bring the testimony of a large sum of money, the capacity of liberal expense in entertainments, the power of serving and obliging the rulers of corporations, of winning over the popular leaders of political clubs, associations, and neighborhoods. It is ten thousand times more necessary to show himself a man of power than a man of integrity, in almost all the elections with which I have been acquainted. Elections, therefore, become a matter of heavy expense; and if contests are frequent, to many they will become a matter of an expense totally ruinous, which no fortunes can bear, but least of all the landed fortunes, incumbered as they often, indeed as they mostly are, with debts, with portions, with jointures, and tied up in the hands of the possessor by the limitations of settlement. It is a material, it is in my opinion a lasting consideration, in all the questions concerning election. Let no one think the charges of elections a trivial matter.

The charge, therefore, of elections ought never to be lost sight of in a question concerning their frequency; because the grand object you seek is independence. Independence of mind will ever be more or less influenced by independence of fortune; and if every three years the exhausting sluices of entertainments, drink-ings, open houses, to say nothing of bribery, are to be periodically drawn up and renewed,—if government favors, for which now, in some shape or other, the whole race of men are candidates, are to be called for upon every occasion, I see that private fortunes will be washed away, and every, even to the least, trace of independence borne down by the torrent. I do not seriously think this Constitution, even to the wrecks of it, could survive five triennial elections. If you are to fight the battle, you must put on the armor of the ministry, you must call in the public to the aid of private money. . . .

Gentlemen, I know, feel the weight of this argument; they agree, that this would be the consequence of more frequent elections, if things were to continue as they are. But they think the greatness and frequency of the evil would itself be a remedy for it,—that, sitting but for a short time, the member would not find it worth while to make such vast expenses, while the fear of their constituents will hold them the more effectually to their duty.

To this I answer, that experience is full against them. This is no new thing; we have had triennial Parliaments; at no period of time were seats more eagerly contested. The expenses of elections ran higher, taking the state of all charges, than they do now. The expense of entertainments was such, that an act, equally severe and ineffectual, was made against it; every monument of the time bears witness of the expense, and most of the acts against corruption in elections were then made; all the writers talked of it and lamented it. Will any one think that a corporation will be contented with a bowl of punch or a piece of beef the less, because elections are every three, instead of every seven years? Will they change their wine for ale, because they are to get more ale three years hence? Don't think it. . . .

A seat in this House, for good purposes, for bad purposes, for no purposes at all, (except the mere consideration derived from being concerned in the public counsels,) will ever be a first-rate object of ambition in England. Ambition is no exact calculator. Avarice itself does not calculate strictly, when it games. One thing is certain,—that in this political game the great lottery of power is that into which men will purchase with millions of chances against them. In Turkey, where the place, where the fortune, where the head itself are so insecure that scarcely any have died in their beds for ages, so that the bowstring is the natural death of bashaws, yet in no country is power and distinction (precarious enough, God knows, in all) sought for with such boundless avidity,—as if the value of place was enhanced by the danger and insecurity of its tenure. Nothing will ever make a seat in this House not an object of desire to numbers by any means or at any charge, but the depriving it of all power and all dignity. This would do it. This is the true and only nostrum for that purpose. But an House of Commons without power and without dignity, either in itself or in its members, is no House of Commons for the purposes of this Constitution.

But they will be afraid to act ill, if they know that the day of their account is always near. I wish it were true; but it is not: here again we have experience, and experience is against us. . . .

The shortness of time in which they are to reap the profits of iniquity is far from checking the avidity of corrupt men; it renders them infinitely more ravenous. They rush violently and precipitately on their object; they lose all regard to decorum. The moments of profits are precious; never are men so wicked as during a general mortality. . . .

Thus, in my opinion, the shortness of a triennial sitting would have the following ill effects: it would make the member more shamelessly and shockingly corrupt; it would increase his dependence on those who could best support him at his election; it would wrack and tear to pieces the fortunes of those who stood upon their own fortunes and their private interest; it would make the electors infinitely more venal; and it would make the whole body of the people, who are, whether they have votes or not, concerned in elections, more lawless, more idle, more debauched; it would utterly destroy the sobriety, the industry, the integrity, the simplicity of all the people, and undermine, I am much afraid, the deepest and best-laid foundations of the commonwealth.

Speech on the Duration of Parliaments (1780). VII, 71–87.

CHAPTER VI

Reform and Tradition

1. Tradition and Change

The root-and-branch revolutionists of the eighteenth century expressed great confidence in the moral goodness of men in general, and in their intellectual competence to select measures dictated by science and reason. Burke did not share this confidence and insisted that our "naked and shivering human nature" needs such comforts and supports as can be provided by the established traditions of an old society. His ideas on prudence as a political virtue, on the nature of society and government, on the importance of manners and religion, are all interrelated with his defense of tradition.

We are afraid to put men to live and trade each on his own private stock of reason; because we suspect that this stock in each man is small, and that the individuals would do better to avail themselves of the general bank and capital of nations and of ages.

Reflections (1790). III, 346.

I feel an insuperable reluctance in giving my hand to destroy any established institution of government, upon a theory, however plausible it may be.

Speech on Mr. Fox's East India Bill (1783). II, 442.

It required a great length of time, very considerable industry and perseverance, no vulgar policy, the union of many men and many tempers, and the concurrence of events which do not happen every day, to build up an independent House of Commons. Its demolition was accomplished in a moment; and it was the work of ordinary hands. But to construct is a matter of skill; to demolish, force and fury are sufficient.

Preface to Motion Relative to the Speech from the Throne (1784). II, 540.

Nothing is more beautiful in the theory of parliaments, than that principle of renovation, and union of permanence and change, that are happily mixed in their constitution:—that in all our changes we are never wholly old or wholly new:—that there are enough of the old to preserve unbroken the traditionary chain of the maxims and policy of our ancestors, and the law and custom of parliament; and enough of the new to invigorate us and bring us to our true character, by being taken fresh from the mass of the people; and the whole, though mostly composed of old members, have, notwithstanding, a new character and may have the advantage of change without the imputation of inconstancy.

Notes for Speech, November 30, 1774.
Correspondence. IV, Appendix, 465.

The people of England well know, that the idea of an inheritance furnishes a sure principle of conservation and a sure principle of transmission; without at all excluding a principle of improvement. It leaves acquisition free; but it secures what it acquires. . . . By a constitutional policy, working after the pattern of nature, we receive, we hold, we transmit our government and our privileges, in the same manner in which we enjoy and transmit our property and our lives. The institutions of policy, the goods of fortune, the gifts of providence, are handed down to us, and from us, in the same course and order. Our political system is placed in a just correspondence and symmetry with the order of the world, and with the mode of existence decreed to a permanent body composed of transitory parts; wherein, by the disposition of a stupendous wisdom, moulding together the great mysterious incorporation of the human race, the whole, at one time, is never old, or middle-aged, or young, but, in a condition of unchangeable constancy, moves on through the varied tenor of perpetual decay, fall, renovation, and progression. Thus, by preserving the method of nature in the conduct of the state, in what we improve, we are never wholly new; in what we retain, we are never wholly obsolete.

Reflections (1790). III, 274–76.

I have taken a view of what has been done by the governing power in France. I have certainly spoke of it with freedom. Those whose principle it is to despise the ancient, permanent sense of mankind, and to set up a scheme of society on new principles, must naturally expect that such of us who think better of the judgment of the human race than of theirs should consider both them and their devices as men and schemes upon their trial. They must take it for granted that we attend much to their reason, but not at all to their authority. They have not one of the great influencing prejudices of mankind in their favor. They avow their hostility to opinion. Of course they must expect no support from that influence, which, with every other authority, they have deposed from the seat of its jurisdiction.

I can never consider this Assembly as anything else than a voluntary association of men who have availed themselves of circumstances to seize upon the power of the state. They have not the sanction and authority of the character under which they first met. They have assumed another of a very different nature, and have completely altered and inverted all the relations in which they originally stood. They do not hold the authority they exercise under any constitutional law of the state. They have departed from the instructions of the people by whom they were sent; which instructions, as the Assembly did not act in virtue of any ancient usage or settled law, were the sole source of their authority. The most considerable of their acts have not been done by great majorities; and in this sort of near divisions, which carry only the constructive authority of the whole, strangers will consider reasons as well as resolutions.

If they had set up this new, experimental government as a necessary substitute for an expelled tyranny, mankind would anticipate the time of prescription [see Chapter VII, section 2], which through long usage mellows into legality governments that were violent in their commencement. All those who have affections which lead them to the conservation of civil order would recognize, even in its cradle, the child as legitimate, which has been produced from those principles of cogent expediency to which all just governments owe their birth, and on which they justify their continuance. But they will be late and reluctant in giving any sort of countenance to the operations of a power which has derived its birth from no law and no necessity, but which, on the contrary, has had its origin in those vices and sinister practices by which the social union is often disturbed and sometimes destroyed. This Assembly has hardly a year's prescription. We have their own word for it that they have made a revolution. To make a revolution is a measure which, *primâ fronte*, requires an apology. To make a revolution is to subvert the ancient state of our country; and no common reasons are called for to justify so violent a proceeding. The sense of mankind authorizes us to examine into the mode of acquiring new power, and to criticize on the use that is made of it, with less awe and reverence than that which is usually conceded to a settled and recognized authority.

In obtaining and securing their power, the Assembly proceeds upon principles the most opposite from those which appear to direct them in the use of it. An observation on this difference will let us into the true spirit of their conduct. Everything which they have done, or continue to do, in order to obtain and keep their power, is by the most common arts. They proceed exactly as their ancestors of ambition have done before them. Trace them through all their artifices, frauds, and violences, you can find nothing at all that is new. They follow precedents and examples with the punctilious exactness of a pleader. They never depart an iota from the authentic formulas of tyranny and usurpation. But in all the regulations relative to the public good the spirit has been the very reverse of this. There they commit the whole to the mercy of untried speculations; they abandon the dearest interests of the public to those loose theories to which none of them would choose to trust the slightest of his private concerns. They make this difference, because in their desire of obtaining and securing power they are thoroughly in earnest; there they travel in the beaten road. The public interests, because about them they have no real solicitude, they abandon wholly to chance: I say to chance, because their schemes have nothing in experience to prove their tendency beneficial.

We must always see with a pity not unmixed with respect the errors of those who are timid and doubtful of themselves with regard to points wherein the happiness of mankind is concerned. But in these gentlemen there is nothing of the tender parental solicitude which fears to cut up the infant for the sake of an experiment. In the vastness of their promises and the confidence of their predictions they far outdo all the boasting of empirics. The arrogance of their pretensions in a manner provokes and challenges us to an inquiry into their foundation.

I am convinced that there are men of considerable parts among the popular leaders in the National Assembly. Some of them display eloquence in their speeches and their writings. This cannot be without powerful and cultivated talents. But eloquence may exist without a proportionable degree of wisdom. When I speak of ability, I am obliged to distinguish. What they have done towards the support of their system bespeaks no ordinary men. In the system itself, taken as the scheme of a republic constructed for procuring the prosperity and security of the citizen, and for promoting the strength and grandeur of the state, I confess myself unable to find out anything which displays, in a single instance, the work of a comprehensive and disposing mind, or even the provisions of a vulgar prudence. Their purpose everywhere seems to have been to evade and slip aside from *difficulty*. This it has been the glory of the great masters in all the arts to confront, and to overcome,—and when they had overcome the first difficulty, to turn it into an instrument for new conquests over new difficulties: thus to enable them to extend the empire of their science, and even to push forward, beyond the reach of their original thoughts, the landmarks of the human understanding itself. Difficulty is a severe instructor, set over us by the supreme ordinance of a parental Guardian and Legislator, who knows us better than we know ourselves, as He loves us better too. *Pater ipse colendi haud facilem esse viam voluit.* ["The great Father himself has willed that the path of tillage should not be easy." Virgil *Georgics* i.121.] He that wrestles with us strengthens our nerves and sharpens our skill. Our antagonist is our helper. This amicable conflict with difficulty obliges us to an intimate acquaintance with our object, and compels us to consider it in all its relations. It will not suffer us to be superficial. It is the want of nerves of understanding for such a task, it is the degenerate fondness for tricking short-cuts and little fallacious facilities, that has in so many parts of the world created governments with arbitrary powers. They have created the late arbitrary monarchy of France. They have created the arbitrary republic of Paris. With them defects in wisdom are to be supplied by the plenitude of force. They get nothing by it. Commencing their labors on a principle of sloth, they have the common fortune of slothful men. The difficulties, which they rather had eluded than escaped, meet them again in their course; they multiply and

thicken on them; they are involved, through a labyrinth of confused detail, in an industry without limit and without direction;
and in conclusion, the whole of their work becomes feeble, vicious, and insecure.

It is this inability to wrestle with difficulty which has obliged
the arbitrary Assembly of France to commence their schemes of
reform with abolition and total destruction.[1] But is it in destroying and pulling down that skill is displayed? Your mob can do
this as well at least as your assemblies. The shallowest understanding, the rudest hand, is more than equal to that task. Rage
and frenzy will pull down more in half an hour than prudence,
deliberation, and foresight can build up in a hundred years. The
errors and defects of old establishments are visible and palpable.
It calls for little ability to point them out; and where absolute
power is given, it requires but a word wholly to abolish the vice
and the establishment together. The same lazy, but restless disposition, which loves sloth and hates quiet, directs these politicians, when they come to work for supplying the place of what
they have destroyed. To make everything the reverse of what
they have seen is quite as easy as to destroy. No difficulties occur
in what has never been tried. Criticism is almost baffled in dis-

---

[1] A leading member of the Assembly, M. Rabaut de St. Étienne, has
expressed the principle of all their proceedings as clearly as possible;
nothing can be more simple:—"*Tous les établissemens en France
couronnent le malheur du peuple: pour le rendre heureux, il faut le
renouveler, changer ses idées, changer ses loix, changer ses mœurs,
. . . . changer les hommes, changer les choses, changer les mots,
. . . . tout détruire; oui, tout détruire; puisque tout est à récréer.*"—
This gentleman was chosen president in an assembly not sitting at
Quinze-Vingt or the *Petites Maisons,* and composed of persons giving
themselves out to be rational beings; but neither his ideas, language,
or conduct differ in the smallest degree from the discourses, opinions,
and actions of those, within and without the Assembly, who direct the
operations of the machine now at work in France. [Burke]

["All the established institutions of France only crown the misery
of the people; to make the people happy it is necessary to renovate it,
to change the ideas, the laws, the morals, . . . change the men, the
things, the words, . . . to destroy everything, yes everything; for
everything must be started anew."]

covering the defects of what has not existed; and eager enthusiasm and cheating hope have all the wide field of imagination, in which they may expatiate with little or no opposition.

At once to preserve and to reform is quite another thing. When the useful parts of an old establishment are kept, and what is superadded is to be fitted to what is retained, a vigorous mind, steady, persevering attention, various powers of comparison and combination, and the resources of an understanding fruitful in expedients are to be exercised; they are to be exercised in a continued conflict with the combined force of opposite vices, with the obstinacy that rejects all improvement, and the levity that is fatigued and disgusted with everything of which it is in possession. But you may object,—"A process of this kind is slow. It is not fit for an Assembly which glories in performing in a few months the work of ages. Such a mode of reforming, possibly, might take up many years." Without question it might; and it ought. It is one of the excellences of a method in which time is amongst the assistants, that its operation is slow, and in some cases almost imperceptible. If circumspection and caution are a part of wisdom, when we work only upon inanimate matter, surely they become a part of duty too, when the subject of our demolition and construction is not brick and timber, but sentient beings, by the sudden alteration of whose state, condition, and habits, multitudes may be rendered miserable. But it seems as if it were the prevalent opinion in Paris, that an unfeeling heart and an undoubting confidence are the sole qualifications for a perfect legislator. Far different are my ideas of that high office. The true law-giver ought to have a heart full of sensibility. He ought to love and respect his kind, and to fear himself. It may be allowed to his temperament to catch his ultimate object with an intuitive glance; but his movements towards it ought to be deliberate. Political arrangement, as it is a work for social ends, is to be only wrought by social means. There mind must conspire with mind. Time is required to produce that union of minds which alone can produce all the good we aim at. Our patience will achieve more than our force. If I might venture to appeal to what is so much out of fashion in Paris,—I mean to experience, —I should tell you, that in my course I have known, and, according to my measure, have coöperated with great men; and I have never yet seen any plan which has not been mended by the observations of those who were much inferior in understanding to the person who took the lead in the business. By a slow, but well-sustained progress, the effect of each step is watched; the good or ill success of the first gives light to us in the second; and so, from light to light, we are conducted with safety through the whole series. We see that the parts of the system do not clash. The evils latent in the most promising contrivances are provided for as they arise. One advantage is as little as possible sacrificed to another. We compensate, we reconcile, we balance. We are enabled to unite into a consistent whole the various anomalies and contending principles that are found in the minds and affairs of men. From hence arises, not an excellence in simplicity, but one far superior, an excellence in composition. Where the great interests of mankind are concerned through a long succession of generations, that succession ought to be admitted into some share in the councils which are so deeply to affect them. If justice requires this, the work itself requires the aid of more minds than one age can furnish. It is from this view of things that the best legislators have been often satisfied with the establishment of some sure, solid, and ruling principle in government,—a power like that which some of the philosophers have called a plastic Nature; and having fixed the principle, they have left it afterwards to its own operation.

To proceed in this manner, that is, to proceed with a presiding principle and a prolific energy, is with me the criterion of profound wisdom. What your politicians think the marks of a bold, hardy genius are only proofs of a deplorable want of ability. By their violent haste, and their defiance of the process of Nature, they are delivered over blindly to every projector and adventurer, to every alchemist and empiric. They despair of turning to account anything that is common. Diet is nothing in their system of remedy. The worst of it is, that this their despair of curing common distempers by regular methods arises not only from defect of comprehension, but, I fear, from some malignity of disposition. Your legislators seem to have taken their opinions of all professions, ranks, and offices from the declamations and buffooneries of satirists,—who would themselves be astonished, if they were held to the letter of their own descriptions. By listening only to these, your leaders regard all things only on the side of their vices and faults, and view those vices and faults under every color of exaggeration. It is undoubtedly true, though it may seem paradoxical,—but, in general, those who are habitually employed in finding and displaying faults are unqualified for the work of reformation; because their minds are not only unfurnished with patterns of the fair and good, but by habit they come to take no delight in the contemplation of those things. By hating vices too much, they come to love men too little. It is therefore not wonderful that they should be indisposed and unable to serve them. From hence arises the complexional disposition of some of your guides to pull everything in pieces. At this malicious game they display the whole of their *quadrimanous* activity. As to the rest, the paradoxes of eloquent writers, brought forth purely as a sport of fancy, to try their talents, to rouse attention, and excite surprise, are taken up by these gentlemen, not in the spirit of the original authors, as means of cultivating their taste and improving their style: these paradoxes become with them serious grounds of action, upon which they proceed in regulating the most important concerns of the state. . . . Mr. Hume told me that he had from Rousseau himself the secret of his principles of composition. That acute, though eccentric observer, had perceived, that, to strike and interest the public, the marvellous must be produced; that the marvellous of the heathen mythology had long since lost its effects; that giants, magicians, fairies, and heroes of romance, which succeeded, had exhausted the portion of credulity which belonged to their age; that now nothing was left to a writer but that species of the marvellous, which might still be produced, and with as great an effect as ever, though in another way,—that is, the marvellous in life, in manners, in characters, and in extraordinary situations, giving rise to new and unlooked-for strokes in politics and morals. I believe, that, were Rousseau alive, and in one of his lucid intervals, he would be shocked at the practical frenzy of his scholars, who in their paradoxes are servile imitators, and even in their incredulity discover an implicit faith.

Men who undertake considerable things, even in a regular way, ought to give us ground to presume ability. But the physician of the state, who, not satisfied with the cure of distempers, undertakes to regenerate constitutions, ought to show uncommon powers. Some very unusual appearances of wisdom ought to display themselves on the face of the designs of those who appeal to no practice and who copy after no model. Has any such been manifested? . . .

It is in the model of the sovereign and presiding part of this new republic that we should expect their grand display. Here they were to prove their title to their proud demands. For the plan itself at large, and for the reasons on which it is grounded, I refer to the journals of the Assembly of the 29th of September, 1789, and to the subsequent proceedings which have made any alterations in the plan. So far as in a matter somewhat confused I can see light, the system remains substantially as it has been originally framed. . . .

Old establishments are tried by their effects. If the people are happy, united, wealthy, and powerful, we presume the rest. We conclude that to be good from whence good is derived. In old establishments various correctives have been found for their aberrations from theory. Indeed, they are the results of various necessities and expediences. They are not often constructed after any theory: theories are rather drawn from them. In them we often see the end best obtained, where the means seem not perfectly reconcilable to what we may fancy was the original scheme. The means taught by experience may be better suited to political ends than those contrived in the original project. They again react upon the primitive constitution, and sometimes improve the design itself, from which they seem to have departed. I think all this might be curiously exemplified in the British Constitution. At worst, the errors and deviations of every kind in reckoning are found and computed, and the ship proceeds in her course. This is the case of old establishments; but in a new and merely theoretic system, it is expected that every contrivance shall appear, on the face of it, to answer its ends, especially where the projectors are no way embarrassed with an endeavor to accommodate the new building to an old one, either in the walls or on the foundations.

Reflections (1790). III, 449–61.

2. Principles of Reform

Burke spent thirty years in the House of Commons, and almost all his activity was in the Opposition. He advocated many reforms, usually without any immediate success. He urged the necessity of reform, but always with wisdom and prudence and with a recognition of continuity in government and the national life. He therefore sharply distinguished between reform and innovation or revolution.

I confess to you, Sir, I never liked this continual talk of resistance and revolution, or the practice of making the extreme medicine of the Constitution its daily bread. It renders the habit of society dangerously valetudinary; it is taking periodical doses of mercury sublimate, and swallowing down repeated provocatives of cantharides to our love of liberty.

Reflections (1790). III, 314.

I wished to warn the people against the greatest of all evils,—a blind and furious spirit of innovation, under the name of reform. I was, indeed, well aware that power rarely reforms itself. So it is, undoubtedly, when all is quiet about it. But I was in hopes that provident fear might prevent fruitless penitence. I trusted that danger might produce at least circumspection. I flattered myself, in a moment like this, that nothing would be added to make authority top-heavy,—that the very moment of an earthquake would not be the time chosen for adding a story to our houses. I hoped to see the surest of all reforms, perhaps the only sure reform,—the ceasing to do ill. In the mean time I wished to the people the wisdom of knowing how to tolerate a condition which none of their efforts can render much more than tolerable. It was a condition, however, in which everything was to be found that could enable them to live to Nature, and, if so they pleased, to live to virtue and to honor.

I do not repent that I thought better of those to whom I wished well than they will suffer me long to think that they deserved. Far from repenting, I would to God that new faculties had been called up in me, in favor not of this or that man, or this or that system, but of the general, vital principle, that, whilst it was in its vigor, produced the state of things transmitted to us from our fathers, but which, through the joint operation of the abuses of authority and liberty, may perish in our hands. I am not of opinion that the race of men, and the commonwealths they create, like the bodies of individuals, grow effete and languid and bloodless, and ossify, by the necessities of their own conformation, and the fatal operation of longevity and time. These analogies between bodies natural and politic, though they may sometimes illustrate arguments, furnish no argument of themselves. They are but too often used, under the color of a specious philosophy, to find apologies for the despair of laziness and pusillanimity, and to excuse the want of all manly efforts, when the exigencies of our country call for them the more loudly.

How often has public calamity been arrested on the very brink of ruin by the seasonable energy of a single man! Have we no such man amongst us? I am as sure as I am of my being, that one vigorous mind, without office, without situation, without public functions of any kind, (at a time when the want of such a thing is felt, as I am sure it is,) I say, one such man, confiding in the aid of God, and full of just reliance in his own fortitude, vigor, enterprise, and perseverance, would first draw to him some few like himself, and then that multitudes, hardly thought to be in existence, would appear and troop about him.

If I saw this auspicious beginning, baffled and frustrated as I am, yet on the very verge of a timely grave, abandoned abroad and desolate at home, stripped of my boast, my hope, my consolation, my helper, my counsellor, and my guide, (you know in part what I have lost, and would to God I could clear myself of all neglect and fault in that loss,) yet thus, even thus, I would rake up the fire under all the ashes that oppress it. I am no longer patient of the public eye; nor am I of force to win my way and to justle and elbow in a crowd. But, even in solitude, something may be done for society. The meditations of the closet have infected senates with a subtle frenzy, and inflamed armies with the brands of the Furies. The cure might come from the same source with the distemper. I would add my part to those who would animate the people (whose hearts are yet right) to new exertions in the old cause.

Novelty is not the only source of zeal. Why should not a Maccabæus and his brethren arise to assert the honor of the ancient law and to defend the temple of their forefathers with as ardent a spirit as can inspire any innovator to destroy the monuments of the piety and the glory of ancient ages? It is not a hazarded assertion, it is a great truth, that, when once things are gone out of their ordinary course, it is by acts out of the ordinary course they can alone be reëstablished. Republican spirit can only be combated by a spirit of the same nature,—of the same nature, but informed with another principle, and pointing to another end. I would persuade a resistance both to the corruption and to the reformation that prevails. It will not be the weaker, but much the stronger, for combating both together. A victory over real corruptions would enable us to baffle the spurious and pretended reformations. I would not wish to excite, or even to tolerate, that kind of evil spirit which evokes the powers of hell to rectify the disorders of the earth. No! I would add my voice with better, and, I trust, more potent charms, to draw down justice and wisdom and fortitude from heaven, for the correction of human vice, and the recalling of human error from the devious ways into which it has been betrayed. I would wish to call the impulses of individuals at once to the aid and to the control of authority. By this, which I call the true republican spirit, paradoxical as it may appear, monarchies alone can be rescued from the imbecility of courts and the madness of the crowd. This republican spirit would not suffer men in high place to bring ruin on their country and on themselves. It would reform, not by destroying, but by saving, the great, the rich, and the powerful. Such a republican spirit we perhaps fondly conceive to have animated the distinguished heroes and patriots of old, who knew no mode of policy but religion and virtue. These they would have paramount to all constitutions; they would not suffer monarchs, or senates, or popular assemblies, under pretences of dignity or authority or freedom, to shake off those moral riders which reason has appointed to govern every sort of rude power. These, in appearance loading them by their weight, do by that pressure augment their essential force. The momentum is increased by the extraneous weight. It is true in moral as it is in mechanical science. It is true, not only in the draught, but in the race. These riders of the great, in effect, hold the reins which guide them in their course, and wear the spur that stimulates them to the goals of honor and of safety. The great must submit to the dominion of prudence and of virtue, or none will long submit to the dominion of the great. . . . This is the feudal tenure which they cannot alter.

Letter to William Elliot (1795). V, 123–27.

When Burke was granted a pension by the Crown in 1796, the wealthy Duke of Bedford, whose great estates had been given his ancestor by Henry VIII, rose in the House of Lords and attacked Burke. Burke published his brilliant retort in "Letter to a Noble Lord." In it he defended against Bedford's insinuations his whole political career, including his proposals for Economical Reform in 1780, which were aimed not only at the wasteful organization of the royal establishment, but even more at the antiquated practices of royal patronage which seriously threatened the independence of the House of Commons.

I knew that there is a manifest, marked distinction, which ill men with ill designs, or weak men incapable of any design, will constantly be confounding,—that is, a marked distinction between change and reformation. The former alters the substance of the objects themselves, and gets rid of all their essential good as well as of all the accidental evil annexed to them. Change is novelty; and whether it is to operate any one of the effects of reformation at all, or whether it may not contradict the very principle upon which reformation is desired, cannot be certainly known beforehand. Reform is not a change in the substance or in the primary modification of the object, but a direct application of a remedy to the grievance complained of. So far as that is removed, all is sure. It stops there; and if it fails, the substance which underwent the operation, at the very worst, is but where it was.

All this, in effect, I think, but am not sure, I have said elsewhere. It cannot at this time be too often repeated, line upon line, precept upon precept, until it comes into the currency of a proverb,—*To innovate is not to reform*. The French revolutionists complained of everything; they refused to reform anything; and they left nothing, no, nothing at all, *unchanged*. The consequences are *before* us,—not in remote history, not in future prognostication: they are about us; they are upon us. They shake the public security; they menace private enjoyment. They dwarf the growth of the young; they break the quiet of the old. If we travel, they stop our way. They infest us in town; they pursue us to the country. Our business is interrupted, our repose is troubled, our pleasures are saddened, our very studies are poisoned and perverted, and knowledge is rendered worse than ignorance, by the enormous evils of this dreadful innovation. . . .

It was, then, not my love, but my hatred to innovation, that produced my plan of reform. Without troubling myself with the exactness of the logical diagram, I considered them as things substantially opposite. It was to prevent that evil, that I proposed the measures which his Grace is pleased, and I am not sorry he is pleased, to recall to my recollection. I had (what I hope that noble Duke will remember in all his operations) a state to preserve, as well as a state to reform. I had a people to gratify, but not to inflame or to mislead. I do not claim half the credit for what I did as for what I prevented from being done. In that situation of the public mind, I did not undertake, as was then proposed, to new-model the House of Commons or the House of Lords, or to change the authority under which any officer of the crown acted, who was suffered at all to exist. Crown, lords, commons, judicial system, system of administration, existed as they had existed before, and in the mode and manner in which they had always existed. My measures were, what I then truly stated them to the House to be, in their intent, healing and mediatorial. A complaint was made of too much influence in the House of Commons: I reduced it in both Houses; and I gave my reasons, article by article, for every reduction, and showed why I thought it safe for the service of the state. I heaved the lead every inch of way I made. A disposition to expense was complained of: to that I opposed, not mere retrenchment, but a system of economy, which would make a random expense, without plan or foresight, in future, not easily practicable. I proceeded upon principles of research to put me in possession of my matter, on principles of method to regulate it, and on principles in the human mind and in civil affairs to secure and perpetuate the operation. I conceived nothing arbitrarily, nor proposed anything to be done by the will and pleasure of others or my own,—but by reason, and by reason only. I have ever abhorred, since the first dawn of my understanding to this its obscure twilight, all the operations of opinion, fancy, inclination, and will, in the affairs of government, where only a sovereign reason, paramount to all forms of legislation and administration, should dictate. Government is made for the very purpose of opposing that reason to will and to caprice, in the reformers or in the reformed, in the governors or in the governed, in kings, in senates, or in people.

Letter to a Noble Lord (1796). V, 185–89.

Burke's statement of his belief in early and moderate reform was expressed in the House of Commons in 1780, long before the French Revolution.

These desires of the people of England . . . are moderate indeed. They only contend that we should interweave some economy with the taxes with which we have chosen to begin the war. They request, not that you should rely upon economy exclusively, but that you should give it rank and precedence, in the order of the ways and means of this single session.

But if it were possible that the desires of our constituents, desires which are at once so natural and so very much tempered and subdued, should have no weight with an House of Commons which has its eye elsewhere, I would turn my eyes to the very quarter to which theirs are directed. I would reason this matter with the House on the mere policy of the question; and I would undertake to prove that an early dereliction of abuse is the direct interest of government,—of government taken abstractedly from its duties, and considered merely as a system intending its own conservation.

If there is any one eminent criterion which above all the rest distinguishes a wise government from an administration weak and improvident, it is this: "well to know the best time and manner of yielding what it is impossible to keep." There have been, Sir, and there are, many who choose to chicane with their situation rather than be instructed by it. Those gentlemen argue against every desire of reformation upon the principles of a criminal prosecution. It is enough for them to justify their adherence to a pernicious system, that it is not of their contrivance, —that it is an inheritance of absurdity, derived to them from their ancestors,—that they can make out a long and unbroken pedigree of mismanagers that have gone before them. They are proud of the antiquity of their house; and they defend their errors as if they were defending their inheritance, afraid of derogating from their nobility, and carefully avoiding a sort of blot in their scutcheon, which they think would degrade them forever. . . .

I do most seriously put it to administration to consider the wisdom of a timely reform. Early reformations are amicable arrangements with a friend in power; late reformations are terms imposed upon a conquered enemy: early reformations are made in cool blood; late reformations are made under a state of inflammation. In that state of things the people behold in government nothing that is respectable. They see the abuse, and they will see nothing else. They fall into the temper of a furious populace provoked at the disorder of a house of ill-fame; they never attempt to correct or regulate; they go to work by the shortest way: they abate the nuisance, they pull down the house.

This is my opinion with regard to the true interest of government. But as it is the interest of government that reformation should be early, it is the interest of the people that it should be temperate. It is their interest, because a temperate reform is permanent, and because it has a principle of growth. Whenever we improve, it is right to leave room for a further improvement. It is right to consider, to look about us, to examine the effect of what we have done. Then we can proceed with confidence, because we can proceed with intelligence. Whereas in hot reformations, in what men more zealous than considerate call *making clear work*, the whole is generally so crude, so harsh, so indigested, mixed with so much imprudence and so much injustice, so contrary to the whole course of human nature and human institutions, that the very people who are most eager for it are among the first to grow disgusted at what they have done. Then some part of the abdicated grievance is recalled from its exile in order to become a corrective of the correction. Then the abuse assumes all the credit and popularity of a reform. The very idea of purity and disinterestedness in politics falls into disrepute, and is considered as a vision of hot and inexperienced men; and thus disorders become incurable, not by the virulence of their own quality, but by the unapt and violent nature of the remedies. A great part, therefore, of my idea of reform is meant to operate gradually: some benefits will come at a nearer, some at a more remote period. We must no more make haste to be rich by parsimony than by intemperate acquisition.

In my opinion, it is our duty, when we have the desires of the people before us, to pursue them, not in the spirit of literal obedience, which may militate with their very principle,—much less to treat them with a peevish and contentious litigation, as if we were adverse parties in a suit. It would, Sir, be most dishonorable for a faithful representative of the Commons to take advantage of any inartificial expression of the people's wishes, in order to frustrate their attainment of what they have an undoubted right to expect. We are under infinite obligations to our constituents, who have raised us to so distinguished a trust, and have imparted such a degree of sanctity to common characters. We ought to walk before them with purity, plainness, and integrity of heart, —with filial love, and not with slavish fear, which is always a low and tricking thing. For my own part, in what I have meditated upon that subject, I cannot, indeed, take upon me to say I have the honor *to follow* the sense of the people. The truth is, *I met it on the way,* while I was pursuing their interest according to my own ideas. I am happy beyond expression to find that my intentions have so far coincided with theirs, that I have not had cause to be in the least scrupulous to sign their petition, conceiving it to express my own opinions, as nearly as general terms can express the object of particular arrangements.

I am therefore satisfied to act as a fair mediator between government and the people, endeavoring to form a plan which should have both an early and a temperate operation. I mean, that it should be substantial, that it should be systematic, that it should rather strike at the first cause of prodigality and corrupt influence than attempt to follow them in all their effects.

Speech on the Plan for Economical Reform (1780). II, 278–82.

In a plan of reformation, it would be one of my maxims, that, when I know of an establishment which may be subservient to useful purposes, and which at the same time, from its discretionary nature, is liable to a very great perversion from those purposes, *I would limit the quantity of the power that might be so abused.* For I am sure that in all such cases the rewards of merit will have very narrow bounds, and that partial or corrupt favor will be infinite.

Speech on the Plan for Economical Reform (1780). II, 328.

One form of government may be better than another, and this difference may be worth a struggle. I think so. I do not mean to treat any of those forms which are often the contrivances of deep human wisdom (not the rights of men, as some people, in my opinion, not very wisely, talk of them) with slight or disrespect; nor do I mean to level them.

A positively vicious and abusive government ought to be changed,—and, if necessary, by violence,—if it cannot be (as sometimes it is the case) reformed. But when the question is concerning the more or the less *perfection* in the organization of a government, the allowance to *means* is not of so much latitude. There is, by the essential fundamental constitution of things, a radical infirmity in all human contrivances; and the weakness is often so attached to the very perfection of our political mechanism, that some defect in it,—something that stops short of its principle,—something that controls, that mitigates, that moderates it,—becomes a necessary corrective to the evils that the theoretic perfection would produce. I am pretty sure it often is so; and this truth may be exemplified abundantly.

Letter to Mons. Dupont, October, 1789.
Correspondence. III, 117.

It would be a dreadful thing if there were any power, in this country, of strength enough to oppose with effect the general wishes of the people. Next to that would be, the people wishing for themselves an object almost as surely destructive to them, as any thing which the worst machinations of their worst enemies could devise.

Letter to Jos. Harford, April 4, 1780.
Correspondence. II, 340.

In great revolutions, and in critical situations like those which France has for some time experienced, great errors are, in a manner, unavoidable. He knows little of mankind, and feels less for them, who is not sensible of this, and who will not make a liberal allowance for our common and inevitable infirmity.

Letter to the Chevalier de Grave, August 24, 1792.
Correspondence. III, 512.

There is another advantage in taking up this business singly and by an arrangement for the single object. It is that you may proceed by *degrees.* We must all obey the great law of change. It is the most powerful law of Nature, and the means perhaps of its conservation. All we can do, and that human wisdom can do, is to provide that the change shall proceed by insensible degrees. This has all the benefits which may be in change, without any of the inconveniences of mutation. Everything is provided for as it arrives. This mode will, on the one hand, prevent the *unfixing old interests at once:* a thing which is apt to breed a black and sullen discontent in those who are at once dispossessed of all their influence and consideration. This gradual course, on the other side, will prevent men long under depression from being intoxicated with a large draught of new power, which they always abuse with a licentious insolence. But, wishing, as I do, the change to be gradual and cautious, I would, in my first steps, lean rather to the side of enlargement than restriction.

Letter to Sir Hercules Langrishe (1792). IV, 301.

I may be unable to lend an helping hand to those who direct the state; but I should be ashamed to make myself one of a noisy multitude to halloo and hearten them into doubtful and dangerous courses. A conscientious man would be cautious how he dealt in blood. He would feel some apprehension at being called to a tremendous account for engaging in so deep a play without any sort of knowledge of the game. It is no excuse for presumptuous ignorance, that it is directed by insolent passion. The poorest being that crawls on earth, contending to save itself from injustice and oppression, is an object respectable in the eyes of God and man. But I cannot conceive any existence under heaven (which in the depths of its wisdom tolerates all sorts of things) that is more truly odious and disgusting than an impotent, helpless creature, without civil wisdom or military skill, without a consciousness of any other qualification for power but his servility to it, bloated with pride and arrogance, calling for battles which he is not to fight, contending for a violent dominion which he can never exercise, and satisfied to be himself mean and miserable, in order to render others contemptible and wretched.

Letter to the Sheriffs of Bristol (1777). II, 206.

CHAPTER VII

Tradition in the English Establishment

1. The English Constitution

The English Constitution is not a written document like that of the United States, but the law and custom accumulated down through the ages. As such it has constantly been growing and changing, and Burke thought the changes had always been for the better. Its merits were due to its long history during which it had incorporated the wisdom and experience of many men and many generations. But Burke feared it could only too easily be destroyed by the willfulness and violent intransigeance of agitators, and especially of imprudent theorists.

Our constitution stands on a nice equipoise, with steep precipices and deep waters upon all sides of it. In removing it from a dangerous leaning towards one side, there may be a risk of oversetting it on the other. Every project of a material change in a government so complicated as ours, combined at the same time with external circumstances still more complicated, is a matter full of difficulties: in which a considerate man will not be too ready to decide; a prudent man too ready to undertake; or an honest man too ready to promise. They do not respect the public nor themselves, who engage for more than they are sure that they ought to attempt, or that they are able to perform.
Thoughts on the Cause of the Present Discontents (1770). I, 520.

In forming a plan for this purpose [of a conciliatory concession to the American Colonies], I endeavored to put myself in that frame of mind which was the most natural and the most reasonable, and which was certainly the most probable means of securing me from all error. I set out with a perfect distrust of my own abilities, a total renunciation of every speculation of my own, and with a profound reverence for the wisdom of our ancestors, who have left us the inheritance of so happy a Constitution and so flourishing an empire, and, what is a thousand times more valuable, the treasury of the maxims and principles which formed the one and obtained the other.

Speech on Conciliation with America (1775). II, 145.

Respecting your wisdom, and valuing your safety, we do not call upon you to trust your existence to your enemies. We do not advise you to an unconditional submission. With satisfaction we assure you that almost all in both Houses (however unhappily they have been deluded, so as not to give any immediate effect to their opinion) disclaim that idea. You can have no friends in whom you cannot rationally confide. But Parliament is your friend from the moment in which, removing its confidence from those who have constantly deceived its good intentions, it adopts the sentiments of those who have made sacrifices, (inferior, indeed, to yours,) but have, however, sacrificed enough to demonstrate the sincerity of their regard and value for your liberty and prosperity.

Arguments may be used to weaken your confidence in that public security; because, from some unpleasant appearances, there is a suspicion that Parliament itself is somewhat fallen from its independent spirit. How far this supposition may be founded in fact we are unwilling to determine. But we are well assured from experience, that, even if all were true that is contended for, and in the extent, too, in which it is argued, yet, as long as the solid and well-disposed forms of this Constitution remain, there ever is within Parliament itself a power of renovating its principles, and effecting a self-reformation, which no other plan of government has ever contained. This Constitution has therefore admitted innumerable improvements, either for the correction of the original scheme, or for removing corruptions, or for bringing its principles better to suit those changes which have successively happened in the circumstances of the nation or in the manners of the people.

We feel that the growth of the colonies is such a change of circumstances, and that our present dispute is an exigency as pressing as any which ever demanded a revision of our government. Public troubles have often called upon this country to look into its Constitution. It has ever been bettered by such a revision.

If our happy and luxuriant increase of dominion, and our diffused population, have outgrown the limits of a Constitution made for a contracted object, we ought to bless God, who has furnished us with this noble occasion for displaying our skill and beneficence in enlarging the scale of rational happiness, and of making the politic generosity of this kingdom as extensive as its fortune. If we set about this great work, on both sides, with the same conciliatory turn of mind, we may now, as in former times, owe even to our mutual mistakes, contentions, and animosities, the lasting concord, freedom, happiness, and glory of this empire.

Address to the British Colonists in North America (1777). VI, 193–94.

Having heard yesterday, by mere accident, that there is an intention of laying before the county meeting *new matter, which is not contained in our petition,* and the consideration of which had been deferred to a fitter time by a majority of our committee in London, permit me to take this method of submitting to you my reasons for thinking, with our committee, that nothing ought to be hastily determined upon the subject.

Our petition arose naturally from distresses which we *felt;* and the requests which we made were in effect nothing more than that such things should be done in Parliament as it was evidently the duty of Parliament to do. But the affair which will be proposed to you by a person of rank and ability is an alteration in the constitution of Parliament itself. It is impossible for you to have a subject before you of more importance, and that requires a more cool and more mature consideration, both on its own account, and for the credit of our sobriety of mind, who are to resolve upon it.

The county will in some way or other be called upon to declare it your opinion, that the House of Commons is not sufficiently numerous, and that the elections are not sufficiently frequent,—that an hundred new knights of the shire ought to be added, and that we are to have a new election once in three years for certain, and as much oftener as the king pleases. Such will be the state of things, if the proposition made shall take effect.

All this may be proper. But, as an honest man, I cannot possibly give my vote for it, until I have considered it more fully. I will not deny that our Constitution may have faults, and that those faults, when found, ought to be corrected; but, on the whole, that Constitution has been our own pride, and an object of admiration to all other nations. It is not everything which appears at first view to be faulty, in such a complicated plan, that is to be determined to be so in reality. To enable us to correct the Constitution, the whole Constitution must be viewed together; and it must be compared with the actual state of the people, and the circumstances of the time. For that which taken singly and by itself may appear to be wrong, when considered with relation to other things, may be perfectly right,—or at least such as ought to be patiently endured, as the means of preventing something that is worse. So far with regard to what at first view may appear a *distemper* in the Constitution. As to the *remedy* of that distemper an equal caution ought to be used; because this latter consideration is not single and separate, no more than the former. There are many things in reformation which would be proper to be done, if other things can be done along with them, but which, if they cannot be so accompanied, ought not to be done at all. I therefore wish, when any new matter of this deep nature is proposed to me, to have the whole scheme distinctly in my view, and full time to consider of it. Please God, I will walk with caution, whenever I am not able clearly to see my way before me.

I am now growing old. I have from my very early youth been conversant in reading and thinking upon the subject of our laws and Constitution, as well as upon those of other times and other countries; I have been for fifteen years a very laborious member of Parliament, and in that time have had great opportunities of seeing with my own eyes the working of the machine of our government, and remarking where it went smoothly and did its business, and where it checked in its movements, or where it damaged its work; I have also had and used the opportunities of conversing with men of the greatest wisdom and fullest experience in those matters; and I do declare to you most solemnly and most truly, that, on the result of all this reading, thinking, experience, and communication, I am not able to come to an immediate resolution in favor of a change of the groundwork of our Constitution, and in particular, that, in the present state of the country, in the present state of our representation, in the present state of our rights and modes of electing, in the present state of the several prevalent interests, in the present state of the affairs and manners of this country, the addition of an hundred knights of the shire, and hurrying election on election, will be things advantageous to liberty or good government.

This is the present condition of my mind; and this is my apology for not going as fast as others may choose to go in this business. I do not by any means reject the propositions; much less do I condemn the gentlemen who, with equal good intentions, with much better abilities, and with infinitely greater personal weight and consideration than mine, are of opinion that this matter ought to be decided upon instantly.

I most heartily wish that the deliberate sense of the kingdom on this great subject should be known. When it is known, it *must* be prevalent. It would be dreadful indeed, if there was any power in the nation capable of resisting its unanimous desire, or even the desire of any very great and decided majority of the people. The people may be deceived in their choice of an object; but I can scarcely conceive any choice they can make to be so very mischievous as the existence of any human force capable of resisting it. It will certainly be the duty of every man, in the situation to which God has called him, to give his best opinion and advice upon the matter: it will *not* be his duty, let him think what he will, to use any violent or any fraudulent means of counteracting the general wish, or even of employing the legal and constructive organ of expressing the people's sense against the sense which they do actually entertain.

In order that the real sense of the people should be known upon so great an affair as this, it is of absolute necessity that timely notice should be given,—that the matter should be prepared in open committees, from a choice into which no class or description of men is to be excluded,—and the subsequent county meetings should be as full and as well attended as possible. Without these precautions, the true sense of the people will ever be uncertain. Sure I am, that no precipitate resolution on a great change in the fundamental constitution of any country can ever be called the real sense of the people.

I trust it will not be taken amiss, if, as an inhabitant and freeholder of this county (one, indeed, among the most inconsiderable,) I assert my right of dissenting (as I do dissent fully and directly) from any resolution whatsoever on the subject of an alteration in the representation and election of the kingdom *at this time*. By preserving this right, and exercising it with temper and moderation, I trust I cannot offend the noble proposer, for whom no man professes or feels more respect and regard than I do. A want of concurrence in *everything* which *can* be proposed will in no sort weaken the energy or distract the efforts of men of upright intentions upon those points in which they are agreed. Assemblies that are met, and with a resolution to be all of a mind, are assemblies that can have no opinion at all of their own. The first proposer of any measure must be their master. I do not know that an amicable variety of sentiment, conducted with mutual good-will, has any sort of resemblance to discord, or that it can give any advantage whatsoever to the enemies of our common cause. On the contrary, a forced and fictitious agreement (which every universal agreement must be) is not becoming the cause of freedom. If, however, any evil should arise from it, (which I confess I do not foresee,) I am happy that those who have brought forward new and arduous matter, when very great doubts and some diversity of opinion must be foreknown, are of authority and weight enough to stand against the consequences.

I humbly lay these my sentiments before the county. They are not taken up to serve any interests of my own, or to be subservient to the interests of any man or set of men under heaven. I could wish to be able to attend our meeting, or that I had time to reason this matter more fully by letter; but I am detained here upon our business: what you have already put upon us is as much as we can do. If we are prevented from going through it with any effect, I fear it will be in part owing not more to the resistance of the enemies of our cause than to our imposing on ourselves such tasks as no human faculties, employed as we are, can be equal to. Our worthy members have shown distinguished ability and zeal in support of our petition. I am just going down to a bill brought in to frustrate a capital part of your desires. The minister is preparing to transfer the cognizance of the public accounts from those whom you and the Constitution have chosen to control them, to unknown persons, creatures of his own. For so much he annihilates Parliament.

Letter to the Buckinghamshire Meeting on Parliamentary Reform (1780). VI, 293–98.

Every age has its own manners, and its politics dependent upon them; and the same attempts will not be made against a constitution fully formed and matured, that were used to destroy it in the cradle, or to resist its growth during its infancy.

Against the being of Parliament, I am satisfied, no designs have ever been entertained since the Revolution [of 1688]. Every one must perceive, that it is strongly the interest of the court, to have some second cause interposed between the ministers and the people. The gentlemen of the House of Commons have an interest equally strong in sustaining the part of that intermediate cause. . . . Accordingly those who have been of the most known devotion to the will and pleasure of a court have, at the same time, been most forward in asserting a high authority in the House of Commons. When they knew who were to use that authority, and how it was to be employed, they thought it never could be carried too far. It must be always the wish of an unconstitutional statesman, that a House of Commons, who are entirely dependent upon him, should have every right of the people entirely dependent upon their pleasure. It was soon discovered, that the forms of a free, and the ends of an arbitrary government, were things not altogether incompatible.

The power of the crown, almost dead and rotten as Prerogative, has grown up anew, with much more strength, and far less odium, under the name of Influence. An influence, which operated without noise and without violence; an influence, which converted the very antagonist into the instrument of power; which contained in itself a perpetual principle of growth and renovation; and which the distresses and the prosperity of the country equally tended to augment, was an admirable substitute for a prerogative, that, being only the offspring of antiquated prejudices, had moulded in its original stamina irresistible principles of decay and dissolution. The ignorance of the people is a bottom but for a temporary system; the interest of active men in the state is a foundation perpetual and infallible. However, some circumstances, arising, it must be confessed, in a great degree from accident, prevented the effects of this influence for a long time from breaking out in a manner capable of exciting any serious apprehensions. Although government was strong and flourished exceedingly, the *court* had drawn far less advantage than one would imagine from this great source of power.

At the Revolution, the crown, deprived, for the ends of the Revolution itself, of many prerogatives, was found too weak to struggle against all the difficulties which pressed so new and unsettled a government. The court was obliged therefore to delegate a part of its power to men of such interest as could support, and of such fidelity as would adhere to, its establishment. Such men were able to draw in a greater number to a concurrence in the common defence. This connection, necessary at first, continued long after convenient; and properly conducted might indeed, in all situations, be an useful instrument of government. At the same time, through the intervention of men of popular weight and character, the people possessed a security for their just proportion of importance in the state. But as the title to the crown grew stronger by long possession, and by the constant increase of its influence, these helps have of late seemed to certain persons no better than incumbrances. The powerful managers for government were not sufficiently submissive to the pleasure of the possessors of immediate and personal favor, sometimes from a confidence in their own strength, natural and acquired; sometimes from a fear of offending their friends, and weakening that lead in the country which gave them a consideration independent of the court. Men acted as if the court could receive, as well as confer, an obligation. The influence of government, thus divided in appearance between the court and the leaders of parties, became in many cases an accession rather to the popular than to the royal scale; and some part of that influence, which would otherwise have been possessed as in a sort of mortmain and unalienable domain, returned again to the great ocean from whence it arose, and circulated among the people. This method, therefore, of governing by men of great natural interest or great acquired consideration was viewed in a very invidious light by the true lovers of absolute monarchy. It is the nature of despotism to abhor power held by any means but its own momentary pleasure; and to annihilate all intermediate situations between boundless strength on its own part, and total debility on the part of the people.

To get rid of all this intermediate and independent importance, and *to secure to the court the unlimited and uncontrolled use of its own vast influence, under the sole direction of its own private favor,* has for some years past been the great object of policy.

If this were compassed, the influence of the crown must of course produce all the effects which the most sanguine partisans of the court could possibly desire. Government might then be carried on without any concurrence on the part of the people; without any attention to the dignity of the greater, or to the affections of the lower sorts.

Thoughts on the Cause of the Present Discontents (1770). I, 434–47.

It is this unnatural infusion of a *system of favoritism* into a government which in a great part of its constitution is popular, that has raised the present ferment in the nation. The people, without entering deeply into its principles, could plainly perceive its effects, in much violence, in a great spirit of innovation, and a general disorder in all the functions of government. . . . This is the fountain of all those bitter waters of which, through an hundred different conduits, we have drunk until we are ready to burst. The discretionary power of the crown in the formation of ministry, abused by bad or weak men, has given rise to a system, which, without directly violating the letter of any law, operates against the spirit of the whole constitution.

A plan of favoritism for our executory government is essentially at variance with the plan of our legislature. One great end undoubtedly of a mixed government like ours, composed of monarchy, and of controls, on the part of the higher people and the lower, is that the prince shall not be able to violate the laws. This is useful indeed and fundamental. But this, even at first view, is no more than a negative advantage; an armor merely defensive. It is therefore next in order, and equal in importance, *that the discretionary powers which are necessarily vested in the monarch, whether for the execution of the laws, or for the nomination to magistracy and office, or for conducting the affairs of peace and war, or for ordering the revenue, should all be exercised upon public principles and national grounds, and not on the likings or prejudices, the intrigues or policies, of a court.* This, I said, is equal in importance to the securing a government according to law. The laws reach but a very little way. Constitute government how you please, infinitely the greater part of it must depend upon the exercise of the powers which are left at large to the prudence and uprightness of ministers of state. Even all the use and potency of the laws depends upon them.

Without them, your commonwealth is no better than a scheme upon paper; and not a living, active, effective constitution. It is possible that through negligence, or ignorance, or design artfully conducted, ministers may suffer one part of government to languish, another to be perverted from its purposes, and every valuable interest of the country to fall into ruin and decay, without possibility of fixing any single act on which a criminal prosecution can be justly grounded. The due arrangement of men in the active part of the state, far from being foreign to the purposes of a wise government, ought to be among its very first and dearest objects. When, therefore, the abettors of the new system tell us, that between them and their opposers there is nothing but a struggle for power, and that therefore we are no ways concerned in it; we must tell those who have the impudence to insult us in this manner, that, of all things, we ought to be the most concerned who, and what sort of men they are that hold the trust of everything that is dear to us. Nothing can render this a point of indifference to the nation, but what must either render us totally desperate, or soothe us into the security of idiots. We must soften into a credulity below the milkiness of infancy to think all men virtuous. We must be tainted with a malignity truly diabolical to believe all the world to be equally wicked and corrupt. Men are in public life as in private, some good, some evil. The elevation of the one, and the depression of the other, are the first objects of all true policy. But that form of government, which, neither in its direct institutions, nor in their immediate tendency, has contrived to throw its affairs into the most trustworthy hands, but has left its whole executory system to be disposed of agreeably to the uncontrolled pleasure of any one man, however excellent or virtuous, is a plan of polity defective not only in that member, but consequentially erroneous in every part of it.

In arbitrary governments, the constitution of the ministry follows the constitution of the legislature. Both the law and the magistrate are the creatures of will. It must be so. Nothing, indeed, will appear more certain, on any tolerable consideration of this matter, than that *every sort of government ought to have its administration correspondent to its legislature.* If it should be otherwise, things must fall into an hideous disorder. The people of a free commonwealth, who have taken such care that their laws should be the result of general consent, cannot be so sense-less as to suffer their executory system to be composed of persons on whom they have no dependence, and whom no proofs of the public love and confidence have recommended to those powers, upon the use of which the very being of the state depends.

The popular election of magistrates, and popular disposition of rewards and honors, is one of the first advantages of a free state. Without it, or something equivalent to it, perhaps the people cannot long enjoy the substance of freedom; certainly none of the vivifying energy of good government. The frame of our commonwealth did not admit of such an actual election: but it provided as well, and (while the spirit of the constitution is preserved) better for all the effects of it than by the method of suffrage in any democratic state whatsoever. It had always, until of late, been held the first duty of Parliament *to refuse to support government, until power was in the hands of persons who were acceptable to the people, or while factions predominated in the court in which the nation had no confidence.* Thus all the good effects of popular election were supposed to be secured to us, without the mischiefs attending on perpetual intrigue, and a distinct canvass for every particular office throughout the body of the people. This was the most noble and refined part of our constitution. The people, by their representatives and grandees, were intrusted with a deliberative power in making laws; the king with the control of his negative. The king was intrusted with the deliberative choice and the election to office; the people had the negative in a Parliamentary refusal to support. Formerly this power of control was what kept ministers in awe of Parliaments, and Parliaments in reverence with the people. If the use of this power of control on the system and persons of administration is gone, everything is lost, Parliament and all. We may assure ourselves, that if Parliament will tamely see evil men take possession of all the strongholds of their country, and allow them time and means to fortify themselves, under a pretence of giving them a fair trial, and upon a hope of discovering, whether they will not be reformed by power, and whether their measures will not be better than their morals; such a Parliament will give countenance to their measures also, whatever that Parliament may pretend, and whatever those measures may be.

Every good political institution must have a preventive operation as well as a remedial. It ought to have a natural tendency to exclude bad men from government, and not to trust for the safety of the state to subsequent punishment alone; punishment, which has ever been tardy and uncertain; and which, when power is suffered in bad hands, may chance to fall rather on the injured than the criminal.

Before men are put forward into the great trusts of the state, they ought by their conduct to have obtained such a degree of estimation in their country, as may be some sort of pledge and security to the public, that they will not abuse those trusts. It is no mean security for a proper use of power, that a man has shown by the general tenor of his actions, that the affection, the good opinion, the confidence of his fellow-citizens have been among the principal objects of his life; and that he has owed none of the gradations of his power or fortune to a settled contempt, or occasional forfeiture of their esteem.

Thoughts on the Cause of the Present Discontents (1770). I, 469–73.

The Revolution Society, which had been formed as an eminently respectable group to commemorate the English Revolution of 1688, had been changed by time and a shift in membership into a more radical political club, which in 1789 saluted the new French Revolution and published the sermon by Dr. Price, an eminent Non-Conformist minister. Dr. Price seemed to Burke to try to justify and glorify the French Revolution by identifying its principles and methods with those of the bloodless Revolution of 1688, of which the English people were so justly proud. Burke therefore felt obligated to clear up this confusion and distinguish between the principles of the two Revolutions.

All circumstances taken together, the French Revolution is the most astonishing that has hitherto happened in the world. The most wonderful things are brought about in many instances by means the most absurd and ridiculous, in the most ridiculous modes, and apparently by the most contemptible instruments. Everything seems out of nature in this strange chaos of levity and ferocity, and of all sorts of crimes jumbled together with all sorts of follies. In viewing this monstrous tragicomic scene, the most opposite passions necessarily succeed and sometimes mix with each other in the mind: alternate contempt and indignation, alternate laughter and tears, alternate scorn and horror.

It cannot, however, be denied that to some this strange scene appeared in quite another point of view. Into them it inspired no other sentiments than those of exultation and rapture. They saw nothing in what has been done in France but a firm and temperate exertion of freedom,—so consistent, on the whole, with morals and with piety as to make it deserving not only of the secular applause of dashing Machiavelian politicians, but to render it a fit theme for all the devout effusions of sacred eloquence.

On the forenoon of the fourth of November last, Doctor Richard Price, a Non-Conforming minister of eminence, preached at the Dissenting meeting-house of the Old Jewry, to his club or society, a very extraordinary miscellaneous sermon, in which there are some good moral and religious sentiments, and not ill expressed, mixed up with a sort of porridge of various political opinions and reflections: but the Revolution in France is the grand ingredient in the caldron. . . .

That sermon is in a strain which I believe has not been heard in this kingdom, in any of the pulpits which are tolerated or encouraged in it, since the year 1648,—when a predecessor of Dr. Price, the Reverend Hugh Peters, made the vault of the king's own chapel at St. James's ring with the honor and privilege of the saints, who, with the "high praises of God in their mouths, and a *two*-edged sword in their hands, were to execute judgment on the heathen, and punishments upon the *people; to* bind their *kings* with chains, and their *nobles* with fetters of iron." . . .[1]

This pulpit style, revived after so long a discontinuance, had to me the air of novelty, and of a novelty not wholly without danger. I do not charge this danger equally to every part of the discourse. The hint given to a noble and reverend lay-divine, who is supposed high in office in one of our universities,[2] and other lay-divines "of *rank* and literature," may be proper and seasonable, though somewhat new. If the noble *Seekers* should find nothing to satisfy their pious fancies in the old staple of

[1] Ps. cxlix. [Burke]
[2] Discourse on the Love of our Country, Nov. 4, 1789, by Dr. Richard Price, 3d edition, p. 17 and 18. [Burke]

the national Church, or in all the rich variety to be found in the well-assorted warehouses of the Dissenting congregations, Dr. Price advises them to improve upon Non-Conformity, and to set up, each of them, a separate meeting-house upon his own particular principles.[3] It is somewhat remarkable that this reverend divine should be so earnest for setting up new churches, and so perfectly indifferent concerning the doctrine which may be taught in them. His zeal is of a curious character. It is not for the propagation of his own opinions, but of any opinions. It is not for the diffusion of truth, but for the spreading of contradiction. Let the noble teachers but dissent, it is no matter from whom or from what. This great point once secured, it is taken for granted their religion will be rational and manly. I doubt whether religion would reap all the benefits which the calculating divine computes from this "great company of great preachers." It would certainly be a valuable addition of nondescripts to the ample collection of known classes, genera, and species, which at present beautify the *hortus siccus* of Dissent. . . .

But I may say of our preacher, "*Utinam nugis tota illa dedisset tempora sævitiæ.*" ["If he had only spent on trifles all that time of violence." Juvenal *Satires* iv.150.] All things in this his fulminating bull are not of so innoxious a tendency. His doctrines affect our Constitution in its vital parts. He tells the Revolution Society, in this political sermon, that his Majesty "is almost the *only* lawful king in the world, because the *only* one who owes his crown to *the choice of his people.*" As to the kings of *the world,* all of whom (except one) this arch-pontiff of the *rights of men,* with all the plenitude and with more than the boldness of the Papal deposing power in its meridian fervor of the twelfth century, puts into one sweeping clause of ban and anathema, and proclaims usurpers by circles of longitude and latitude over the whole globe, it behooves them to consider how they admit into

---

[3] "Those who dislike that mode of worship which is prescribed by public authority ought, if they can find *no* worship *out* of the Church which they approve, *to set up a separate worship for themselves;* and by doing this, and giving an example of a rational and manly worship, men of *weight* from their *rank* and literature may do the greatest service to society and the world."—P. 18, Dr. Price's Sermon. [Burke]

their territories these apostolic missionaries, who are to tell their subjects they are not lawful kings. That is their concern. It is ours, as a domestic interest of some moment, seriously to consider the solidity of the *only* principle upon which these gentlemen acknowledge a king of Great Britain to be entitled to their allegiance.

This doctrine, as applied to the prince now on the British throne, either is nonsense, and therefore neither true nor false, or it affirms a most unfounded, dangerous, illegal, and unconstitutional position. According to this spiritual doctor of politics, if his Majesty does not owe his crown to the choice of his people, he is no *lawful* king. Now nothing can be more untrue than that the crown of this kingdom is so held by his Majesty. Therefore, if you follow their rule, the king of Great Britain, who most certainly does not owe his high office to any form of popular election, is in no respect better than the rest of the gang of usurpers, who reign, or rather rob, all over the face of this our miserable world, without any sort of right or title to the allegiance of their people. The policy of this general doctrine, so qualified, is evident enough. The propagators of this political gospel are in hopes their abstract principle (their principle that a popular choice is necessary to the legal existence of the sovereign magistracy) would be overlooked, whilst the king of Great Britain was not affected by it. In the mean time the ears of their congregations would be gradually habituated to it, as if it were a first principle admitted without dispute. For the present it would only operate as a theory, pickled in the preserving juices of pulpit eloquence, and laid by for future use. . . .

At some time or other, to be sure, all the beginners of dynasties were chosen by those who called them to govern. There is ground enough for the opinion that all the kingdoms of Europe were at a remote period elective, with more or fewer limitations in the objects of choice. But whatever kings might have been here or elsewhere a thousand years ago, or in whatever manner the ruling dynasties of England or France may have begun, the king of Great Britain is at this day king by a fixed rule of succession, according to the laws of his country; and whilst the legal conditions of the compact of sovereignty are performed by him, (as they are performed,) he holds his crown in contempt of the choice of the Revolution Society, who have not a single vote for a king amongst them, either individually or collectively: though I make no doubt they would soon erect themselves into an electoral college, if things were ripe to give effect to their claim. . . .

Whatever may be the success of evasion in explaining away the gross error of *fact*, which supposes that his Majesty (though he holds it in concurrence with the wishes) owes his crown to the choice of his people, yet nothing can evade their full, explicit declaration concerning the principle of a right in the people to choose,—which right is directly maintained, and tenaciously adhered to. All the oblique insinuations concerning election bottom in this proposition, and are referable to it. Lest the foundation of the king's exclusive legal title should pass for a mere rant of adulatory freedom, the political divine proceeds dogmatically to assert,[4] that, by the principles of the Revolution, the people of England have acquired three fundamental rights, all of which, with him, compose one system, and lie together in one short sentence: namely, that we have acquired a right

1. "To choose our own governors."
2. "To cashier them for misconduct."
3. "To frame a government for ourselves."

This new, and hitherto unheard-of bill of rights, though made in the name of the whole people, belongs to those gentlemen and their faction only. The body of the people of England have no share in it. They utterly disclaim it. They will resist the practical assertion of it with their lives and fortunes. They are bound to do so by the laws of their country, made at the time of that very Revolution which is appealed to in favor of the fictitious rights claimed by the society which abuses its name.

These gentlemen of the Old Jewry, in all their reasonings on the Revolution of 1688, have a revolution which happened in England about forty years before, and the late French Revolution, so much before their eyes and in their hearts, that they are constantly confounding all the three together. It is necessary that we should separate what they confound. We must recall their erring fancies to the *acts* of the Revolution which we revere, for the discovery of its true *principles*. If the *principles* of the Revolution of 1688 are anywhere to be found, it is in the statute

---

[4] P. 34, Discourse on the Love of our Country, by Dr. Price. [Burke]

called the *Declaration of Right*. In that most wise, sober, and considerate declaration, drawn up by great lawyers and great statesmen, and not by warm and inexperienced enthusiasts, not one word is said, nor one suggestion made, of a general right "to choose our own *governors*, to cashier them for misconduct, and to *form* a government for *ourselves*."

This Declaration of Right (the act of the 1st of William and Mary, sess. 2, ch. 2) is the corner-stone of our Constitution, as reinforced, explained, improved, and in its fundamental principles forever settled. It is called "An act for declaring the rights and liberties of the subject, and for *settling* the *succession* of the crown." You will observe that these rights and this succession are declared in one body, and bound indissolubly together.

A few years after this period, a second opportunity offered for asserting a right of election to the crown. On the prospect of a total failure of issue from King William, and from the princess, afterwards Queen Anne, the consideration of the settlement of the crown, and of a further security for the liberties of the people, again came before the legislature. Did they this second time make any provision for legalizing the crown on the spurious Revolution principles of the Old Jewry? No. They followed the principles which prevailed in the Declaration of Right; indicating with more precision the persons who were to inherit in the Protestant line. This act also incorporated, by the same policy, our liberties and an hereditary succession in the same act. Instead of a right to choose our own governors, they declared that the *succession* in that line (the Protestant line drawn from James the First) was absolutely necessary "for the peace, quiet, and security of the realm," and that it was equally urgent on them "to maintain a *certainty in the succession* thereof, to which the subjects may safely have recourse for their protection." Both these acts, in which are heard the unerring, unambiguous oracles of Revolution policy, instead of countenancing the delusive gypsy predictions of a "right to choose our governors," prove to a demonstration how totally adverse the wisdom of the nation was from turning a case of necessity into a rule of law.

Unquestionably there was at the Revolution, in the person of King William, a small and a temporary deviation from the strict order of a regular hereditary succession; but it is against all genuine principles of jurisprudence to draw a principle from a law made in a special case and regarding an individual person. *Privilegium non transit in exemplum.* ["A special case does not make a general rule."] If ever there was a time favorable for establishing the principle that a king of popular choice was the only legal king, without all doubt it was at the Revolution. Its not being done at that time is a proof that the nation was of opinion it ought not to be done at any time. There is no person so completely ignorant of our history as not to know that the majority in Parliament, of both parties, were so little disposed to anything resembling that principle, that at first they were determined to place the vacant crown, not on the head of the Prince of Orange, but on that of his wife, Mary, daughter of King James, the eldest born of the issue of that king, which they acknowledged as undoubtedly his. It would be to repeat a very trite story, to recall to your memory all those circumstances which demonstrated that their accepting King William was not properly a *choice;* but to all those who did not wish in effect to recall King James, or to deluge their country in blood, and again to bring their religion, laws, and liberties into the peril they had just escaped, it was an act of *necessity,* in the strictest moral sense in which necessity can be taken.

In the very act in which, for a time, and in a single case, Parliament departed from the strict order of inheritance, in favor of a prince who, though not next, was, however, very near in the line of succession, it is curious to observe how Lord Somers, who drew the bill called the Declaration of Right, has comported himself on that delicate occasion. It is curious to observe with what address this temporary solution of continuity is kept from the eye; whilst all that could be found in this act of necessity to countenance the idea of an hereditary succession is brought forward, and fostered, and made the most of, by this great man, and by the legislature who followed him. Quitting the dry, imperative style of an act of Parliament, he makes the Lords and Commons fall to a pious legislative ejaculation, and declare that they consider it "as a marvellous providence, and merciful goodness of God to this nation, to preserve their said Majesties' *royal* persons most happily to reign over us *on the throne of their ancestors,* for which, from the bottom of their hearts, they return their humblest thanks and praises." The legislature plainly had in view the Act of Recognition of the first of Queen Elizabeth, chap.

3rd, and of that of James the First, chap. 1st, both acts strongly declaratory of the inheritable nature of the crown; and in many parts they follow, with a nearly literal precision, the words, and even the form of thanksgiving which is found in these old declaratory statutes.

The two Houses, in the act of King William, did not thank God that they had found a fair opportunity to assert a right to choose their own governors, much less to make an election the *only lawful* title to the crown. Their having been in a condition to avoid the very appearance of it, as much as possible, was by them considered as a providential escape. They threw a politic, well-wrought veil over every circumstance tending to weaken the rights which in the meliorated order of succession they meant to perpetuate, or which might furnish a precedent for any future departure from what they had then settled forever. Accordingly, that they might not relax the nerves of their monarchy, and that they might preserve a close conformity to the practice of their ancestors, as it appeared in the declaratory statutes of Queen Mary [5] and Queen Elizabeth, in the next clause they vest, by recognition, in their Majesties *all* the legal prerogatives of the crown, declaring "that in them they are most *fully*, rightfully, and *entirely* invested, incorporated, united, and annexed." In the clause which follows, for preventing questions, by reason of any pretended titles to the crown, they declare (observing also in this the traditionary language, along with the traditionary policy of the nation, and repeating as from a rubric the language of the preceding acts of Elizabeth and James) that on the preserving "a *certainty* in the SUCCESSION thereof the unity, peace, and tranquillity of this nation doth, under God, wholly depend."

They knew that a doubtful title of succession would but too much resemble an election, and that an election would be utterly destructive of the "unity, peace, and tranquillity of this nation," which they thought to be considerations of some moment. To provide for these objects, and therefore to exclude forever the Old Jewry doctrine of "a right to choose our own governors," they follow with a clause containing a most solemn pledge, taken from the preceding act of Queen Elizabeth,—as solemn a pledge

[5] 1st Mary, sess. 3, ch. 1. [Burke]

as ever was or can be given in favor of an hereditary succession, and as solemn a renunciation as could be made of the principles by this society imputed to them:—"The Lords Spiritual and Temporal, and Commons, do, in the name of all the people aforesaid, most humbly and faithfully submit *themselves, their heirs, and posterities forever;* and do faithfully promise that they will stand to, maintain, and defend their said Majesties, and also the *limitation of the crown,* herein specified and contained, to the utmost of their powers," &c., &c.

So far is it from being true that we acquired a right by the Revolution to elect our kings, that, if we had possessed it before, the English nation did at that time most solemnly renounce and abdicate it, for themselves, and for all their posterity forever. These gentlemen may value themselves as much as they please on their Whig principles; but I never desire to be thought a better Whig than Lord Somers, or to understand the principles of the Revolution better than those by whom it was brought about, or to read in the Declaration of Right any mysteries unknown to those whose penetrating style has engraved in our ordinances, and in our hearts, the words and spirit of that immortal law.

It is true, that, aided with the powers derived from force and opportunity, the nation was at that time, in some sense, free to take what course it pleased for filling the throne,—but only free to do so upon the same grounds on which they might have wholly abolished their monarchy, and every other part of their Constitution. However, they did not think such bold changes within their commission. It is, indeed, difficult, perhaps impossible, to give limits to the mere *abstract* competence of the supreme power, such as was exercised by Parliament at that time; but the limits of a *moral* competence, subjecting, even in powers more indisputably sovereign, occasional will to permanent reason, and to the steady maxims of faith, justice, and fixed fundamental policy, are perfectly intelligible, and perfectly binding upon those who exercise any authority, under any name, or under any title, in the state. The House of Lords, for instance, is not morally competent to dissolve the House of Commons,—no, nor even to dissolve itself, nor to abdicate, if it would, its portion in the legislature of the kingdom. Though a king may abdicate for his own person, he cannot abdicate for the monarchy. By as strong, or by a stronger reason, the House of Commons cannot renounce its share of authority. The engagement and pact of society, which generally goes by the name of the Constitution, forbids such invasion and such surrender. The constituent parts of a state are obliged to hold their public faith with each other, and with all those who derive any serious interest under their engagements, as much as the whole state is bound to keep its faith with separate communities: otherwise, competence and power would soon be confounded, and no law be left but the will of a prevailing force. On this principle, the succession of the crown has always been what it now is, an hereditary succession by law: in the old line it was a succession by the Common Law; in the new by the statute law, operating on the principles of the Common Law, not changing the substance, but regulating the mode and describing the persons. Both these descriptions of law are of the same force, and are derived from an equal authority, emanating from the common agreement and original compact of the state, *communi sponsione reipublicæ* [the consent of the whole commonwealth], and as such are equally binding on king, and people too, as long as the terms are observed, and they continue the same body politic.

It is far from impossible to reconcile, if we do not suffer ourselves to be entangled in the mazes of metaphysic sophistry, the use both of a fixed rule and an occasional deviation,—the sacredness of an hereditary principle of succession in our government with a power of change in its application in cases of extreme emergency. Even in that extremity, (if we take the measure of our rights by our exercise of them at the Revolution,) the change is to be confined to the peccant part only,—to the part which produced the necessary deviation; and even then it is to be effected without a decomposition of the whole civil and political mass, for the purpose of originating a new civil order out of the first elements of society.

A state without the means of some change is without the means of its conservation. Without such means it might even risk the loss of that part of the Constitution which it wished the most religiously to preserve. The two principles of conservation and correction operated strongly at the two critical periods of the Restoration and Revolution, when England found itself without a king. At both those periods the nation had lost the bond of union in their ancient edifice: they did not, however, dissolve the whole fabric. On the contrary, in both cases they regenerated the deficient part of the old Constitution through the parts which were not impaired. They kept these old parts exactly as they were, that the part recovered might be suited to them. They acted by the ancient organized states in the shape of their old organization, and not by the organic *moleculæ* of a disbanded people. At no time, perhaps, did the sovereign legislature manifest a more tender regard to that fundamental principle of British constitutional policy than at the time of the Revolution, when it deviated from the direct line of hereditary succession. The crown was carried somewhat out of the line in which it had before moved; but the new line was derived from the same stock. It was still a line of hereditary descent; still an hereditary descent in the same blood, though an hereditary descent qualified with Protestantism. When the legislature altered the direction, but kept the principle, they showed that they held it inviolable.

On this principle, the law of inheritance had admitted some amendment in the old time, and long before the era of the Revolution. Some time after the Conquest great questions arose upon the legal principles of hereditary descent. It became a matter of doubt whether the heir *per capita* or the heir *per stirpes* [6] was to succeed; but whether the heir *per capita* gave way when the heirdom *per stirpes* took place, or the Catholic heir when the Protestant was preferred, the inheritable principle survived with a sort of immortality through all transmigrations. . . . This is the spirit of our Constitution, not only in its settled course, but in all its revolutions. Whoever came in, or however he came in, whether he obtained the crown by law or by force, the hereditary succession was either continued or adopted.

The gentlemen of the Society for Revolutions see nothing in that of 1688 but the deviation from the Constitution; and they take the deviation from the principle for the principle. They have little regard to the obvious consequences of their doctrine, though they may see that it leaves positive authority in very few of the positive institutions of this country. When such an unwarrantable

---

[6] Roman legal terms for two different methods of inheritance of titles and estates within the family.

maxim is once established, that no throne is lawful but the elective, no one act of the princes who preceded this era of fictitious
election can be valid. Do these theorists mean to imitate some of
their predecessors, who dragged the bodies of our ancient sovereigns out of the quiet of their tombs? Do they mean to attaint
and disable backwards all the kings that have reigned before the
Revolution, and consequently to stain the throne of England with
the blot of a continual usurpation? Do they mean to invalidate,
annul, or to call into question, together with the titles of the
whole line of our kings, that great body of our statute law which
passed under those whom they treat as usurpers? to annul laws
of inestimable value to our liberties,—of as great value at least
as any which have passed at or since the period of the Revolution? If kings who did not owe their crown to the choice of their
people had no title to make laws, what will become of the statute
De tallagio non concedendo? [7] of the *Petition of Right?* of the
act of *Habeas Corpus?* Do these new doctors of the rights of
men presume to assert that King James the Second, who came to
the crown as next of blood, according to the rules of a then unqualified succession, was not to all intents and purposes a lawful
king of England, before he had done any of those acts which
were justly construed into an abdication of his crown? If he was
not, much trouble in Parliament might have been saved at the
period these gentlemen commemorate. But King James was a bad
king with a good title, and not an usurper. The princes who succeeded according to the act of Parliament which settled the crown
on the Electress Sophia and on her descendants, being Protestants, came in as much by a title of inheritance as King James
did. He came in according to the law, as it stood at his accession
to the crown; and the princes of the House of Brunswick came
to the inheritance of the crown, not by election, but by the law,
as it stood at their several accessions, of Protestant descent and
inheritance, as I hope I have shown sufficiently. . . .

No experience has taught us that in any other course or
method than that of an *hereditary crown* our liberties can be
regularly perpetuated and preserved sacred as our *hereditary*

---

[7] The statute held that no tallage, or tax on the demesne lands
of the king, could be laid without the consent of the people.

right. An irregular, convulsive movement may be necessary to throw off an irregular, convulsive disease. But the course of succession is the healthy habit of the British Constitution. Was it that the legislature wanted, at the act for the limitation of the crown in the Hanoverian line, drawn through the female descendants of James the First, a due sense of the inconveniences of having two or three, or possibly more, foreigners in succession to the British throne? No!—they had a due sense of the evils which might happen from such foreign rule, and more than a due sense of them. But a more decisive proof cannot be given of the full conviction of the British nation that the principles of the Revolution did not authorize them to elect kings at their pleasure, and without any attention to the ancient fundamental principles of our government, than their continuing to adopt a plan of hereditary Protestant succession in the old line, with all the dangers and all the inconveniences of its being a foreign line full before their eyes, and operating with the utmost force upon their minds.

A few years ago I should be ashamed to overload a matter so capable of supporting itself by the then unnecessary support of any argument; but this seditious, unconstitutional doctrine is now publicly taught, avowed, and printed. The dislike I feel to revolutions, the signals for which have so often been given from pulpits,—the spirit of change that is gone abroad,—the total contempt which prevails with you, and may come to prevail with us, of all ancient institutions, when set in opposition to a present sense of convenience, or to the bent of a present inclination,—all these considerations make it not unadvisable, in my opinion, to call back our attention to the true principles of our own domestic laws, that you, my French friend, should begin to know, and that we should continue to cherish them. We ought not, on either side of the water, to suffer ourselves to be imposed upon by the counterfeit wares which some persons, by a double fraud, export to you in illicit bottoms, as raw commodities of British growth, though wholly alien to our soil, in order afterwards to smuggle them back again into this country, manufactured after the newest Paris fashion of an improved liberty.

The people of England will not ape the fashions they have never tried, nor go back to those which they have found mischievous on trial. They look upon the legal hereditary succession of their crown as among their rights, not as among their wrongs, —as a benefit, not as a grievance,—as a security for their liberty, not as a badge of servitude. They look on the frame of their commonwealth, *such as it stands,* to be of inestimable value; and they conceive the undisturbed succession of the crown to be a pledge of the stability and perpetuity of all the other members of our Constitution.

I shall beg leave, before I go any further, to take notice of some paltry artifices which the abettors of election as the only lawful title to the crown are ready to employ, in order to render the support of the just principles of our Constitution a task somewhat invidious. These sophisters substitute a fictitious cause, and feigned personages, in whose favor they suppose you engaged, whenever you defend the inheritable nature of the crown. It is common with them to dispute as if they were in a conflict with some of those exploded fanatics of slavery who formerly maintained, what I believe no creature now maintains, "that the crown is held by divine, hereditary, and indefeasible right." These old fanatics of single arbitrary power dogmatized as if hereditary royalty was the only lawful government in the world, —just as our new fanatics of popular arbitrary power maintain that a popular election is the sole lawful source of authority. The old prerogative enthusiasts, it is true, did speculate foolishly, and perhaps impiously too, as if monarchy had more of a divine sanction than any other mode of government,—and as if a right to govern by inheritance were in strictness *indefeasible* in every person who should be found in the succession to a throne, and under every circumstance, which no civil or political right can be. But an absurd opinion concerning the king's hereditary right to the crown does not prejudice one that is rational, and bottomed upon solid principles of law and policy. If all the absurd theories of lawyers and divines were to vitiate the objects in which they are conversant, we should have no law and no religion left in the world. But an absurd theory on one side of a question forms no justification for alleging a false fact or promulgating mischievous maxims on the other.

The second claim of the Revolution Society is "a right of cashiering their governors for *misconduct.*" Perhaps the apprehensions our ancestors entertained of forming such a precedent as that "of cashiering for misconduct" was the cause that the declaration of the act which implied the abdication of King James was, if it had any fault, rather too guarded and too circumstantial.[8] But all this guard, and all this accumulation of circumstances, serves to show the spirit of caution which predominated in the national councils, in a situation in which men irritated by oppression, and elevated by a triumph over it, are apt to abandon themselves to violent and extreme courses; it shows the anxiety of the great men who influenced the conduct of affairs at that great event to make the Revolution a parent of settlement, and not a nursery of future revolutions.

No government could stand a moment, if it could be blown down with anything so loose and indefinite as an opinion of *"misconduct."* They who led at the Revolution grounded their virtual abdication of King James upon no such light and uncertain principle. They charged him with nothing less than a design, confirmed by a multitude of illegal overt acts, to *subvert the Protestant Church and State,* and their *fundamental,* unquestionable laws and liberties: they charged him with having broken the *original contract* between king and people. This was more than *misconduct.* A grave and overruling necessity obliged them to take the step they took, and took with infinite reluctance, as under that most rigorous of all laws. Their trust for the future preservation of the Constitution was not in future revolutions. The grand policy of all their regulations was to render it almost impracticable for any future sovereign to compel the states of the kingdom to have again recourse to those violent remedies. . . . The rule laid down for government in the Declaration of Right, the constant inspection of Parliament, the practical claim of impeachment, they thought infinitely a better security not only for their constitutional liberty, but against the vices of administration, than the reservation of a right so difficult in the practice,

---

[8] "That King James the Second, having endeavored to *subvert the Constitution* of the kingdom, by breaking the *original contract* between king and people, and, by the advice of Jesuits and other wicked persons, having violated the *fundamental* laws, and *having withdrawn himself out of the kingdom,* hath *abdicated* the government, and the throne is thereby *vacant."* [Burke]

so uncertain in the issue, and often so mischievous in the consequences, as that "cashiering their governors."

Dr. Price, in this sermon, condemns, very properly, the practice of gross adulatory addresses to kings. Instead of this fulsome style, he proposes that his Majesty should be told, on occasions of congratulation, that "he is to consider himself as more properly the servant than the sovereign of his people." For a compliment, this new form of address does not seem to be very soothing. Those who are servants in name, as well as in effect, do not like to be told of their situation, their duty, and their obligations. The slave in the old play tells his master, "*Hæc commemoratio est quasi exprobratio.*" It is not pleasant as compliment; it is not wholesome as instruction. After all, if the king were to bring himself to echo this new kind of address, to adopt it in terms, and even to take the appellation of Servant of the People as his royal style, how either he or we should be much mended by it I cannot imagine. I have seen very assuming letters signed, "Your most obedient, humble servant." The proudest domination that ever was endured on earth took a title of still greater humility than that which is now proposed for sovereigns by the Apostle of Liberty. Kings and nations were trampled upon by the foot of one calling himself "The Servant of Servants"; and mandates for deposing sovereigns were sealed with the signet of "The Fisherman."

I should have considered all this as no more than a sort of flippant, vain discourse, in which, as in an unsavory fume, several persons suffer the spirit of liberty to evaporate, if it were not plainly in support of the idea, and a part of the scheme, of "cashiering kings for misconduct." In that light it is worth some observation.

Kings, in one sense, are undoubtedly the servants of the people, because their power has no other rational end than that of the general advantage; but it is not true that they are, in the ordinary sense, (by our Constitution, at least,) anything like servants,— the essence of whose situation is to obey the commands of some other, and to be removable at pleasure. But the king of Great Britain obeys no other person; all other persons are individually, and collectively too, under him, and owe to him a legal obedience. The law, which knows neither to flatter nor to insult, calls this high magistrate, not our servant, as this humble divine calls him, but *"our sovereign lord the king";* and we, on our parts, have learned to speak only the primitive language of the law, and not the confused jargon of their Babylonian pulpits.

As he is not to obey us, but we are to obey the law in him, our Constitution has made no sort of provision towards rendering him, as a servant, in any degree responsible. Our Constitution knows nothing of a magistrate like the *Justicia* of Aragon,—nor of any court legally appointed, nor of any process legally settled, for submitting the king to the responsibility belonging to all servants. In this he is not distinguished from the commons and the lords, who, in their several public capacities, can never be called to an account for their conduct; although the Revolution Society chooses to assert, in direct opposition to one of the wisest and most beautiful parts of our Constitution, that "a king is no more than the first servant of the public, created by it, *and responsible to it.*"

Ill would our ancestors at the Revolution have deserved their fame for wisdom, if they had found no security for their freedom, but in rendering their government feeble in its operations and precarious in its tenure,—if they had been able to contrive no better remedy against arbitrary power than civil confusion. Let these gentlemen state who that *representative* public is to whom they will affirm the king, as a servant, to be responsible. It will be then time enough for me to produce to them the positive statute law which affirms that he is not.

The ceremony of cashiering kings, of which these gentlemen talk so much at their ease, can rarely, if ever, be performed without force. It then becomes a case of war, and not of constitution. Laws are commanded to hold their tongues amongst arms; and tribunals fall to the ground with the peace they are no longer able to uphold. The Revolution of 1688 was obtained by a just war, in the only case in which any war, and much more a civil war, can be just. *"Justa bella quibus* NECESSARIA." The question of dethroning, or, if these gentlemen like the phrase better, "cashiering kings," will always be, as it has always been, an extraordinary question of state, and wholly out of the law: a question (like all other questions of state) of dispositions, and of means, and of probable consequences, rather than of positive rights. As it was not made for common abuses, so it is not to be agitated by common minds. The speculative line of demarcation, where obedience ought to end and resistance must begin, is faint, obscure, and not easily definable. It is not a single act or a single event which determines it. Governments must be abused and deranged indeed, before it can be thought of; and the prospect of the future must be as bad as the experience of the past. When things are in that lamentable condition, the nature of the disease is to indicate the remedy to those whom Nature has qualified to administer in extremities this critical, ambiguous, bitter potion to a distempered state. Times and occasions and provocations will teach their own lessons. The wise will determine from the gravity of the case; the irritable, from sensibility to oppression; the high-minded, from disdain and indignation at abusive power in unworthy hands; the brave and bold, from the love of honorable danger in a generous cause: but, with or without right, a revolution will be the very last resource of the thinking and the good.

The third head of right asserted by the pulpit of the Old Jewry, namely, the "right to form a government for ourselves," has, at least, as little countenance from anything done at the Revolution, either in precedent or principle, as the two first of their claims. The Revolution was made to preserve our *ancient* indisputable laws and liberties, and that *ancient* constitution of government which is our only security for law and liberty. If you are desirous of knowing the spirit of our Constitution, and the policy which predominated in that great period which has secured it to this hour, pray look for both in our histories, in our records, in our acts of Parliament and journals of Parliament, and not in the sermons of the Old Jewry, and the after-dinner toasts of the Revolution Society. In the former you will find other ideas and another language. Such a claim is as ill-suited to our temper and wishes as it is unsupported by any appearance of authority. The very idea of the fabrication of a new government is enough to fill us with disgust and horror. We wished at the period of the Revolution, and do now wish, to derive all we possess as *an inheritance from our forefathers*. Upon that body and stock of inheritance we have taken care not to inoculate any scion alien to the nature of the original plant. All the reformations we have hitherto made have proceeded upon the principle of reference to antiquity; and I hope, nay, I am persuaded, that all those which possibly may be made hereafter will be carefully formed upon analogical precedent, authority, and example.

Our oldest reformation is that of Magna Charta. You will see that Sir Edward Coke, that great oracle of our law, and indeed all the great men who follow him, to Blackstone,[9] are industrious to prove the pedigree of our liberties. They endeavor to prove that the ancient charter, the Magna Charta of King John, was connected with another positive charter from Henry the First, and that both the one and the other were nothing more than a reaffirmance of the still more ancient standing law of the kingdom. In the matter of fact, for the greater part, these authors appear to be in the right; perhaps not always: but if the lawyers mistake in some particulars, it proves my position still the more strongly; because it demonstrates the powerful prepossession towards antiquity with which the minds of all our lawyers and legislators, and of all the people whom they wish to influence, have been always filled, and the stationary policy of this kingdom in considering their most sacred rights and franchises as an *inheritance*.

In the famous law of the 3rd of Charles the First, called the *Petition of Right*, the Parliament says to the king, "Your subjects have *inherited* this freedom": claiming their franchises, not on abstract principles, "as the rights of men," but as the rights of Englishmen, and as a patrimony derived from their forefathers. Selden, and the other profoundly learned men who drew this Petition of Right, were as well acquainted, at least, with all the general theories concerning the "rights of men" as any of the discoursers in our pulpits or on your tribune: full as well as Dr. Price, or as the Abbé Sièyes. But, for reasons worthy of that practical wisdom which superseded their theoretic science, they preferred this positive, recorded, *hereditary* title to all which can be dear to the man and the citizen to that vague, speculative right which exposed their sure inheritance to be scrambled for and torn to pieces by every wild, litigious spirit.

The same policy pervades all the laws which have since been made for the preservation of our liberties. In the 1st of William and Mary, in the famous statute called the Declaration of Right,

---

[9] See Blackstone's Magna Charta, printed at Oxford, 1759. [Burke]

the two Houses utter not a syllable of "a right to frame a government for themselves." You will see that their whole care was to secure the religion, laws, and liberties that had been long possessed, and had been lately endangered. "Taking into their most serious consideration the *best* means for making such an establishment that their religion, laws, and liberties might not be in danger of being again subverted," they auspicate all their proceedings by stating as some of those *best* means, "in the *first place*," to do "as their *ancestors in like cases have usually* done for vindicating their *ancient* rights and liberties, to *declare*";—and then they pray the king and queen "that it may be *declared* and enacted that *all and singular* the rights and liberties *asserted and declared* are the true *ancient* and indubitable rights and liberties of the people of this kingdom."

You will observe, that, from Magna Charta to the Declaration of Right, it has been the uniform policy of our Constitution to claim and assert our liberties as an *entailed inheritance* derived to us from our forefathers, and to be transmitted to our posterity,—as an estate specially belonging to the people of this kingdom, without any reference whatever to any other more general or prior right. By this means our Constitution preserves an unity in so great a diversity of its parts. We have an inheritable crown, an inheritable peerage, and a House of Commons and a people inheriting privileges, franchises, and liberties from a long line of ancestors.

This policy appears to me to be the result of profound reflection,—or rather the happy effect of following Nature, which is wisdom without reflection, and above it. A spirit of innovation is generally the result of a selfish temper and confined views. People will not look forward to posterity, who never look backward to their ancestors. Besides, the people of England well know that the idea of inheritance furnishes a sure principle of conservation, and a sure principle of transmission, without at all excluding a principle of improvement. It leaves acquisition free; but it secures what it acquires. Whatever advantages are obtained by a state proceeding on these maxims are locked fast as in a sort of family settlement, grasped as in a kind of mortmain forever. By a constitutional policy working after the pattern of Nature, we receive, we hold, we transmit our government and our privileges, in the same manner in which we enjoy and transmit our property and our lives. The institutions of policy, the goods of fortune, the gifts of Providence, are handed down to us, and from us, in the same course and order. Our political system is placed in a just correspondence and symmetry with the order of the world, and with the mode of existence decreed to a permanent body composed of transitory parts,—wherein, by the disposition of a stupendous wisdom, moulding together the great mysterious incorporation of the human race, the whole, at one time, is never old or middle-aged or young, but, in a condition of unchangeable constancy, moves on through the varied tenor of perpetual decay, fall, renovation, and progression. Thus, by preserving the method of Nature in the conduct of the state, in what we improve we are never wholly new, in what we retain we are never wholly obsolete. By adhering in this manner and on those principles to our forefathers, we are guided, not by the superstition of antiquarians, but by the spirit of philosophic analogy. In this choice of inheritance we have given to our frame of polity the image of a relation in blood: binding up the Constitution of our country with our dearest domestic ties; adopting our fundamental laws into the bosom of our family affections; keeping inseparable, and cherishing with the warmth of all their combined and mutually reflected charities, our state, our hearths, our sepulchres, and our altars.

Through the same plan of a conformity to Nature in our artificial institutions, and by calling in the aid of her unerring and powerful instincts to fortify the fallible and feeble contrivances of our reason, we have derived several other, and those no small benefits, from considering our liberties in the light of an inheritance. Always acting as if in the presence of canonized forefathers, the spirit of freedom, leading in itself to misrule and excess, is tempered with an awful gravity. This idea of a liberal descent inspires us with a sense of habitual native dignity, which prevents that upstart insolence almost inevitably adhering to and disgracing those who are the first acquirers of any distinction. By this means our liberty becomes a noble freedom. It carries an imposing and majestic aspect. It has a pedigree and illustrating ancestors. It has its bearings and its ensigns armorial. It has its gallery of portraits, its monumental inscriptions, its records, evidences, and titles. We procure reverence to our civil institutions on the principle upon which Nature teaches us to revere individual men: on account of their age, and on account of those from whom they are descended. All your sophisters cannot produce anything better adapted to preserve a rational and manly freedom than the course that we have pursued, who have chosen our nature rather than our speculations, our breasts rather than our inventions, for the great conservatories and magazines of our rights and privileges.

Reflections (1790). III, 242–76.

2. Prescription and Property

In 1782 William Pitt moved in the Commons for a committee to inquire into the state of representation in the House, with the expectation of bringing in a bill for extending the suffrage and redistributing the seats more nearly on a basis of population. In his speech against the motion Burke took his stand on the theory of virtual representation, or representation by interests rather than by geography or population. Part of his argument was that the authority of any government is essentially prescriptive, one of Burke's most important beliefs. The doctrine of prescription, familiar in English and American common law, is that immemorial use and enjoyment of a thing constitutes a valid claim of title to it.

We have now discovered, at the close of the eighteenth century, that the Constitution of England, which for a series of ages had been the proud distinction of this country, always the admiration and sometimes the envy of the wise and learned in every other nation,—we have discovered that this boasted Constitution, in the most boasted part of it, is a gross imposition upon the understanding of mankind, an insult to their feelings, and acting by contrivances destructive to the best and most valuable interests of the people. Our political architects have taken a survey of the fabric of the British Constitution. It is singular that they report nothing against the crown, nothing against the lords: but in the House of Commons everything is unsound; it is ruinous in every part; it is infested by the dry rot, and ready to tumble about our ears without their immediate help. You know by the faults they find what are their ideas of the alteration. As all government stands upon opinion, they know that the way utterly to destroy it is to remove that opinion, to take away all reverence, all confidence from it; and then, at the first blast of public discontent and popular tumult, it tumbles to the ground.

In considering this question, they who oppose it oppose it on different grounds. One is in the nature of a previous question: that some alterations may be expedient, but that this is not the time for making them. The other is, that no essential alterations are at all wanting, and that neither *now* nor at *any* time is it prudent or safe to be meddling with the fundamental principles and ancient tried usages of our Constitution,—that our representation is as nearly perfect as the necessary imperfection of human affairs and of human creatures will suffer it to be,—and that it is a subject of prudent and honest use and thankful enjoyment, and not of captious criticism and rash experiment.

On the other side there are two parties, who proceed on two grounds, in my opinion, as they state them, utterly irreconcilable. The one is juridical, the other political. The one is in the nature of a claim of right, on the supposed rights of man as man: this party desire the decision of a suit. The other ground, as far as I can divine what it directly means, is, that the representation is not so politically framed as to answer the theory of its institution. As to the claim of *right,* the meanest petitioner, the most gross and ignorant, is as good as the best: in some respects his claim is more favorable, on account of his ignorance; his weakness, his poverty, and distress only add to his titles; he sues *in forma pauperis;* he ought to be a favorite of the court. But when the *other* ground is taken, when the question is political, when a new constitution is to be made on a sound theory of government, then the presumptuous pride of didactic ignorance is to be excluded from the counsel in this high and arduous matter, which often bids defiance to the experience of the wisest. The first claims a personal representation; the latter rejects it with scorn and fervor. The language of the first party is plain and intelligible; they who plead an absolute right cannot be satisfied with anything short of personal representation, because all *natural* rights must be the rights of individuals, as by *nature* there is no such thing as politic or corporate personality: all these ideas are mere fictions of law, they are creatures of voluntary institution; men as men are individuals, and nothing else. They, therefore, who reject the principle of natural and personal representation are essentially and eternally at variance with those who claim it. As to the first sort of reformers, it is ridiculous to talk to them of the British Constitution upon any or upon all of its bases: for they lay it down, that every man ought to govern, himself, and that, where he cannot go, himself, he must send his representative; that all other government is usurpation, and is so far from having a claim to our obedience, it is not only our right, but our duty, to resist it. Nine tenths of the reformers argue thus,— that is, on the natural right.

It is impossible not to make some reflection on the nature of this claim, or avoid a comparison between the extent of the principle and the present object of the demand. If this claim be founded, it is clear to what it goes. The House of Commons, in that light, undoubtedly, is no representative of the people, as a collection of individuals. Nobody pretends it, nobody can justify such an assertion. When you come to examine into this claim of right, founded on the right of self-government in each individual, you find the thing demanded infinitely short of the principle of the demand. What! *one third* only of the legislature, and of the government no share at all? What sort of treaty of partition is this for those who have an inherent right to the whole? Give them all they ask, and your grant is still a cheat: for how comes only a third to be their younger-children's fortune in this settlement? How came they neither to have the choice of kings, or lords, or judges, or generals, or admirals, or bishops, or priests, or ministers, or justices of peace? Why, what have you to answer in favor of the prior rights of the crown and peerage but this: Our Constitution is a prescriptive constitution; it is a constitution whose sole authority is, that it has existed time out of mind? It is settled in these *two* portions against one, legislatively,—and in the whole of the judicature, the whole of the federal capacity, of the executive, the prudential, and the financial administration, in one alone. Nor was your House of Lords and the prerogatives of the crown settled on any adjudication in favor of natural rights: for they could never be so partitioned. Your king, your lords, your judges, your juries, grand and little, all are prescriptive; and what proves it is the disputes, not yet concluded, and never near becoming so, when any of them first originated. Prescription is the most solid of all titles, not only to property, but, which is to secure that property, to government. They harmonize with each other, and give mutual aid to one another. It is accompanied with another ground of authority in the constitution of the human mind, presumption. It is a presumption in favor of any settled scheme of government against any untried project, that a nation has long existed and flourished under it. It is a better presumption even of the *choice* of a nation,—far better than any sudden and temporary arrangement by actual election. Because a nation is not an idea only of local extent and individual momentary aggregation, but it is an idea of continuity which extends in time as well as in numbers and in space. And this is a choice not of one day or one set of people, not a tumultuary and giddy choice; it is a deliberate election of ages and of generations; it is a constitution made by what is ten thousand times better than choice; it is made by the peculiar circumstances, occasions, tempers, dispositions, and moral, civil, and social habitudes of the people, which disclose themselves only in a long space of time. It is a vestment which accommodates itself to the body. Nor is prescription of government formed upon blind, unmeaning prejudices. For man is a most unwise and a most wise being. The individual is foolish; the multitude, for the moment, is foolish, when they act without deliberation; but the species is wise, and, when time is given to it, as a species, it almost always acts right.

The reason for the crown as it is, for the lords as they are, is my reason for the commons as they are, the electors as they are. Now if the crown, and the lords, and the judicatures are all prescriptive, so is the House of Commons of the very same origin, and of no other. We and our electors have their powers and privileges both made and circumscribed by prescription, as much to the full as the other parts; and as such we have always claimed them, and on no other title. The House of Commons is a legislative body corporate by prescription, not made upon any given theory, but existing prescriptively,—just like the rest. This prescription has made it essentially what it is, an aggregate collection of three parts, knights, citizens, burgesses. The question is, whether this has been always so, since the House of Commons has taken its present shape and circumstances, and has been an essential operative part of the Constitution,—which, I take it, it has been for at least five hundred years.

This I resolve to myself in the affirmative: and then another

question arises:—Whether this House stands firm upon its ancient foundations, and is not, by time and accidents, so declined
from its perpendicular as to want the hand of the wise and experienced architects of the day to set it upright again, and to
prop and buttress it up for duration;—whether it continues true
to the principles upon which it has hitherto stood;—whether this
be *de facto* the constitution of the House of Commons, as it has
been since the time that the House of Commons has without dispute become a necessary and an efficient part of the British Constitution. To ask whether a thing which has always been the
same stands to its usual principle seems to me to be perfectly
absurd: for how do you know the principles, but from the construction? and if that remains the same, the principles remain the
same. It is true that to say your Constitution is what it has been
is no sufficient defence for those who say it is a bad constitution.
It is an answer to those who say that it is a degenerate constitution. To those who say it is a bad one, I answer, Look to its
effects. In all moral machinery, the moral results are its test.

On what grounds do we go to restore our Constitution to what
it has been at some given period, or to reform and reconstruct
it upon principles more conformable to a sound theory of government? A prescriptive government, such as ours, never was the
work of any legislator, never was made upon any foregone
theory. It seems to me a preposterous way of reasoning, and a
perfect confusion of ideas, to take the theories which learned and
speculative men have made from that government, and then,
supposing it made on those theories which were made from it,
to accuse the government as not corresponding with them. I do
not vilify theory and speculation: no, because that would be to
vilify reason itself. . . . No,—whenever I speak against theory,
I mean always a weak, erroneous, fallacious, unfounded, or imperfect theory; and one of the ways of discovering that it is a
false theory is by comparing it with practice. This is the true
touchstone of all theories which regard man and the affairs of
men,—Does it suit his nature in general?—does it suit his nature
as modified by his habits?

The more frequently this affair is discussed, the stronger the
case appears to the sense and the feelings of mankind. I have
no more doubt than I entertain of my existence, that this very
thing, which is stated as an horrible thing, is the means of the

preservation of our Constitution whilst it lasts,—of curing it
of many of the disorders which, attending every species of institution, would attend the principle of an exact local representation,
or a representation on the principle of numbers. If you reject
personal representation, you are pushed upon expedience; and
then what they wish us to do is, to prefer their speculations on
that subject to the happy experience of this country, of a growing liberty and a growing prosperity for five hundred years.
Whatever respect I have for their talents, this, for one, I will
not do. Then what is the standard of expedience? Expedience
is that which is good for the community, and good for every
individual in it. Now this expedience is the *desideratum*, to be
sought either without the experience of means or with that experience. If without, as in case of the fabrication of a new commonwealth, I will hear the learned arguing what promises to
be expedient; but if we are to judge of a commonwealth actually
existing, the first thing I inquire is, What has been *found* expedient or inexpedient? And I will not take their *promise* rather
than the *performance* of the Constitution.

But no, this was not the cause of the discontents. I went
through most of the northern parts,—the Yorkshire election was
then raging; the year before, through most of the western coun-
ties,—Bath, Bristol, Gloucester: not one word, either in the towns
or country, on the subject of representation; much on the receipt
tax, something on Mr. Fox's ambition; much greater apprehension of danger from thence than from want of representation. One would think that the ballast of the ship was shifted
with us, and that our Constitution had the gunwale under water.
But can you fairly and distinctly point out what one evil or
grievance has happened which you can refer to the representative not following the opinion of his constituents? What one
symptom do we find of this inequality? But it is not an arithmeti-
cal inequality with which we ought to trouble ourselves. If there
be a moral, a political equality, this is the *desideratum* in our
Constitution, and in every constitution in the world. Moral inequality is as between places and between classes. Now, I ask,
what advantage do you find that the places which abound in
representation possess over others in which it is more scanty,
in security for freedom, in security for justice, or in any one
of those means of procuring temporal prosperity and eternal

happiness, the ends for which society was formed? Are the local interests of Cornwall and Wiltshire, for instance, their roads, canals, their prisons, their police, better than Yorkshire, Warwickshire, or Staffordshire? Warwick has members: is Warwick or Stafford more opulent, happy, or free than Newcastle, or than Birmingham? Is Wiltshire the pampered favorite, whilst Yorkshire, like the child of the bondwoman, is turned out to the desert? This is like the unhappy persons who live, if they can be said to live, in the statical chair,—who are ever feeling their pulse, and who do not judge of health by the aptitude of the body to perform its functions, but by their ideas of what ought to be the true balance between the several secretions. Is a committee of Cornwall, &c., thronged, and the others deserted? No. You have an equal representation, because you have men equally interested in the prosperity of the whole, who are involved in the general interest and the general sympathy; and, perhaps, these places furnishing a superfluity of public agents and administrators, (whether in strictness they are representatives or not I do not mean to inquire, but they are agents and administrators,) they will stand clearer of local interests, passions, prejudices, and cabals than the others, and therefore preserve the balance of the parts, and with a more general view and a more steady hand than the rest. . . .

In every political proposal we must not leave out of the question the political views and object of the proposer; and these we discover, not by what he says, but by the principles he lays down. "I mean," says he, "a moderate and temperate reform: that is, I mean to do as little good as possible." If the Constitution be what you represent it, and there be no danger in the change, you do wrong not to make the reform commensurate to the abuse. Fine reformer, indeed! generous donor! What is the cause of this parsimony of the liberty which you dole out to the people? Why all this limitation in giving blessings and benefits to mankind? You admit that there is an extreme in liberty, which may be infinitely noxious to those who are to receive it, and which in the end will leave them no liberty at all. I think so, too. They know it, and they feel it. The question is, then, What is the standard of that extreme? What that gentleman, and the associations, or some parts of their phalanxes, think proper? Then our liberties are in their pleasure; it depends on their arbitrary will how far I shall be free. I will have none of that freedom. If, therefore, the standard of moderation be sought for, I will seek for it. Where? Not in their fancies, nor in my own: I will seek for it where I know it is to be found,—in the Constitution I actually enjoy. Here it says to an encroaching prerogative,—"Your sceptre has its length; you cannot add an hair to your head, or a gem to your crown, but what an eternal law has given to it." Here it says to an overweening peerage,— "Your pride finds banks that it cannot overflow": here to a tumultuous and giddy people,—"There is a bound to the raging of the sea." Our Constitution is like our island, which uses and restrains its subject sea; in vain the waves roar. In that Constitution, I know, and exultingly I feel, both that I am free, and that I am not free dangerously to myself or to others. I know that no power on earth, acting as I ought to do, can touch my life, my liberty, or my property. I have that inward and dignified consciousness of my own security and independence, which constitutes, and is the only thing which does constitute, the proud and comfortable sentiment of freedom in the human breast. I know, too, and I bless God for, my safe mediocrity: I know, that, if I possessed all the talents of the gentlemen on the side of the House I sit, and on the other, I cannot, by royal favor, or by popular delusion, or by oligarchical cabal, elevate myself above a certain very limited point, so as to endanger my own fall, or the ruin of my country. I know there is an order that keeps things fast in their place: it is made to us, and we are made to it. Why not ask another wife, other children, another body, another mind? . . .

There is a difference between a moral or political exposure of a public evil relative to the administration of government, whether in men or systems, and a declaration of defects, real or supposed, in the fundamental constitution of your country. The first may be cured in the individual by the motives of religion, virtue, honor, fear, shame, or interest. Men may be made to abandon also false systems, by exposing their absurdity or mischievous tendency to their own better thoughts, or to the contempt or indignation of the public; and after all, if they should exist, and exist uncorrected, they only disgrace individuals as fugitive opinions. But it is quite otherwise with the frame and constitution of the state: if that is disgraced, patriotism is destroyed in its very source. No man has ever willingly obeyed, much less was desirous of defending with his blood, a mischievous and absurd scheme of government. Our first, our dearest, most comprehensive relation, our country, is gone.

It suggests melancholy reflections, in consequence of the strange course we have long held, that we are now no longer quarrelling about the character, or about the conduct of men, or the tenor of measures, but we are grown out of humor with the English Constitution itself: this is become the object of the animosity of Englishmen. This Constitution in former days used to be the admiration and the envy of the world: it was the pattern for politicians, the theme of the eloquent, the meditation of the philosopher, in every part of the world. As to Englishmen, it was their pride, their consolation. By it they lived, for it they were ready to die. Its defects, if it had any, were partly covered by partiality, and partly borne by prudence. Now all its excellencies are forgot, its faults are now forcibly dragged into day, exaggerated by every artifice of representation. It is despised and rejected of men, and every device and invention of ingenuity or idleness set up in opposition or in preference to it. It is to this humor, and it is to the measures growing out of it, that I set myself (I hope not alone) in the most determined opposition.

Speech on Reform of Representation of the Commons in Parliament (1782). VII, 91–103.

There is a sacred veil to be drawn over the beginnings of all governments. Ours in India had an origin like those which time has sanctified by obscurity. Time, in the origin of most governments, has thrown this mysterious veil over them; prudence and discretion make it necessary to throw something of the same drapery over more recent foundations, in which otherwise the fortune, the genius, the talents, and military virtue of this nation never shone more conspicuously. But whatever necessity might hide or excuse or palliate, in the acquisition of power, a wise nation, when it has once made a revolution upon its own principles and for its own ends, rests there. The first step to empire is revolution, by which power is conferred; the next is good laws, good order, good institutions, to give that power stability.

Speech on Impeachment of Warren Hastings, February 16, 1788. IX, 401–2.

There must be some impulse, besides public spirit, to put private interest into motion along with it. Moneyed men ought to be allowed to set a value on their money: if they did not, there could be no moneyed men. This desire of accumulation is a principle without which the means of their service to the state could not exist. The love of lucre, though sometimes carried to a ridiculous, sometimes to a vicious excess, is the grand cause of prosperity to all states. In this natural, this reasonable, this powerful, this prolific principle, it is for the satirist to expose the ridiculous,—it is for the moralist to censure the vicious,— it is for the sympathetic heart to reprobate the hard and cruel,— it is for the judge to animadvert on the fraud, the extortion, and the oppression; but it is for the statesman to employ it as he finds it, with all its concomitant excellencies, with all its imperfections on its head. It is his part, in this case, as it is in all other cases, where he is to make use of the general energies of Nature, to take them as he finds them.

Third Letter on a Regicide Peace (1796–97). V, 455.

As far as my share of a public trust goes, I am in trust religiously to maintain the rights and properties of all descriptions of people in the possessions which they legally hold, and in the rule by which alone they can be secure in any possession. I do not find myself at liberty, either as a man or as a trustee for men, to take a vested property from one man and give it to another, because I think that the portion of one is too great, and that of another too small. From my first juvenile rudiments of speculative study, to the grey hairs of my present experience, I have never learned anything else. I can never be taught anything else by *reason;* and when *force* comes, I shall consider whether I am to submit to it, or how I am to resist it. This I am very sure of, that an early guard against the manifest tendency of a contrary doctrine, is the only way by which those who love order can be prepared to resist such force.

The calling men by the names of "pampered and luxurious prelates" is, in you, no more than a mark of your dislike to intemperance and idle expense. But in others it is used for other purposes; it is often used to extinguish the sense of justice in our minds, and the natural feelings of humanity in our bosoms. In them, such abusive language is used to mitigate the cruel effects of reducing men of opulent condition, and their innumerable dependants, to the last distress. If I were to adopt the plan of a spoliatory reformation, I should probably employ it; but it would aggravate, instead of extenuating guilt, in overturning the sacred principles of property.

Sir, I say that church and state, and human society too (for which church and state are made) are subverted by such doctrines, joined to such practices, as leave no foundation for property in long possessions. My dear Captain Mercer, it is not my calling the use you make of your plate, in your house either of dwelling or of prayer, "pageantry and hypocrisy," that can justify me in taking from you your property, and your liberty to use your own property according to your own ideas of ornament. When you find me attempting to break into your house to take your plate under any pretence whatsoever,—but most of all, under pretence of purity of religion and Christian charity, —shoot me for a robber and an hypocrite, as in that case I shall certainly be. The true Christian religion never taught me any such practices; nor did the religion of my nature, nor any religion, nor any law.

Let those who have never abstained from a full meal, and as much wine as they could swallow, for a single day of their whole lives, satirize "luxurious and pampered prelates" if they will. Let them abuse such prelates, and such lords, and such "squires" provided it be only to correct their vices. I care not much about the language of this moral satire, if they go no further than satire. But there are occasions when the language of Falstaff, reproaching the Londoners whom he robbed in their way to Canterbury, with their gorbellies and city-luxury, is not so becoming. It is not calling the landed estates, possessed by old *prescriptive* rights, "the accumulations of ignorance and superstition," that can support me in shaking that grand title which supersedes every other title, and which all my studies of general jurisprudence have taught me to consider as one principal cause of the formation of states;—I mean the ascertaining and securing of *prescription.* "But these are donations made in ages of ignorance and superstition." Be it so;—it proves that they were made long ago; and this is prescription, and this gives right and title. It is possible that many estates about you were obtained by arms; a thing almost as bad as superstition, and not much short of ignorance;—but it is old violence; and that which might be wrong in the beginning, is consecrated by time and becomes law-

ful. This may be superstition in me, and ignorance; but I had rather remain in ignorance and superstition than be enlightened and purified out of the first principles of law and natural justice.
Letter to Captain Mercer, February 26, 1790.
Correspondence. III, 142–45.

If I conceive rightly of the spirit of the present combination [of European powers], it is not at war with France, but with Jacobinism. . . . We are at war with a *principle*, and with an example, which there is no shutting out by fortresses, or excluding by territorial limits. . . . In the whole circle of military arrangements and of political expedients, I fear that there cannot be found any sort of *merely defensive plan* of the least force, against the effect of the *example* which has been given in France. That *example* has shown, for the first time in the history of the world, that it is very possible to subvert the whole frame and order of the best constructed states, by corrupting the common people with the spoil of the superior classes. . . . It is the contempt of property, and the setting up against its principle certain pretended advantages of the state (which, by the way, exists only for its conservation), that has led to all the other evils which have ruined France, and brought all Europe into the most imminent danger. The beginning of the whole mischief was a false idea that there is a difference in property, according to the description of the persons who held it under the laws; and that the despoiling a minister of religion, is not the same robbery with the pillage of other men. They who, through weakness, gave way to the ill-designs of bad men in that confiscation, were not long before they practically found their error. The spoil of the royal domain soon followed the seizure of the estates of the church. The *appanages* of the king's brothers immediately came on the heels of the usurpation of the royal domain; the property of the nobility survived but a short time the *appanages* of the princes of the blood-royal. At length the monied and the movable property tumbled on the ruin of the immovable property;—and at this day, no magazine, from the warehouses of the East India Company to the grocer's and the baker's shop, possesses the smallest degree of safety.
Letter to the Comte de Mercy, August, 1793.
Correspondence. IV, 138–43.

The Chancellor of France, at the opening of the States, said, in a tone of oratorial flourish, that all occupations were honorable. If he meant only that no honest employment was disgraceful, he would not have gone beyond the truth. But in asserting that anything is honorable, we imply some distinction in its favor. The occupation of a hair-dresser, or of a working tallow-chandler, cannot be a matter of honor to any person,—to say nothing of a number of other more servile employments. Such descriptions of men ought not to suffer oppression from the state; but the state suffers oppression, if such as they, either individually or collectively, are permitted to rule. In this you think you are combating prejudice, but you are at war with Nature.[10]

I do not, my dear Sir, conceive you to be of that sophistical, captious spirit, or of that uncandid dulness, as to require, for every general observation or sentiment, an explicit detail of the correctives and exceptions which reason will presume to be included in all the general propositions which come from reasonable men. You do not imagine that I wish to confine power, authority, and distinction to blood and names and titles. No, Sir. There is no qualification for government but virtue and wisdom, actual or presumptive. Wherever they are actually found, they have, in whatever state, condition, profession, or trade, the passport of Heaven to human place and honor. Woe to the country which would madly and impiously reject the service of the

---

[10] Ecclesiasticus, chap. xxxviii. ver. 24, 25. "The wisdom of a learned man cometh by opportunity of leisure: and he that hath little business shall become wise. How can he get wisdom that holdeth the plough, and that glorieth in the goad; that driveth oxen, and is occupied in their labors, and whose talk is of bullocks?"

Ver. 27. "So every carpenter and workmaster, that laboreth night and day," &c.

Ver. 33. "They shall not be sought for in public counsel, nor sit high in the congregation: they shall not sit on the judge's seat, nor understand the sentence of judgment: they cannot declare justice and judgment, and they shall not be found where parables are spoken."

Ver. 34. "But they will maintain the state of the world."

I do not determine whether this book be canonical, as the Gallican Church (till lately) has considered it, or apocryphal, as here it is taken. I am sure it contains a great deal of sense and truth. [Burke]

talents and virtues, civil, military, or religious, that are given to grace and to serve it; and would condemn to obscurity everything formed to diffuse lustre and glory around a state! Woe to that country, too, that, passing into the opposite extreme, considers a low education, a mean, contracted view of things, a sordid, mercenary occupation, as a preferable title to command! Everything ought to be open,—but not indifferently to every man. No rotation, no appointment by lot, no mode of election operating in the spirit of sortition or rotation, can be generally good in a government conversant in extensive objects; because they have no tendency, direct or indirect, to select the man with a view to the duty, or to accommodate the one to the other. I do not hesitate to say that the road to eminence and power, from obscure condition, ought not to be made too easy, nor a thing too much of course. If rare merit be the rarest of all rare things, it ought to pass through some sort of probation. The temple of honor ought to be seated on an eminence. If it be opened through virtue, let it be remembered, too, that virtue is never tried but by some difficulty and some struggle.

Nothing is a due and adequate representation of a state, that does not represent its ability, as well as its property. But as ability is a vigorous and active principle, and as property is sluggish, inert, and timid, it never can be safe from the invasions of ability, unless it be, out of all proportion, predominant in the representation. It must be represented, too, in great masses of accumulation, or it is not rightly protected. The characteristic essence of property, formed out of the combined principles of its acquisition and conservation, is to be *unequal*. The great masses, therefore, which excite envy, and tempt rapacity, must be put out of the possibility of danger. Then they form a natural rampart about the lesser properties in all their gradations. The same quantity of property which is by the natural course of things divided among many has not the same operation. Its defensive power is weakened as it is diffused. In this diffusion each man's portion is less than what, in the eagerness of his desires, he may flatter himself to obtain by dissipating the accumulations of others. The plunder of the few would, indeed, give but a share inconceivably small in the distribution to the many. But the many are not capable of making this calculation; and those who lead them to rapine never intend this distribution.

The power of perpetuating our property in our families is one of the most valuable and interesting circumstances belonging to it, and that which tends the most to the perpetuation of society itself. It makes our weakness subservient to our virtue; it grafts benevolence even upon avarice. The possessors of family wealth, and of the distinction which attends hereditary possession, (as most concerned in it,) are the natural securities for this transmission. With us the House of Peers is formed upon this principle. It is wholly composed of hereditary property and hereditary distinction, and made, therefore, the third of the legislature, and, in the last event, the sole judge of all property in all its subdivisions. The House of Commons, too, though not necessarily, yet in fact, is always so composed, in the far greater part. Let those large proprietors be what they will, (and they have their chance of being amongst the best,) they are, at the very worst, the ballast in the vessel of the commonwealth. For though hereditary wealth, and the rank which goes with it, are too much idolized by creeping sycophants, and the blind, abject admirers of power, they are too rashly slighted in shallow speculations of the petulant, assuming, shortsighted coxcombs of philosophy. Some decent, regulated preëminence, some preference (not exclusive appropriation) given to birth, is neither unnatural, nor unjust, nor impolitic.

It is said that twenty-four millions ought to prevail over two hundred thousand. True; if the constitution of a kingdom be a problem of arithmetic. This sort of discourse does well enough with the lamp-post for its second: to men who *may* reason calmly it is ridiculous. The will of the many, and their interest, must very often differ; and great will be the difference when they make an evil choice. A government of five hundred country attorneys and obscure curates is not good for twenty-four millions of men, though it were chosen by eight-and-forty millions; nor is it the better for being guided by a dozen of persons of quality who have betrayed their trust in order to obtain that power. At present, you seem in everything to have strayed out of the high road of Nature.

Reflections (1790). III, 296–99.

I know that tyranny seldom attacks the poor,—never in the first instance. They are not its proper prey. It falls upon the wealthy

and great, whom, by rendering them objects of envy, and otherwise obnoxious to the multitude, they the more easily destroy;
and when they are destroyed, that multitude which was led to
that ill work by the arts of bad men, is itself undone forever. I
hate tyranny, at least I think so; but I hate it most of all where
most are concerned in it. The tyranny of the multitude is but a
multiplied tyranny.

Letter to Captain Mercer, February 26, 1790.
Correspondence. III, 146–47.

If wealth is the obedient and laborious slave of virtue, and of
public honor, then wealth is in its place and has its use; but if
this order is changed, and honor is to be sacrificed to the conservation of riches, riches, which have neither eyes nor hands,
nor anything truly vital in them, cannot long survive the being
of their vivifying powers, their legitimate masters, and their potent protectors. If we command our wealth, we shall be rich and
free; if our wealth commands us, we are poor indeed.

First Letter on a Regicide Peace (1796). V, 242.

It is not the confiscation of our Church property from this example in France that I dread, though I think this would be no
trifling evil. The great source of my solicitude is, lest it should
ever be considered in England as the policy of a state to seek a
resource in confiscations of any kind, or that any one description
of citizens should be brought to regard any of the others as their
proper prey.[11] Nations are wading deeper and deeper into an

---

[11] "Si plures sunt ii quibus improbe datum est, quam illi quibus
injuste ademptum est, idcirco plus etiam valent? Non enim numero
hæc judicantur, sed pondere. Quam autem habet æquitatem, ut
agrum multis annis, aut etiam sæculis ante possessum, qui nullum
habuit habeat, qui autem habuit amittat? Ac, propter hoc injuriæ
genus, Lacedæmonii Lysandrum Ephorum expulerunt; Agin regem
(quod nunquam antea apud eos acciderat) necaverunt; exque eo
tempore tantæ discordiæ secutæ sunt, ut et tyranni exsisterent, et
optimates exterminarentur, et preclarissime constituta respublica dilabe-
retur. Nec vero solum ipsa cecidit, sed etiam reliquam Græciam
evertit contagionibus malorum, quæ a Lacedæmoniis profectæ mana-
runt latius."—After speaking of the conduct of the model of true

ocean of boundless debt. Public debts, which at first were a security to governments, by interesting many in the public tranquillity, are likely in their excess to become the means of their subversion. If governments provide for these debts by heavy impositions, they perish by becoming odious to the people. If they do not provide for them, they will be undone by the efforts of the most dangerous of all parties: I mean an extensive, discontented moneyed interest, injured and not destroyed. The men who compose this interest look for their security, in the first instance, to the fidelity of government; in the second, to its power. If they find the old governments effete, worn out, and

---

patriots, Aratus of Sicyon, which was in a very different spirit, he says,—"Sic par est agere cum civibus; non (ut bis jam vidimus) hastam in foro ponere et bona civium voci subjicere præconis. At ille Græcus (id quod fuit sapientis et præstantis viri) omnibus consulendum esse putavit: eaque est summa ratio et sapientia boni civis, commoda civium non divellere, sed omnes eadem æquitate continere." —Cic. Off. 1. 2. [Burke] ["Though the number of those who unjustly benefit by the levelling of estates be greater than those who are injuriously robbed, yet it does not follow that they are more powerful; for it is not the number, but the quality of the persons that must be given weight in this case. Moreover, what reason or equity is there when those who have held estates for many years, even ages, suddenly have nothing, and those who had nothing suddenly come into possession? For such partial and injurious proceedings the Spartans once banished Lysander, one of the Ephori, and put to death Agis their king, for the same reason, actions unprecedented in that city. This brought on such grievous contentions and discords in the state that tyranny and oppression got the upper hand amongst them; the nobles were banished from their native country, and the best-constituted republic on earth was utterly dissolved and brought into confusion. . . . Aratus of Sicyon, on the other hand, had the true way of dealing with citizens, and not (as has been twice practised among us in Rome) to make sale of their goods in the public auctions and have them cried up by the voice of the common crier. But this famous Grecian, as was the duty of a wise and distinguished person, thought he should consider the good of all; and indeed every magistrate who proceeds upon principles of reason and prudence, will not act partially on the interests of his people, but will govern them all by the same rule and standard of justice and equity."—Cicero De Officiis ii.22–23.]

with their springs relaxed, so as not to be of sufficient vigor for
their purposes, they may seek new ones that shall be possessed
of more energy; and this energy will be derived, not from an
acquisition of resources, but from a contempt of justice. Revolutions are favorable to confiscation; and it is impossible to know
under what obnoxious names the next confiscations will be authorized. I am sure that the principles predominant in France
extend to very many persons, and descriptions of persons, in all
countries, who think their innoxious indolence their security. This
kind of innocence in proprietors may be argued into inutility;
and inutility into an unfitness for their estates. Many parts of
Europe are in open disorder. In many others there is a hollow
murmuring under ground; a confused movement is felt, that
threatens a general earthquake in the political world. Already
confederacies and correspondences of the most extraordinary nature are forming in several countries.[12] In such a state of things
we ought to hold ourselves upon our guard. In all mutations (if
mutations must be) the circumstance which will serve most to
blunt the edge of their mischief, and to promote what good may
be in them, is, that they should find us with our minds tenacious
of justice and tender of property.

But it will be argued, that this confiscation in France ought
not to alarm other nations. They say it is not made from wanton
rapacity; that it is a great measure of national policy, adopted,to
remove an extensive, inveterate, superstitious mischief.—It is
with the greatest difficulty that I am able to separate policy from
justice. Justice is itself the great standing policy of civil society;
and any eminent departure from it, under any circumstances,
lies under the suspicion of being no policy at all.

When men are encouraged to go into a certain mode of life
by the existing laws, and protected in that mode as in a lawful
occupation,—when they have accommodated all their ideas and
all their habits to it,—when the law had long made their adherence to its rules a ground of reputation, and their departure
from them a ground of disgrace and even of penalty,—I am sure

---

[12] See two books entitled, "Einige Originalschriften des Illuminatenordens,"—"System und Folgen des Illuminatenordens." Mün-
chen, 1787. [Burke]

it is unjust in legislature, by an arbitrary act, to offer a sudden violence to their minds and their feelings, forcibly to degrade them from their state and condition, and to stigmatize with shame and infamy that character and those customs which before had been made the measure of their happiness and honor. If to this be added an expulsion from their habitations and a confiscation of all their goods, I am not sagacious enough to discover how this despotic sport made of the feelings, consciences, prejudices, and properties of men can be discriminated from the rankest tyranny.

If the injustice of the course pursued in France be clear, the policy of the measure, that is, the public benefit to be expected from it, ought to be at least as evident, and at least as important. To a man who acts under the influence of no passion, who has nothing in view in his projects but the public good, a great difference will immediately strike him, between what policy would dictate on the original introduction of such institutions, and on a question of their total abolition, where they have cast their roots wide and deep, and where, by long habit, things more valuable than themselves are so adapted to them, and in a manner interwoven with them, that the one cannot be destroyed without notably impairing the other. He might be embarrassed, if the case were really such as sophisters represent it in their paltry style of debating. But in this, as in most questions of state, there is a middle. There is something else than the mere alternative of absolute destruction or unreformed existence. *Spartam nactus es; hanc exorna.* ["You were born in Sparta; accept it and be a credit to it." An old Latin proverb.] This is, in my opinion, a rule of profound sense, and ought never to depart from the mind of an honest reformer. I cannot conceive how any man can have brought himself to that pitch of presumption, to consider his country as nothing but *carte blanche,* upon which he may scribble whatever he pleases. A man full of warm, speculative benevolence may wish his society otherwise constituted than he finds it; but a good patriot, and a true politician, always considers how he shall make the most of the existing materials of his country. A disposition to preserve, and an ability to improve, taken together, would be my standard of a statesman. Everything else is vulgar in the conception, perilous in the execution.

There are moments in the fortune of states, when particular men are called to make improvements by great mental exertion. In those moments, even when they seem to enjoy the confidence of their prince and country, and to be invested with full authority, they have not always apt instruments. A politician, to do great things, looks for a *power,* what our workmen call a *purchase;* and if he finds that power, in politics as in mechanics, he cannot be at a loss to apply it. In the monastic institutions, in my opinion, was found a great *power* for the mechanism of politic benevolence. There were revenues with a public direction; there were men wholly set apart and dedicated to public purposes, without any other than public ties and public principles,—men without the possibility of converting the estate of the community into a private fortune,—men denied to self-interests, whose avarice is for some community,—men to whom personal poverty is honor, and implicit obedience stands in the place of freedom. In vain shall a man look to the possibility of making such things when he wants them. The winds blow as they list. These institutions are the products of enthusiasm; they are the instruments of wisdom. Wisdom cannot create materials; they are the gifts of Nature or of chance; her pride is in the use. The perennial existence of bodies corporate and their fortunes are things particularly suited to a man who has long views,—who meditates designs that require time in fashioning, and which propose duration when they are accomplished. He is not deserving to rank high, or even to be mentioned in the order of great statesmen, who, having obtained the command and direction of such a power as existed in the wealth, the discipline, and the habits of such corporations as those which you have rashly destroyed, cannot find any way of converting it to the great and lasting benefit of his country. On the view of this subject, a thousand uses suggest themselves to a contriving mind. To destroy any power growing wild from the rank productive force of the human mind is almost tantamount, in the moral world, to the destruction of the apparently active properties of bodies in the material. It would be like the attempt to destroy (if it were in our competence to destroy) the expansive force of fixed air in nitre, or the power of steam, or of electricity, or of magnetism. These energies always existed in Nature, and they were always discernible. They seemed, some of them unserviceable, some noxious, some no better than a sport to children,—until contemplative ability, combining with practic skill, tamed their wild nature, subdued them to use, and rendered them at once the most powerful and the most tractable agents, in subservience to the great views and designs of men. Did fifty thousand persons, whose mental and whose bodily labor you might direct, and so many hundred thousand a year of a revenue, which was neither lazy nor superstitious, appear too big for your abilities to wield? Had you no way of using the men, but by converting monks into pensioners? Had you no way of turning the revenue to account, but through the improvident resources of a spendthrift sale? If you were thus destitute of mental funds, the proceeding is in its natural course. Your politicians do not understand their trade; and therefore they sell their tools.

Reflections (1790). III, 436–42.

I live in an inverted order. They who ought to have succeeded me are gone before me. They who should have been to me as posterity are in the place of ancestors. I owe to the dearest relation (which ever must subsist in memory) that act of piety which he would have performed to me: I owe it to him to show that he was not descended, as the Duke of Bedford would have it, from an unworthy parent.

The crown has considered me after long service: the crown has paid the Duke of Bedford by advance. He has had a long credit for any service which he may perform hereafter. He is secure, and long may he be secure, in his advance, whether he performs any services or not. But let him take care how he endangers the safety of that Constitution which secures his own utility or his own insignificance, or how he discourages those who take up even puny arms to defend an order of things which, like the sun of heaven, shines alike on the useful and the worthless. His grants are ingrafted on the public law of Europe, covered with the awful hoar of innumerable ages. They are guarded by the sacred rules of prescription, found in that full treasury of jurisprudence from which the jejuneness and penury of our municipal law has by degrees been enriched and strengthened. This prescription I had my share (a very full share) in bringing to its perfection.[13] The Duke of Bedford will stand as long as prescriptive law endures,—as long as the great, stable laws of property, common to us with all civilized nations, are kept in their integrity, and without the smallest intermixture of the laws, maxims, principles, or precedents of the Grand Revolution. They are secure against all changes but one. The whole Revolutionary system, institutes, digest, code, novels, text, gloss, comment, are not only not the same, but they are the very reverse, and the reverse fundamentally, of all the laws on which civil life has hitherto been upheld in all the governments of the world. The learned professors of the Rights of Man regard prescription not as a title to bar all claim set up against old possession, but they look on prescription as itself a bar against the possessor and proprietor. They hold an immemorial possession to be no more than a long continued and therefore an aggravated injustice.

Such are *their* ideas, such *their* religion, and such *their* law. But as to *our* country and *our* race, as long as the well-compacted structure of our Church and State, the sanctuary, the holy of holies of that ancient law, defended by reverence, defended by power, a fortress at once and a temple,[14] shall stand inviolate on the brow of the British Sion,—as long as the British monarchy, not more limited than fenced by the orders of the state, shall, like the proud Keep of Windsor, rising in the majesty of proportion, and girt with the double belt of its kindred and coëval towers, as long as this awful structure shall oversee and guard the subjected land,—so long the mounds and dikes of the low, fat, Bedford level will have nothing to fear from all the pickaxes of all the levellers of France. As long as our sovereign lord the king, and his faithful subjects, the lords and commons of this realm,—the triple cord which no man can break,—the solemn, sworn, constitutional frank-pledge of this nation,—the firm guaranties of each other's being and each other's rights,—the joint and several securities, each in its place and order, for every kind and every quality of property and of dignity,—as long as these

---

[13] Sir George Savile's act, called The *Nullum Tempus* Act. [Burke]
[14] "Templum in modum arcis."—TACITUS, of the temple of Jerusalem. [Burke] [*History* v.12.]

endure, so long the Duke of Bedford is safe, and we are all safe together,—the high from the blights of envy and the spoliations of rapacity, the low from the iron hand of oppression and the insolent spurn of contempt. Amen! and so be it! and so it will be. . . .

But if the rude inroad of Gallic tumult, with its sophistical rights of man to falsify the account, and its sword as a make-weight to throw into the scale, shall be introduced into our city by a misguided populace, set on by proud great men, themselves blinded and intoxicated by a frantic ambition, we shall all of us perish and be overwhelmed in a common ruin. If a great storm blow on our coast, it will cast the whales on the strand, as well as the periwinkles. His Grace will not survive the poor grantee he despises,—no, not for a twelvemonth. If the great look for safety in the services they render to this Gallic cause, it is to be foolish even above the weight of privilege allowed to wealth. If his Grace be one of these whom they endeavor to proselytize, he ought to be aware of the character of the sect whose doctrines he is invited to embrace.

Letter to a Noble Lord (1796). V, 209–11.

CHAPTER VIII

Jacobinism

The Jacobin Clubs became the most powerful party among the French Revolutionists of 1789, and Burke used their popular nickname to designate the theories and policies of the Revolutionary movement in general. Their party, with Robespierre as leader, was chiefly responsible for the Reign of Terror in 1793–94. Burke had much to say against their violence and cruelty, but he probably feared more what he thought was the insidious danger of their philosophical principles, which had already been expounded and popularized by the pre-Revolutionary French "philosophes." In England William Godwin's *Political Justice*, published in 1793 and attracting many young disciples, including Wordsworth and later Shelley, presented a political theory similar and somewhat indebted to the French philosophy that Burke attacked. Burke charged that this philosophy was false in theory, dangerous in practice, and dehumanizing its adherents into hardhearted "metaphysicians" or theorizers.

What is Jacobinism? It is an attempt (hitherto but too successful) to eradicate prejudice out of the minds of men, for the purpose of putting all power and authority into the hands of the persons capable of occasionally enlightening the minds of the people. For this purpose the Jacobins have resolved to destroy the whole frame and fabric of the old societies of the world, and to regenerate them after their fashion. To obtain an army for this purpose, they everywhere engage the poor by holding out to them as a bribe the spoils of the rich. This I take to be a fair description of the principles and leading maxims of the enlightened of our day who are commonly called Jacobins.

Letter to William Smith (1795). VI, 367.

The example of what is done by France is too important not to have a vast and extensive influence; and that example, backed with its power, must bear with great force on those who are near it, especially on those who shall recognize the pretended republic on the principle upon which it now stands. It is not an old structure, which you have found as it is, and are not to dispute of the original end and design with which it had been so fashioned. It is a recent wrong, and can plead no prescription. It violates the rights upon which not only the community of France, but those on which all communities are founded. The principles on which they proceed are *general* principles, and are as true [or false] in England as in any other country. They who (though with the purest intentions) recognize the authority of these regicides and robbers upon principle justify their acts, and establish them as precedents. It is a question not between France and England; it is a question between property and force. The property claims; and its claim has been allowed. The property of the nation is the nation. They who massacre, plunder, and expel the body of the proprietary are murderers and robbers. The state, in its essence, must be moral and just: and it may be so, though a tyrant or usurper should be accidentally at the head of it. This is a thing to be lamented: but this notwithstanding, the body of the commonwealth may remain in all its integrity and be perfectly sound in its composition. The present case is different. It is not a revolution in government. It is not the victory of party over party. It is a destruction and decomposition of the whole society; which never can be made of right by any faction, however powerful, nor without terrible consequences to all about it, both in the act and in the example. This pretended republic is founded in crimes, and exists by wrong and robbery; and wrong and robbery, far from a title to anything, is war with mankind. To be at peace with robbery is to be an accomplice with it.

First Letter on a Regicide Peace (1796). V, 324–26.

They [the English Whig Jacobins] are sublime metaphysicians; and the horrible consequences produced by their speculations affect them not at all. They only ask whether the proposition be true?—Whether it produces good or evil, is no part of their concern.

Letter to William Weddell, January 31, 1792.
Correspondence. III, 409.

These philosophers are fanatics: independent of any interest, which, if it operated alone, would make them much more tractable, they are carried with such an headlong rage towards every desperate trial that they would sacrifice the whole human race to the slightest of their experiments. . . . I have lived long and variously in the world. Without any considerable pretensions to literature in myself, I have aspired to the love of letters. I have lived for a great many years in habitudes with those who professed them. I can form a tolerable estimate of what is likely to happen from a character chiefly dependent for fame and fortune on knowledge and talent, as well in its morbid and perverted state as in that which is sound and natural. Naturally, men so formed and finished are the first gifts of Providence to the world. But when they have once thrown off the fear of God, which was in all ages too often the case, and the fear of man, which is now the case, and when in that state they come to understand one another, and to act in corps, a more dreadful calamity cannot arise out of hell to scourge mankind. Nothing can be conceived more hard than the heart of a thorough-bred metaphysician. It comes nearer to the cold malignity of a wicked spirit than to the frailty and passion of a man. It is like that of the Principle of Evil himself, incorporeal, pure, unmixed, dephlegmated, defecated evil. It is no easy operation to eradicate humanity from the human breast. What Shakspeare calls the "compunctious visitings of Nature" will sometimes knock at their hearts, and protest against their murderous speculations. But they have a means of compounding with their nature. Their humanity is not dissolved; they only give it a long prorogation. They are ready to declare that they do not think two thousand years too long a period for the good that they pursue. It is remarkable that they never see any way to their projected good but by the road of some evil. Their imagination is not fatigued with the contemplation of human suffering through the wild waste of centuries added to centuries of misery and desolation. Their humanity is at their horizon,—and, like the horizon, it always flies before them. The geometricians and the chemists bring, the one from the dry bones of their diagrams, and the other from the soot of their furnaces, dispositions that make them worse than indifferent about those feelings and habitudes which are the supports of the moral world. Ambition is come upon them suddenly; they are intoxicated with it, and it has rendered them fearless of the danger which may from thence arise to others or to themselves.

These philosophers consider men in their experiments no more than they do mice in an air-pump or in a recipient of mephitic gas.

Letter to a Noble Lord (1796). V, 215–17.

Instead of the religion and the law by which they were in a great politic communion with the Christian world, they have constructed their republic on three bases, all fundamentally opposite to those on which the communities of Europe are built. Its foundation is laid in Regicide, in Jacobinism, and in Atheism; and it has joined to those principles a body of systematic manners which secures their operation.

If I am asked how I would be understood in the use of these terms, Regicide, Jacobinism, Atheism, and a system of correspondent manners, and their establishment, I will tell you.

I call a commonwealth *Regicide* which lays it down as a fixed law of Nature and a fundamental right of man, that all government, not being a democracy, is an usurpation,[1]—that all kings, as such, are usurpers, and, for being kings, may and ought to be put to death, with their wives, families, and adherents. The commonwealth which acts uniformly upon those principles, and which, after abolishing every festival of religion, chooses the most flagrant act of a murderous regicide treason for a feast of eternal commemoration, and which forces all her people to observe it,— this I call *Regicide by Establishment.*

Jacobinism is the revolt of the enterprising talents of a country against its property. When private men form themselves into

[1] Nothing could be more solemn than their promulgation of this principle, as a preamble to the destructive code of their famous articles for the decomposition of society, into whatever country they should enter. "La Convention Nationale, après avoir entendu le rapport de ses comités de finances, de la guerre, et diplomatiques réunis, fidèle *au principe de souveraineté de peuples, qui ne lui permet pas de reconnoître aucune institution qui y porte atteinte,*" &c., &c. *Décret sur le Rapport de Cambon,* Dec. 18, 1792. And see the subsequent proclamation. [Burke] ["The National Convention, after having heard the report of their united committees on finance, war, and diplomacy, faithful to the principle of the sovereignty of the people, which does not permit it to recognize any institution which is injurious to it," etc.]

associations for the purpose of destroying the preëxisting laws and institutions of their country,—when they secure to themselves an army by dividing amongst the people of no property the estates of the ancient and lawful proprietors,—when a state recognizes those acts,—when it does not make confiscations for crimes, but makes crimes for confiscations,—when it has its principal strength and all its resources in such a violation of property, —when it stands chiefly upon such a violation, massacring by judgments, or otherwise, those who make any struggle for their old legal government, and their legal, hereditary, or acquired possessions,—I call this *Jacobinism by Establishment.*

I call it *Atheism by Establishment,* when any state, as such, shall not acknowledge the existence of God as a moral governor of the world,—when it shall offer to Him no religious or moral worship,—when it shall abolish the Christian religion by a regular decree,—when it shall persecute, with a cold, unrelenting, steady cruelty, by every mode of confiscation, imprisonment, exile, and death, all its ministers,—when it shall generally shut up or pull down churches,—when the few buildings which remain of this kind shall be opened only for the purpose of making a profane apotheosis of monsters whose vices and crimes have no parallel amongst men, and whom all other men consider as objects of general detestation and the severest animadversion of law. When, in the place of the religion of social benevolence and of individual self-denial, in mockery of all religion, they institute impious, blasphemous, indecent theatric rites, in honor of their vitiated, perverted reason, and erect altars to the personification of their own corrupted and bloody republic,—when schools and seminaries are founded at public expense to poison mankind, from generation to generation, with the horrible maxims of this impiety,—when, wearied out with incessant martyrdom, and the cries of a people hungering and thirsting for religion, they permit it only as a tolerated evil,—I call this *Atheism by Establishment.*

When to these establishments of Regicide, of Jacobinism, and of Atheism, you add the *correspondent system of manners,* no doubt can be left on the mind of a thinking man concerning their determined hostility to the human race. Manners are of more importance than laws. Upon them, in a great measure, the laws depend. The law touches us but here and there, and now and then. Manners are what vex or soothe, corrupt or purify, exalt or debase, barbarize or refine us, by a constant, steady, uniform, insensible operation, like that of the air we breathe in. They give their whole form and color to our lives. According to their quality, they aid morals, they supply them, or they totally destroy them. Of this the new French legislators were aware; therefore, with the same method, and under the same authority, they settled a system of manners, the most licentious, prostitute, and abandoned that ever has been known, and at the same time the most coarse, rude, savage, and ferocious. Nothing in the Revolution, no, not to a phrase or a gesture, not to the fashion of a hat or a shoe, was left to accident. All has been the result of design; all has been matter of institution. No mechanical means could be devised in favor of this incredible system of wickedness and vice, that has not been employed. The noblest passions, the love of glory, the love of country, have been debauched into means of its preservation and its propagation. All sorts of shows and exhibitions, calculated to inflame and vitiate the imagination and pervert the moral sense, have been contrived. They have sometimes brought forth five or six hundred drunken women calling at the bar of the Assembly for the blood of their own children, as being Royalists or Constitutionalists. Sometimes they have got a body of wretches, calling themselves fathers, to demand the murder of their sons, boasting that Rome had but one Brutus, but that they could show five hundred. There were instances in which they inverted and retaliated the impiety, and produced sons who called for the execution of their parents. The foundation of their republic is laid in moral paradoxes. Their patriotism is always prodigy. All those instances to be found in history, whether real or fabulous, of a doubtful public spirit, at which morality is perplexed, reason is staggered, and from which affrighted Nature recoils, are their chosen and almost sole examples for the instruction of their youth.

The whole drift of their institution is contrary to that of the wise legislators of all countries, who aimed at improving instincts into morals, and at grafting the virtues on the stock of the natural affections. They, on the contrary, have omitted no pains to eradicate every benevolent and noble propensity in the mind of men. In their culture it is a rule always to graft virtues on vices. They think everything unworthy of the name of public virtue, unless it indicates violence on the private. All their new institutions (and with them everything is new) strike at the root of our social nature. Other legislators, knowing that marriage is the origin of all relations, and consequently the first element of all duties, have endeavored by every art to make it sacred. The Christian religion, by confining it to the pairs, and by rendering that relation indissoluble, has by these two things done more towards the peace, happiness, settlement, and civilization of the world than by any other part in this whole scheme of Divine wisdom. The direct contrary course has been taken in the synagogue of Antichrist,—I mean in that forge and manufactory of all evil, the sect which predominated in the Constituent Assembly of 1789. Those monsters employed the same or greater industry to desecrate and degrade that state, which other legislators have used to render it holy and honorable. By a strange, uncalled-for declaration, they pronounced that marriage was no better than a common civil contract. It was one of their ordinary tricks, to put their sentiments into the mouths of certain personated characters, which they theatrically exhibited at the bar of what ought to be a serious assembly. One of these was brought out in the figure of a prostitute, whom they called by the affected name of "a mother without being a wife." This creature they made to call for a repeal of the incapacities which in civilized states are put upon bastards. The prostitutes of the Assembly gave to this their puppet the sanction of their greater impudence. In consequence of the principles laid down, and the manners authorized, bastards were not long after put on the footing of the issue of lawful unions. Proceeding in the spirit of the first authors of their Constitution, succeeding Assemblies went the full length of the principle, and gave a license to divorce at the mere pleasure of either party, and at a month's notice. With them the matrimonial connection is brought into so degraded a state of concubinage, that I believe none of the wretches in London who keep warehouses of infamy would give out one of their victims to private custody on so short and insolent a tenure. There was, indeed, a kind of profligate equity in giving to women the same licentious power. The reason they assigned was as infamous as the act: declaring that women had been too long under the tyranny of parents and of husbands. It is not necessary to observe upon the horrible consequences of taking one half of the species wholly out of the guardianship and protection of the other.

The practice of divorce, though in some countries permitted, has been discouraged in all. In the East, polygamy and divorce are in discredit; and the manners correct the laws. In Rome, whilst Rome was in its integrity, the few causes allowed for divorce amounted in effect to a prohibition. They were only three. The arbitrary was totally excluded; and accordingly some hundreds of years passed without a single example of that kind. When manners were corrupted, the laws were relaxed; as the latter always follow the former, when they are not able to regulate them or to vanquish them. Of this circumstance the legislators of vice and crime were pleased to take notice, as an inducement to adopt their regulation: holding out an hope that the permission would as rarely be made use of. They knew the contrary to be true; and they had taken good care that the laws should be well seconded by the manners. Their law of divorce, like all their laws, had not for its object the relief of domestic uneasiness, but the total corruption of all morals, the total disconnection of social life.

First Letter on a Regicide Peace (1796). V, 308–14.

My ideas and my principles led me, in this contest, to encounter France, not as a state, but as a faction. The vast territorial extent of that country, its immense population, its riches of production, its riches of commerce and convention, the whole aggregate mass of what in ordinary cases constitutes the force of a state, to me were but objects of secondary consideration. They might be balanced; and they have been often more than balanced. Great as these things are, they are not what make the faction formidable. It is the faction that makes them truly dreadful. That faction is the evil spirit that possesses the body of France,—that informs it as a soul,—that stamps upon its ambition, and upon all its pursuits, a characteristic mark, which strongly distinguishes them from the same general passions and the same general views in other men and in other communities. It is that spirit which inspires into them a new, a pernicious, a desolating activity. Constituted as France was ten years ago, it was not in that France to shake, to shatter, and to overwhelm Europe in the manner that we behold. A sure destruction impends over those infatuated princes who, in the conflict with this new and unheard-of power, proceed as if they were engaged in a war that bore a resemblance

to their former contests, or that they can make peace in the spirit
of their former arrangements of pacification. Here the beaten
path is the very reverse of the safe road.

As to me, I was always steadily of opinion that this disorder
was not in its nature intermittent. I conceived that the contest,
once begun, could not be laid down again, to be resumed at our
discretion, but that our first struggle with this evil would also
be our last. I never thought we could make peace with the system; because it was not for the sake of an object we pursued in
rivalry with each other, but with the system itself that we were
at war. As I understood the matter, we were at war, not with its
conduct, but with its existence,—convinced that its existence and
its hostility were the same.

The faction is not local or territorial. It is a general evil. Where
it least appears in action, it is still full of life. In its sleep it
recruits its strength and prepares its exertion. Its spirit lies deep
in the corruptions of our common nature. The social order which
restrains it feeds it. It exists in every country in Europe, and
among all orders of men in every country, who look up to France
as to a common head. The centre is there. The circumference is
the world of Europe, wherever the race of Europe may be settled.
Everywhere else the faction is militant; in France it is trium-
phant. In France is the bank of deposit and the bank of circulation of all the pernicious principles that are forming in every
state. It will be a folly scarcely deserving of pity, and too mischievous for contempt, to think of restraining it in any other
country whilst it is predominant there. War, instead of being the
cause of its force, has suspended its operation. It has given a
reprieve, at least, to the Christian world.

The true nature of a Jacobin war, in the beginning, was by
most of the Christian powers felt, acknowledged, and even in the
most precise manner declared. In the joint manifesto published
by the Emperor and the King of Prussia, on the 4th of August,
1792, it is expressed in the clearest terms, and on principles which
could not fail, if they had adhered to them, of classing those
monarchs with the first benefactors of mankind. This manifesto
was published, as they themselves express it, "to lay open to the
present generation, as well as to posterity, their motives, their
intentions, and the *disinterestedness* of their personal views:
taking up arms for the purpose of preserving social and political

order amongst all civilized nations, and to secure to *each* state its religion, happiness, independence, territories, and real constitution."—"On this ground they hoped that all empires and all states would be unanimous, and, becoming the firm guardians of the happiness of mankind, that they could not fail to unite their efforts to rescue a numerous nation from its own fury, to preserve Europe from the return of barbarism, and the universe from the subversion and anarchy with which it was threatened." The whole of that noble performance ought to be read at the first meeting of any congress which may assemble for the purpose of pacification. In that piece "these powers expressly renounce all views of personal aggrandizement," and confine themselves to objects worthy of so generous, so heroic, and so perfectly wise and politic an enterprise. It was to the principles of this confederation, and to no other, that we wished our sovereign and our country to accede, as a part of the commonwealth of Europe. To these principles, with some trifling exceptions and limitations, they did fully accede.[2] And all our friends who took office acceded to the ministry, (whether wisely or not,) as I always understood the matter, on the faith and on the principles of that declaration.

As long as these powers flattered themselves that the menace of force would produce the effect of force, they acted on those declarations; but when their menaces failed of success, their efforts took a new direction. It did not appear to them that virtue and heroism ought to be purchased by millions of rix-dollars. It is a dreadful truth, but it is a truth that cannot be concealed: in ability, in dexterity, in the distinctness of their views, the Jacobins are our superiors. They saw the thing right from the very beginning. Whatever were the first motives to the war among politicians, they saw that in its spirit, and for its objects, it was a *civil war;* and as such they pursued it. It is a war between the partisans of the ancient civil, moral, and political order of Europe against a sect of fanatical and ambitious atheists which means to change them all. It is not France extending a foreign empire over other nations: it is a sect aiming at universal empire, and beginning with the conquest of France. The leaders of that sect

---

[2] See Declaration, Whitehall, Oct. 29, 1793. [Burke]

secured *the centre of Europe;* and that secured, they knew, that, whatever might be the event of battles and sieges, their *cause* was victorious. Whether its territory had a little more or a little less peeled from its surface, or whether an island or two was detached from its commerce, to them was of little moment. The conquest of France was a glorious acquisition. That once well laid as a basis of empire, opportunities never could be wanting to regain or to replace what had been lost, and dreadfully to avenge themselves on the faction of their adversaries.

They saw it was *a civil war.* It was their business to persuade their adversaries that it ought to be a *foreign* war.

Second Letter on a Regicide Peace (1796). V, 342–46.

When I contemplate the scheme on which France is formed, and when I compare it with these systems with which it is and ever must be in conflict, those things which seem as defects in her polity are the very things which make me tremble. The states of the Christian world have grown up to their present magnitude in a great length of time and by a great variety of accidents. They have been improved to what we see them with greater or less degrees of felicity and skill. Not one of them has been formed upon a regular plan or with any unity of design. As their constitutions are not systematical, they have not been directed to any *peculiar* end, eminently distinguished, and superseding every other. The objects which they embrace are of the greatest possible variety, and have become in a manner infinite. In all these old countries, the state has been made to the people, and not the people conformed to the state. Every state has pursued not only every sort of social advantage, but it has cultivated the welfare of every individual. His wants, his wishes, even his tastes, have been consulted. This comprehensive scheme virtually produced a degree of personal liberty in forms the most adverse to it. That liberty was found, under monarchies styled absolute, in a degree unknown to the ancient commonwealths. From hence the powers of all our modern states meet, in all their movements, with some obstruction. It is therefore no wonder, that when these states are to be considered as machines to operate for some one great end, that this dissipated and balanced force is not easily concentred, or made to bear with the whole force of the nation upon one point.

The British state is, without question, that which pursues the greatest variety of ends, and is the least disposed to sacrifice any one of them to another or to the whole. It aims at taking in the entire circle of human desires, and securing for them their fair enjoyment. Our legislature has been ever closely connected, in its most efficient part, with individual feeling and individual interest. Personal liberty, the most lively of these feelings and the most important of these interests, which in other European countries has rather arisen from the system of manners and the habitudes of life than from the laws of the state, (in which it flourished more from neglect than attention,) in England has been a direct object of government.

On this principle, England would be the weakest power in the whole system. Fortunately, however, the great riches of this kingdom, arising from a variety of causes, and the disposition of the people, which is as great to spend as to accumulate, has easily afforded a disposable surplus that gives a mighty momentum to the state. This difficulty, with these advantages to overcome it, has called forth the talents of the English financiers, who, by the surplus of industry poured out by prodigality, have outdone everything which has been accomplished in other nations. The present minister has outdone his predecessors, and, as a minister of revenue, is far above my power of praise. But still there are cases in which England feels more than several others (though they all feel) the perplexity of an immense body of balanced advantages and of individual demands, and of some irregularity in the whole mass.

France differs essentially from all those governments which are formed without system, which exist by habit, and which are confused with the multitude and with the complexity of their pursuits. What now stands as government in France is struck out at a heat. The design is wicked, immoral, impious, oppressive: but it is spirited and daring; it is systematic; it is simple in its principle; it has unity and consistency in perfection. In that country, entirely to cut off a branch of commerce, to extinguish a manufacture, to destroy the circulation of money, to violate credit, to suspend the course of agriculture, even to burn a city or to lay waste a province of their own, does not cost them a moment's anxiety. To them the will, the wish, the want, the liberty, the toil, the blood of individuals, is as nothing. Individuality is left out of their scheme of government. The state is all in all. Everything is referred to the production of force; afterwards, everything is trusted to the use of it. It is military in its principle, in its maxims, in its spirit, and in all its movements. The state has dominion and conquest for its sole objects,— dominion over minds by proselytism, over bodies by arms.

Thus constituted, with an immense body of natural means, which are lessened in their amount only to be increased in their effect, France has, since the accomplishment of the Revolution, a complete unity in its direction. It has destroyed every resource of the state which depends upon opinion and the good-will of individuals. The riches of convention disappear. The advantages of Nature in some measure remain; even these, I admit, are astonishingly lessened; the command over what remains is complete and absolute. We go about asking when assignats [paper money] will expire, and we laugh at the last price of them. But what signifies the fate of those tickets of despotism? The despotism will find despotic means of supply. They have found the short cut to the productions of Nature, while others, in pursuit of them, are obliged to wind through the labyrinth of a very intricate state of society. They seize upon the fruit of the labor; they seize upon the laborer himself. Were France but half of what it is in population, in compactness, in applicability of its force, situated as it is, and being what it is, it would be too strong for most of the states of Europe, constituted as they are, and proceeding as they proceed. Would it be wise to estimate what the world of Europe, as well as the world of Asia, had to dread from Genghiz Khân, upon a contemplation of the resources of the cold and barren spot in the remotest Tartary from whence first issued that scourge of the human race? Ought we to judge from the excise and stamp duties of the rocks, or from the paper circulation of the sands of Arabia, the power by which Mahomet and his tribes laid hold at once on the two most powerful empires of the world, beat one of them totally to the ground, broke to pieces the other, and, in not much longer space of time than I have lived, overturned governments, laws, manners, religion, and extended an empire from the Indus to the Pyrenees?

Material resources never have supplied, nor ever can supply, the want of unity in design and constancy in pursuit. But unity in design and perseverance and boldness in pursuit have never wanted resources, and never will. We have not considered as we ought the dreadful energy of a state in which the property has nothing to do with the government. Reflect, my dear Sir, reflect again and again, on a government in which the property is in complete subjection, and where nothing rules but the mind of desperate men. The condition of a commonwealth not governed by its property was a combination of things which the learned and ingenious speculator, Harrington, who has tossed about society into all forms, never could imagine to be possible. We have seen it; the world has felt it; and if the world will shut their eyes to this state of things, they will feel it more. The rulers there have found their resources in crimes. The discovery is dreadful, the mine exhaustless. They have everything to gain, and they have nothing to lose. They have a boundless inheritance in hope, and there is no medium for them betwixt the highest elevation and death with infamy. Never can they, who, from the miserable servitude of the desk, have been raised to empire, again submit to the bondage of a starving bureau, or the profit of copying music, or writing *plaidoyers* by the sheet. It has made me often smile in bitterness, when I have heard talk of an indemnity to such men, provided they returned to their allegiance.

From all this what is my inference? It is, that this new system of robbery in France cannot be rendered safe by any art; that it *must* be destroyed, or that it will destroy all Europe; that to destroy that enemy, by some means or other, the force opposed to it should be made to bear some analogy and resemblance to the force and spirit which that system exerts; that war ought to be made against it in its vulnerable parts. These are my inferences. In one word, with this republic nothing independent can coexist. The errors of Louis the Sixteenth were more pardonable to prudence than any of those of the same kind into which the allied courts may fall. They have the benefit of his dreadful example. . . .

Louis the Sixteenth was a diligent reader of history. But the very lamp of prudence blinded him. The guide of human life led him astray. A silent revolution in the moral world preceded the political, and prepared it. It became of more importance than ever what examples were given, and what measures were adopted. Their causes no longer lurked in the recesses of cabinets or in the private conspiracies of the factious. They were no longer to be controlled by the force and influence of the grandees, who formerly had been able to stir up troubles by their discontents and to quiet them by their corruption. The chain of subordination, even in cabal and sedition, was broken in its most important links. It was no longer the great and the populace. Other interests were formed, other dependencies, other connections, other communications. The middle classes had swelled far beyond their former proportion. Like whatever is the most effectively rich and great in society, these classes became the seat of all the active politics, and the preponderating weight to decide on them. There were all the energies by which fortune is acquired; there the consequence of their success. There were all the talents which assert their pretensions, and are impatient of the place which settled society prescribes to them. These descriptions had got between the great and the populace; and the influence on the lower classes was with them. The spirit of ambition had taken possession of this class as violently as ever it had done of any other. They felt the importance of this situation. The correspondence of the moneyed and the mercantile world, the literary intercourse of academies, but above all, the press, of which they had in a manner entire possession, made a kind of electric communication everywhere. The press, in reality, has made every government, in its spirit, almost democratic. Without the great, the first movements in this revolution could not, perhaps, have been given. But the spirit of ambition, now for the first time connected with the spirit of speculation, was not to be restrained at will. There was no longer any means of arresting a principle in its course. When Louis the Sixteenth, under the influence of the enemies to monarchy, meant to found but one republic, he set up two; when he meant to take away half the crown of his neighbor, he lost the whole of his own.[3] Louis the Sixteenth could not with impunity countenance a new republic. Yet between his throne and that dangerous lodgment for an enemy, which he had erected, he had the whole Atlantic for a ditch. He had for an outwork the English nation itself, friendly to liberty, adverse to that mode of it. He was surrounded by a rampart of monarchies, most of them allied to him, and generally

[3] Burke refers to French assistance to the American Colonies.

under his influence. Yet even thus secured, a republic erected under his auspices, and dependent on his power, became fatal to his throne. The very money which he had lent to support this republic, by a good faith which to him operated as perfidy, was punctually paid to his enemies, and became a resource in the hands of his assassins.

With this example before their eyes, do any ministers in England, do any ministers in Austria, really flatter themselves that they can erect, not on the remote shores of the Atlantic, but in their view, in their vicinity, in absolute contact with one of them, not a commercial, but a martial republic,—a republic not of simple husbandmen or fishermen, but of intriguers, and of warriors,—a republic of a character the most restless, the most enterprising, the most impious, the most fierce and bloody, the most hypocritical and perfidious, the most bold and daring, that ever has been seen, or indeed that can be conceived to exist, without bringing on their own certain ruin?

Such is the republic to which we are going to give a place in civilized fellowship,—the republic which, with joint consent, we are going to establish in the centre of Europe, in a post that overlooks and commands every other state, and which eminently confronts and menaces this kingdom.

Second Letter on a Regicide Peace (1796). V, 373–82.

1. The New Morality of France and Rousseau

Those who have made the exhibition of the fourteenth of July are capable of every evil. They do not commit crimes for their designs; but they form designs that they may commit crimes. It is not their necessity, but their nature, that impels them. They are modern philosophers, which when you say of them, you express everything that is ignoble, savage, and hard-hearted.

Besides the sure tokens which are given by the spirit of their particular arrangements, there are some characteristic lineaments in the general policy of your tumultuous despotism, which, in my opinion, indicate, beyond a doubt, that no revolution whatsoever *in their disposition* is to be expected: I mean their scheme of educating the rising generation, the principles which they intend to instil and the sympathies which they wish to form in the mind at the season in which it is the most susceptible. Instead of forming their young minds to that docility, to that modesty, which are the grace and charm of youth, to an admiration of famous examples, and to an averseness to anything which approaches to pride, petulance, and self-conceit, (distempers to which that time of life is of itself sufficiently liable,) they artificially foment these evil dispositions, and even form them into springs of action. Nothing ought to be more weighed than the nature of books recommended by public authority. So recommended, they soon form the character of the age. Uncertain indeed is the efficacy, limited indeed is the extent, of a virtuous institution. But if education takes in *vice* as any part of its system, there is no doubt but that it will operate with abundant energy, and to an extent indefinite. The magistrate, who in favor of freedom thinks himself obliged to suffer all sorts of publications, is under a stricter duty than any other well to consider what sort of writers he shall authorize, and shall recommend by the strongest of all sanctions, that is, by public honors and rewards. He ought to be cautious how he recommends authors of mixed or ambiguous morality. He ought to be fearful of putting into the hands of youth writers indulgent to the peculiarities of their own complexion, lest they should teach the humors of the professor, rather than the principles of the science. He ought, above all, to be cautious in recommending any writer who has carried marks of a deranged understanding: for where there is no sound reason, there can be no real virtue; and madness is ever vicious and malignant.

The Assembly proceeds on maxims the very reverse of these. The Assembly recommends to its youth a study of the bold experimenters in morality. Everybody knows that there is a great dispute amongst their leaders, which of them is the best resemblance of Rousseau. In truth, they all resemble him. His blood they transfuse into their minds and into their manners. Him they study; him they meditate; him they turn over in all the time they can spare from the laborious mischief of the day or the debauches of the night. Rousseau is their canon of holy writ; in his life he is their canon of Polycletus; he is their standard figure of perfection. To this man and this writer, as a pattern to authors and to Frenchmen, the foundries of Paris are now running for statues, with the kettles of their poor and the bells of their churches. If an author had written like a great genius on geometry, though his practical and speculative morals were vicious in the extreme, it might appear that in voting the statue they honored only the geometrician. But Rousseau is a moralist or he is nothing. It is impossible, therefore, putting the circumstances together, to mistake their design in choosing the author with whom they have begun to recommend a course of studies.

Their great problem is, to find a substitute for all the principles which hitherto have been employed to regulate the human will and action. They find dispositions in the mind of such force and quality as may fit men, far better than the old morality, for the purposes of such a state as theirs, and may go much further in supporting their power and destroying their enemies. They have therefore chosen a selfish, flattering, seductive, ostentatious vice, in the place of plain duty. True humility, the basis of the Christian system, is the low, but deep and firm foundation of all real virtue. But this, as very painful in the practice, and little imposing in the appearance, they have totally discarded. Their object is to merge all natural and all social sentiment in inordinate vanity. In a small degree, and conversant in little things, vanity is of little moment. When full-grown, it is the worst of vices, and the occasional mimic of them all. It makes the whole man false. It leaves nothing sincere or trustworthy about him. His best qualities are poisoned and perverted by it, and operate exactly as the worst. When your lords had many writers as immoral as the object of their statue (such as Voltaire and others) they chose Rousseau, because in him that peculiar vice which they wished to erect into ruling virtue was by far the most conspicuous.

We have had the great professor and founder of *the philosophy of vanity* in England [in 1766-67]. As I had good opportunities of knowing his proceedings almost from day to day, he left no doubt on my mind that he entertained no principle, either to influence his heart or to guide his understanding, but *vanity*. With this vice he was possessed to a degree little short of madness. It is from the same deranged, eccentric vanity, that this, the insane Socrates of the National Assembly, was impelled to publish a mad confession of his mad faults, and to attempt a new sort of glory from bringing hardily to light the obscure and vulgar vices which we know may sometimes be blended with eminent talents. He has not observed on the nature of vanity who does not know that it is omnivorous,—that it has no choice in its food,—that it is fond to talk even of its own faults and vices, as what will excite surprise and draw attention, and what will pass at worst for openness and candor.

It was this abuse and perversion, which vanity makes even of hypocrisy, which has driven Rousseau to record a life not so much as checkered or spotted here and there with virtues, or even distinguished by a single good action. It is such a life he chooses to offer to the attention of mankind. It is such a life that, with a wild defiance, he flings in the face of his Creator, whom he acknowledges only to brave. Your Assembly, knowing how much more powerful example is found than precept, has chosen this man (by his own account without a single virtue) for a model. To him they erect their first statue. From him they commence their series of honors and distinctions.

It is that new-invented virtue which your masters canonize that led their moral hero constantly to exhaust the stores of his powerful rhetoric in the expression of universal benevolence, whilst his heart was incapable of harboring one spark of common parental affection. Benevolence to the whole species, and want of feeling for every individual with whom the professors come in contact, form the character of the new philosophy. Setting up for an unsocial independence, this their hero of vanity refuses the just price of common labor, as well as the tribute which opulence owes to genius, and which, when paid, honors the giver and the receiver; and then he pleads his beggary as an excuse for his crimes. He melts with tenderness for those only who touch him by the remotest relation, and then, without one natural pang, casts away, as a sort of offal and excrement, the spawn of his disgustful amours, and sends his children to the hospital of foundlings. The bear loves, licks, and forms her young: but bears are not philosophers. Vanity, however, finds its account in reversing the train of our natural feelings. Thousands admire the sentimental writer; the affectionate father is hardly known in his parish.

Under this philosophic instructor in *the ethics of vanity*, they have attempted in France a regeneration of the moral constitution of man. Statesmen like your present rulers exist by everything which is spurious, fictitious, and false,—by everything which takes the man from his house, and sets him on a stage,—which makes him up an artificial creature, with painted, theatric sentiments, fit to be seen by the glare of candle-light, and formed to be contemplated at a due distance. Vanity is too apt to prevail in all of us, and in all countries. To the improvement of Frenchmen, it seems not absolutely necessary that it should be taught upon system. But it is plain that the present rebellion was its legitimate offspring, and it is piously fed by that rebellion with a daily dole.

If the system of institution recommended by the Assembly is false and theatric, it is because their system of government is of the same character. To that, and to that alone, it is strictly conformable. To understand either, we must connect the morals with the politics of the legislators. Your practical philosophers, systematic in everything, have wisely begun at the source. As the relation between parents and children is the first among the elements of vulgar, natural morality,[4] they erect statues to a wild, ferocious, low-minded, hard-hearted father, of fine general feelings,—a lover of his kind, but a hater of his kindred. Your masters reject the duties of this vulgar relation, as contrary to liberty, as not founded in the social compact, and not binding according to the rights of men; because the relation is not, of course, the result of *free election*,—never so on the side of the children, not always on the part of the parents.

The next relation which they regenerate by their statues to Rousseau is that which is next in sanctity to that of a father. They differ from those old-fashioned thinkers who considered pedagogues as sober and venerable characters, and allied to the

---

[4] "Filiola tua te delectari lætor, et probari tibi φυσικὴν esse τὴν πρὸς τὰ τέκνα: etenim, si hæc non est, nulla potest homini esse ad hominem naturæ adjunctio: qua sublata, vitæ societas tollitur. Valete, Patron [Rousseau] et tui condiscipuli [L'Assemblée Nationale]!" —Cic. Ep. ad Atticum. [Burke] ["I am glad you take such delight in your daughter, and have been converted to the doctrine that sex is a natural instinct for having children. For in the absence of this instinct there can be no natural tie uniting man and man, and, without that, social life is impossible." Cicero *Letters to Atticus* vii.2. Cicero was bantering Atticus for his earlier adherence to the Epicurean doctrine that sex is mere self-gratification.]

parental. The moralists of the dark times *præceptorem sancti voluere parentis esse loco* [would have the teacher in the sacred position of a parent]. In this age of light they teach the people that preceptors ought to be in the place of gallants. They systematically corrupt a very corruptible race, (for some time a growing nuisance amongst you,)—a set of pert, petulant literators, to whom, instead of their proper, but severe, unostentatious duties, they assign the brilliant part of men of wit and pleasure, of gay, young, military sparks, and danglers at toilets. They call on the rising generation in France to take a sympathy in the adventures and fortunes, and they endeavor to engage their sensibility on the side, of pedagogues who betray the most awful family trusts and vitiate their female pupils. They teach the people that the debauchers of virgins, almost in the arms of their parents, may be safe inmates in their house, and even fit guardians of the honor of those husbands who succeed legally to the office which the young literators had preoccupied without asking leave of law or conscience.

Thus they dispose of all the family relations of parents and children, husbands and wives. Through this same instructor, by whom they corrupt the morals, they corrupt the taste. Taste and elegance, though they are reckoned only among the smaller and secondary morals, yet are of no mean importance in the regulation of life. A moral taste is not of force to turn vice into virtue; but it recommends virtue with something like the blandishments of pleasure, and it infinitely abates the evils of vice. Rousseau, a writer of great force and vivacity, is totally destitute of taste in any sense of the word. Your masters, who are his scholars, conceive that all refinement has an aristocratic character. The last age had exhausted all its powers in giving a grace and nobleness to our natural appetites, and in raising them into a higher class and order than seemed justly to belong to them. Through Rousseau, your masters are resolved to destroy these aristocratic prejudices. The passion called love has so general and powerful an influence, it makes so much of the entertainment, and indeed so much the occupation, of that part of life which decides the character forever, that the mode and the principles on which it engages the sympathy and strikes the imagination become of the utmost importance to the morals and manners of every society. Your rulers were well aware of this; and in their system of changing your manners to accommodate them to their politics, they found nothing so convenient as Rousseau. Through him they teach men to love after the fashion of philosophers: that is, they teach to men, to Frenchmen, a love without gallantry,—a love without anything of that fine flower of youthfulness and gentility which places it, if not among the virtues, among the ornaments of life. Instead of this passion, naturally allied to grace and manners, they infuse into their youth an unfashioned, indelicate, sour, gloomy, ferocious medley of pedantry and lewdness,—of metaphysical speculations blended with the coarsest sensuality. Such is the general morality of the passions to be found in their famous philosopher, in his famous work of philosophic gallantry, the *Nouvelle Éloise.*

When the fence from the gallantry of preceptors is broken down, and your families are no longer protected by decent pride and salutary domestic prejudice, there is but one step to a frightful corruption. The rulers in the National Assembly are in good hopes that the females of the first families in France may become an easy prey to dancing-masters, fiddlers, pattern-drawers, friseurs, and valets-de-chambre, and other active citizens of that description, who, having the entry into your houses, and being half domesticated by their situation, may be blended with you by regular and irregular relations. By a law they have made these people their equals. By adopting the sentiments of Rousseau they have made them your rivals. In this manner these great legislators complete their plan of levelling, and establish their rights of men on a sure foundation.

I am certain that the writings of Rousseau lead directly to this kind of shameful evil. I have often wondered how he comes to be so much more admired and followed on the Continent than he is here. Perhaps a secret charm in the language may have its share in this extraordinary difference. We certainly perceive, and to a degree we feel, in this writer, a style glowing, animated, enthusiastic, at the same time that we find it lax, diffuse, and not in the best taste of composition,—all the members of the piece being pretty equally labored and expanded, without any due selection or subordination of parts. He is generally too much on the stretch, and his manner has little variety. We cannot rest upon any of his works, though they contain observations which occasionally discover a considerable insight into human nature.

But his doctrines, on the whole, are so inapplicable to real life
and manners, that we never dream of drawing from them any
rule for laws or conduct, or for fortifying or illustrating anything
by a reference to his opinions. They have with us the fate of
older paradoxes:—

> Cum ventum ad *verum* est, *sensus moresque* repugnant,
> Atque ipsa utilitas, justi prope mater et æqui.

[Horace said that those who would like to believe that there is
no gradation in offences find themselves in real difficulty "when
they turn to realities; they have against them the consensus of
opinion, moral feeling, and even the good of the public, which
one can almost call the mother of justice and equity." Horace
Satires I.iii.96–97.]

Perhaps bold speculations are more acceptable because more
new to you than to us, who have been long since satiated with
them. We continue, as in the two last ages, to read, more generally than I believe is now done on the Continent, the authors
of sound antiquity. These occupy our minds; they give us another taste and turn; and will not suffer us to be more than
transiently amused with paradoxical morality. It is not that I
consider this writer as wholly destitute of just notions. Amongst
his irregularities, it must be reckoned that he is sometimes moral,
and moral in a very sublime strain. But the *general spirit and
tendency* of his works is mischievous,—and the more mischievous
for this mixture: for perfect depravity of sentiment is not reconcilable with eloquence; and the mind (though corruptible, not
complexionally vicious) would reject and throw off with disgust
a lesson of pure and unmixed evil. These writers make even virtue
a pander to vice.

However, I less consider the author than the system of the
Assembly in perverting morality through his means. This I confess makes me nearly despair of any attempt upon the minds of
their followers, through reason, honor, or conscience. The great
object of your tyrants is to destroy the gentlemen of France;
and for that purpose they destroy, to the best of their power, all
the effect of those relations which may render considerable men
powerful or even safe. To destroy that order, they vitiate the
whole community. That no means may exist of confederating

against their tyranny, by the false sympathies of this *Nouvelle Éloise* they endeavor to subvert those principles of domestic trust and fidelity which form the discipline of social life. They propagate principles by which every servant may think it, if not his duty, at least his privilege, to betray his master. By these principles, every considerable father of a family loses the sanctuary of his house. *Debet sua cuique domus esse perfugium tutissimum* [Every man's home should be his place of refuge], says the law, which your legislators have taken so much pains first to decry, then to repeal. They destroy all the tranquillity and security of domestic life: turning the asylum of the house into a gloomy prison, where the father of the family must drag out a miserable existence, endangered in proportion to the apparent means of his safety,—where he is worse than solitary in a crowd of domestics, and more apprehensive from his servants and inmates than from the hired, bloodthirsty mob without doors who are ready to pull him to the *lanterne.*

It is thus, and for the same end, that they endeavor to destroy that tribunal of conscience which exists independently of edicts and decrees. Your despots govern by terror. They know that he who fears God fears nothing else; and therefore they eradicate from the mind, through their Voltaire, their Helvétius, and the rest of that infamous gang, that only sort of fear which generates true courage. Their object is, that their fellow-citizens may be under the dominion of no awe but that of their Committee of Research and of their *lanterne.*

Having found the advantage of assassination in the formation of their tyranny, it is the grand resource in which they trust for the support of it. Whoever opposes any of their proceedings, or is suspected of a design to oppose them, is to answer it with his life, or the lives of his wife and children. This infamous, cruel, and cowardly practice of assassination they have the impudence to call *merciful.* They boast that they operated their usurpation rather by terror than by force, and that a few seasonable murders have prevented the bloodshed of many battles. There is no doubt they will extend these acts of mercy whenever they see an occasion. Dreadful, however, will be the consequences of their attempt to avoid the evils of war by the merciful policy of murder.

Letter to a Member of the National Assembly (1791). **IV,** 23–34.

In his essay "On the Function of Criticism" Matthew Arnold commented on the following passage: "That return of Burke upon himself has always seemed to me one of the finest things in English literature, or indeed in any literature. That is what I call living by ideas."

What is to be done?

It would be presumption in me to do more than to make a case. Many things occur. But as they, like all political measures, depend on dispositions, tempers, means, and external circumstances, for all their effect, not being well assured of these, I do not know how to let loose any speculations of mine on the subject. The evil is stated, in my opinion, as it exists. The remedy must be where power, wisdom, and information, I hope, are more united with good intentions than they can be with me. I have done with this subject, I believe, forever. It has given me many anxious moments for the two last years. If a great change is to be made in human affairs, the minds of men will be fitted to it, the general opinions and feelings will draw that way. Every fear, every hope, will forward it; and then they who persist in opposing this mighty current in human affairs will appear rather to resist the decrees of Providence itself than the mere designs of men. They will not be resolute and firm, but perverse and obstinate.

Thoughts on French Affairs (1791). IV, 377.

CHAPTER IX

Aesthetics: The Psychology of the Sublime

In 1757, before he entered on his political career, Burke published a small volume entitled *A Philosophical Enquiry into the Origin of our Ideas of the Sublime and Beautiful*. The most original and influential idea advanced in this treatise was that there is an element of fear in our enjoyment of the sublime. The acuteness of observation and analysis which distinguishes his later political writings is already evident in this essay, which had a considerable influence. For studies of its historical importance, see Samuel H. Monk, *The Sublime: A Study of Critical Theories in XVIII-Century England* (New York, 1935) and the edition of the *Enquiry* by J. T. Boulton (New York, 1958).

The passion caused by the great and sublime in *nature*, when those causes operate most powerfully, is astonishment: and astonishment is that state of the soul in which all its motions are suspended, with some degree of horror. In this case the mind is so entirely filled with its object, that it cannot entertain any other, nor by consequence reason on that object which employs it. Hence arises the great power of the sublime, that, far from being produced by them, it anticipates our reasonings, and hurries us on by an irresistible force. Astonishment, as I have said, is the effect of the sublime in its highest degree; the inferior effects are admiration, reverence, and respect.

No passion so effectually robs the mind of all its powers of acting and reasoning as *fear*. For fear being an apprehension of pain or death, it operates in a manner that resembles actual pain. Whatever therefore is terrible, with regard to sight, is sublime too, whether this cause of terror be endued with greatness of dimensions or not; for it is impossible to look on anything as trifling, or contemptible, that may be dangerous. There are many animals, who, though far from being large, are yet capable of raising ideas of the sublime, because they are considered as objects of terror. As serpents and poisonous animals of almost all kinds. And to things of great dimensions, if we annex an adventitious idea of terror, they become without comparison greater. A level plain of a vast extent on land, is certainly no mean idea; the prospect of such a plain may be as extensive as a prospect of the ocean; but can it ever fill the mind with anything so great as the ocean itself? This is owing to several causes; but it is owing to none more than this, that the ocean is an object of no small terror. Indeed terror is in all cases whatsoever, either more openly or latently, the ruling principle of the sublime. Several languages bear a strong testimony to the affinity of these ideas. They frequently use the same word to signify indifferently the modes of astonishment or admiration and those of terror. Θάμβος is in Greek either fear or wonder; δεινός is terrible or respectable; αἰδέω, to reverence or to fear. *Vereor* in Latin is what αἰδέω is in Greek. The Romans used the verb *stupeo*, a term which strongly marks the state of an astonished mind, to express the effect either of simple fear, or of astonishment; the word *attonitus* (thunderstruck) is equally expressive of the alliance of these ideas; and do not the French *étonnement*, and the English *astonishment* and *amazement*, point out as clearly the kindred emotions which attend fear and wonder? They who have a more general knowledge of languages, could produce, I make no doubt, many other and equally striking examples.

To make anything very terrible, obscurity seems in general to be necessary. When we know the full extent of any danger, when we can accustom our eyes to it, a great deal of the apprehension vanishes. Every one will be sensible of this, who considers how greatly night adds to our dread, in all cases of danger, and how much the notions of ghosts and goblins, of which none can form clear ideas, affect minds which give credit to the popular tales concerning such sorts of beings. Those despotic governments which are founded on the passions of men, and principally upon the passion of fear, keep their chief as much as may be from the public eye. The policy has been the same in many cases of religion. Almost all the heathen temples were dark. Even in the barbarous temples of the Americans at this day, they keep their idol in a dark part of the hut, which is consecrated to his worship. For this purpose too the Druids performed all their ceremonies in the bosom of the darkest woods, and in the shade of the oldest and most spreading oaks. No person seems better to have understood the secret of heightening, or of setting terrible things, if I may use the expression, in their strongest light, by the force of a judicious obscurity than Milton. His description of death in the second book is admirably studied; it is astonishing with what a gloomy pomp, with what a significant and expressive uncertainty of strokes and coloring, he has finished the portrait of the king of terrors:

> "The other shape,
> If shape it might be called that shape had none
> Distinguishable, in member, joint, or limb;
> Or substance might be called that shadow seemed;
> For each seemed either; black he stood as night;
> Fierce as ten furies; terrible as hell;
> And shook a deadly dart. What seemed his head
> The likeness of a kingly crown had on."
>
> *Paradise Lost*, II, 666–73.

In this description all is dark, uncertain, confused, terrible, and sublime to the last degree.

It is one thing to make an idea clear, and another to make it *affecting* to the imagination. If I make a drawing of a palace, or a temple, or a landscape, I present a very clear idea of those objects; but then (allowing for the effect of imitation which is something) my picture can at most affect only as the palace, temple, or landscape, would have affected in the reality. On the other hand, the most lively and spirited verbal description I can give raises a very obscure and imperfect *idea* of such objects; but then it is in my power to raise a stronger *emotion* by the description than I could do by the best painting. This experience constantly evinces. The proper manner of conveying the *affections* of the mind from one to another is by words; there is a great insufficiency in all other methods of communication; and so far is a clearness of imagery from being absolutely necessary to an influence upon the passions, that they may be considerably operated upon, without presenting any image at all, by certain sounds adapted to that purpose; of which we have a sufficient proof in the acknowledged and powerful effects of instrumental music. In reality, a great clearness helps but little towards affecting the passions, as it is in some sort an enemy to all enthusiasms whatsoever.

There are two verses in Horace's Art of Poetry that seem to contradict this opinion; for which reason I shall take a little more pains in clearing it up. The verses are,

> Segnius irritant animos demissa per aures,
> Quam quæ sunt oculis subjecta fidelibus.

["No doubt we receive less vivid impressions by ear than by the eye, which is a faithful witness." Horace *Ars Poetica* ii. 180–81.]

On this the Abbé du Bos [1] founds a criticism, wherein he gives painting the preference to poetry in the article of moving the passions; principally on account of the greater *clearness* of the ideas it represents. I believe this excellent judge was led into this mistake (if it be a mistake) by his system; to which he found it more conformable than I imagine it will be found to experience. I know several who admire and love painting, and yet who regard the objects of their admiration in that art with coolness enough in comparison of that warmth with which they are animated by affecting pieces of poetry or rhetoric. Among the common sort of people, I never could perceive that painting had much influence on their passions. It is true that the best sorts of painting, as well as the best sorts of poetry, are not much understood in that sphere. But it is most certain that their passions are very strongly roused by a fanatic preacher, or by the ballads of Chevy Chase, or the Children in the Wood, and by other little popular poems and tales that are current in that rank of life. I do not know of any paintings, bad or good, that produce the same effect. So that poetry, with all its obscurity, has a more general, as well as a more powerful dominion over the passions, than the other art. And I think there are reasons in nature, why the obscure idea, when properly conveyed, should be more affecting than the clear. It is our ignorance of things that causes all our admiration, and chiefly excites our passions. Knowledge and acquaintance make the most striking causes affect but little. It is thus with the vulgar; and all men are as the vulgar in what they do not understand.

---

[1] *Réflexions Critiques* (Paris, 1719). Vol. I, sect. 40.

The ideas of eternity, and infinity, are among the most affecting we have: and yet perhaps there is nothing of which we really understand so little, as of infinity and eternity. We do not anywhere meet a more sublime description than this justly-celebrated one of Milton, wherein he gives the portrait of Satan with a dignity so suitable to the subject:

> "He above the rest
> In shape and gesture proudly eminent
> Stood like a tower; his form had yet not lost
> All her original brightness, nor appeared
> Less than archangel ruined, and th' excess
> Of glory obscured: as when the sun new risen
> Looks through the horizontal misty air
> Shorn of his beams; or from behind the moon
> In dim eclipse disastrous twilight sheds
> On half the nations; and with fear of change
> Perplexes monarchs."
>
> *Paradise Lost,* I, 589–99.

Here is a very noble picture; and in what does this poetical picture consist? In images of a tower, an archangel, the sun rising through mists, or in an eclipse, the ruin of monarchs and the revolutions of kingdoms. The mind is hurried out of itself, by a crowd of great and confused images; which affect because they are crowded and confused. For separate them, and you lose much of the greatness; and join them, and you infallibly lose the clearness. The images raised by poetry are always of this obscure kind; though in general the effects of poetry are by no means to be attributed to the images it raises; which point we shall examine more at large hereafter.[2] But painting, when we have allowed for the pleasure of imitation, can only affect simply by the images it presents; and even in painting, a judicious obscurity in some things contributes to the effect of the picture; because the images in painting are exactly similar to those in nature; and in nature, dark, confused, uncertain images have a greater power on the fancy to form the grander passions, than those have which

---

[2] Part V of the *Enquiry.*

are more clear and determinate. But where and when this observation may be applied to practice, and how far it shall be extended, will be better deduced from the nature of the subject,
and from the occasion, than from any rules that can be given.

I am sensible that this idea has met with opposition, and is
likely still to be rejected by several. But let it be considered that
hardly anything can strike the mind with its greatness, which
does not make some sort of approach towards infinity; which
nothing can do whilst we are able to perceive its bounds; but
to see an object distinctly, and to perceive its bounds, is one
and the same thing. A clear idea is therefore another name for
a little idea. There is a passage in the book of Job amazingly
sublime, and this sublimity is principally due to the terrible uncertainty of the thing described: *In thoughts from the visions of
the night, when deep sleep falleth upon men, fear came upon me
and trembling, which made all my bones to shake. Then a spirit
passed before my face. The hair of my flesh stood up. It stood
still,* but I could not discern the form thereof; *an image was before mine eyes; there was silence; and I heard a voice,—Shall
mortal man be more just than God?* [3] We are first prepared with
the utmost solemnity for the vision; we are first terrified, before
we are let even into the obscure cause of our emotion: but when
this grand cause of terror makes its appearance, what is it? Is it
not wrapt up in the shades of its own incomprehensible darkness,
more awful, more striking, more terrible, than the liveliest description, than the clearest painting, could possibly represent it?
When painters have attempted to give us clear representations
of these very fanciful and terrible ideas, they have, I think, almost
always failed; insomuch that I have been at a loss, in all the
pictures I have seen of hell, to determine whether the painter did
not intend something ludicrous. Several painters have handled a
subject of this kind, with a view of assembling as many horrid
phantoms as their imagination could suggest; but all the designs
I have chanced to meet of the temptations of St. Anthony were
rather a sort of odd, wild grotesques, than anything capable of
producing a serious passion. In all these subjects poetry is very
happy. Its apparitions, its chimeras, its harpies, its allegorical

[3] *Job* iv:13–17.

figures, are grand and affecting; and though Virgil's Fame [4] and Homer's Discord [5] are obscure, they are magnificent figures. These figures in painting would be clear enough, but I fear they might become ridiculous.

Besides those things which *directly* suggest the idea of danger, and those which produce a similar effect from a mechanical cause, I know of nothing sublime, which is not some modification of power. And this branch rises, as naturally as the other two branches, from terror, the common stock of everything that is sublime. The idea of power, at first view, seems of the class of those indifferent ones, which may equally belong to pain or to pleasure. But in reality, the affection arising from the idea of vast power is extremely remote from that neutral character. For first, we must remember that the idea of pain, in its highest degree, is much stronger than the highest degree of pleasure; and that it preserves the same superiority through all the subordinate gradations. From hence it is, that where the chances for equal degrees of suffering or enjoyment are in any sort equal, the idea of the suffering must always be prevalent. And indeed the ideas of pain, and, above all, of death, are so very affecting, that whilst we remain in the presence of whatever is supposed to have the power of inflicting either, it is impossible to be perfectly free from terror. Again, we know by experience, that, for the enjoyment of pleasure, no great efforts of power are at all necessary; nay, we know that such efforts would go a great way towards destroying our satisfaction: for pleasure must be stolen, and not forced upon us; pleasure follows the will; and therefore we are generally affected with it by many things of a force greatly inferior to our own. But pain is always inflicted by a power in some way superior, because we never submit to pain willingly. So that strength, violence, pain, and terror, are ideas that rush in upon the mind together. Look at a man, or any other animal of prodigious strength, and what is your idea before reflection? Is it that this strength will be subservient to you, to your ease, to your pleasure, to your interest in any sense? No; the emotion you feel is, lest this enormous strength should be employed to the pur-

---

[4] Latin *Fama*, or Rumor. *Æneid* iv.173 ff.

[5] Greek Ἔρις. *Iliad* iv.440 and xx.48.

poses of rapine and destruction. That power derives all its sublimity from the terror with which it is generally accompanied, will appear evidently from its effect in the very few cases, in which it may be possible to strip a considerable degree of strength of its ability to hurt. When you do this, you spoil it of everything sublime, and it immediately becomes contemptible. An ox is a creature of vast strength; but he is an innocent creature, extremely serviceable, and not at all dangerous; for which reason the idea of an ox is by no means grand. A bull is strong too; but his strength is of another kind; often very destructive, seldom (at least amongst us) of any use in our business; the idea of a bull is therefore great, and it has frequently a place in sublime descriptions, and elevating comparisons. Let us look at another strong animal, in the two distinct lights in which we may consider him. The horse in the light of an useful beast, fit for the plough, the road, the draft; in every social useful light, the horse has nothing sublime; but is it thus that we are affected with him, *whose neck is clothed with thunder, the glory of whose nostrils is terrible, who swalloweth the ground with fierceness and rage, neither believeth that it is the sound of the trumpet?* In this description, the useful character of the horse entirely disappears, and the terrible and sublime blaze out together. We have continually about us animals of a strength that is considerable, but not pernicious. Amongst these we never look for the sublime; it comes upon us in the gloomy forest, and in the howling wilderness, in the form of the lion, the tiger, the panther, or rhinoceros. Whenever strength is only useful, and employed for our benefit or our pleasure, then it is never sublime; for nothing can act agreeably to us, that does not act in conformity to our will; but to act agreeably to our will, it must be subject to us, and therefore can never be the cause of a grand and commanding conception. The description of the wild ass, in Job, is worked up into no small sublimity, merely by insisting on his freedom, and his setting mankind at defiance; otherwise the description of such an animal could have had nothing noble in it. *Who hath loosed* (says he) *the bands of the wild ass? whose house I have made the wilderness and the barren land his dwellings. He scorneth the multitude of the city, neither regardeth he the voice of the driver. The range of the mountains is his pasture.* The magnificent description of the unicorn and of leviathan, in the same book, is full of the same heightening circumstances: *Will the unicorn be willing to serve thee? canst thou bind the unicorn with his band in the furrow? wilt thou trust him because his strength is great?—Canst thou draw out leviathan with an hook? will he make a covenant with thee? wilt thou take him for a servant forever? shall not one be cast down even at the sight of him?* [6] In short, wheresoever we find strength, and in what light soever we look upon power, we shall all along observe the sublime the concomitant of terror, and contempt the attendant on a strength that is subservient and innoxious. The race of dogs, in many of their kinds, have generally a competent degree of strength and swiftness; and they exert these and other valuable qualities which they possess, greatly to our convenience and pleasure. Dogs are indeed the most social, affectionate, and amiable animals of the whole brute creation; but love approaches much nearer to contempt than is commonly imagined; and accordingly, though we caress dogs, we borrow from them an appellation of the most despicable kind, when we employ terms of reproach; and this appellation is the common mark of the last vileness and contempt in every language. Wolves have not more strength than several species of dogs; but, on account of their unmanageable fierceness, the idea of a wolf is not despicable; it is not excluded from grand descriptions and similitudes. Thus we are affected by strength, which is *natural* power. The power which arises from institution in kings and commanders, has the same connection with terror. Sovereigns are frequently addressed with the title of *dread majesty.* And it may be observed, that young persons, little acquainted with the world, and who have not been used to approach men in power, are commonly struck with an awe which takes away the free use of their faculties. *When I prepared my seat in the street,* (says Job,) *the young men saw me, and hid themselves.* Indeed so natural is this timidity with regard to power, and so strongly does it inhere in our constitution, that very few are able to conquer it, but by mixing much in the business of the great world, or by using no small violence to their natural dispositions. I know some people are of opinion, that no awe, no degree of terror, accompanies the idea

[6] *Job* xxxix, xli.

of power; and have hazarded to affirm, that we can contemplate the idea of God himself without any such emotion. I purposely avoided, when I first considered this subject, to introduce the idea of that great and tremendous Being, as an example in an argument so light as this; though it frequently occurred to me, not as an objection to, but as a strong confirmation of, my notions in this matter. I hope, in what I am going to say, I shall avoid presumption, where it is almost impossible for any mortal to speak with strict propriety. I say then, that whilst we consider the Godhead merely as he is an object of the understanding, which forms a complex idea of power, wisdom, justice, goodness, all stretched to a degree far exceeding the bounds of our comprehension, whilst we consider the divinity in this refined and abstracted light, the imagination and passions are little or nothing affected. But because we are bound, by the condition of our nature, to ascend to these pure and intellectual ideas, through the medium of sensible images, and to judge of these divine qualities by their evident acts and exertions, it becomes extremely hard to disentangle our idea of the cause from the effect by which we are led to know it. Thus, when we contemplate the Deity, his attributes and their operation, coming united on the mind, form a sort of sensible image, and as such are capable of affecting the imagination. Now, though in a just idea of the Deity, perhaps none of his attributes are predominant, yet, to our imagination, his power is by far the most striking. Some reflection, some comparing, is necessary to satisfy us of his wisdom, his justice, and his goodness. To be struck with his power, it is only necessary that we should open our eyes. But whilst we contemplate so vast an object, under the arm, as it were, of almighty power, and invested upon every side with omnipresence, we shrink into the minuteness of our own nature, and are, in a manner, annihilated before him. And though a consideration of his other attributes may relieve, in some measure, our apprehensions; yet no conviction of the justice with which it is exercised, nor the mercy with which it is tempered, can wholly remove the terror that naturally arises from a force which nothing can withstand. If we rejoice, we rejoice with trembling; and even whilst we are receiving benefits, we cannot but shudder at a power which can confer benefits of such mighty importance. When the prophet David contemplated the wonders of wisdom and power which are displayed in the economy of man, he seems to be struck with a sort of divine horror, and cries out, *fearfully and wonderfully am I made!* An heathen poet has a sentiment of a similar nature; Horace looks upon it as the last effort of philosophical fortitude, to behold without terror and amazement, this immense and glorious fabric of the universe:

> Hunc solem, et stellas, et decedentia certis
> Tempora momentis, sunt qui formidine nulla
> Imbuti spectent.

["Could anyone behold the sun, the stars, the regular march of the seasons, without being filled with fear?" Horace *Epistolae* I.vi.3–5.]

Lucretius is a poet not to be suspected of giving way to superstitious terrors; yet, when he supposes the whole mechanism of nature laid open by the master of his philosophy, his transport on this magnificent view, which he has represented in the colors of such bold and lively poetry, is overcast with a shade of secret dread and horror:

> His ibi me rebus quædam divina voluptas
> Percipit, atque horror; quod sic natura, tua vi
> Tam manifesta patens, ex omni parte retecta est.

["A kind of divine pleasure, joined with horror, comes over me as I see Epicurus lay open the ways of nature and reveal all its aspects." Lucretius *De Rerum Natura* iii. 28–30.]

But the Scripture alone can supply ideas answerable to the majesty of this subject. In the Scripture, wherever God is represented as appearing or speaking, everything terrible in nature is called up to heighten the awe and solemnity of the Divine presence. The Psalms, and the prophetical books, are crowded with instances of this kind. *The earth shook*, (says the Psalmist,) *the heavens also dropped at the presence of the Lord.*[7] And what is remarkable, the painting preserves the same character, not only when he is supposed descending to take vengeance upon the

---

[7] *Psalms* xviii:7–9.

wicked, but even when he exerts the like plenitude of power in acts of beneficence to mankind. *Tremble, thou earth! at the presence of the Lord; at the presence of the God of Jacob; which turned the rock into standing water, the flint into a fountain of waters!* [8] It were endless to enumerate all the passages, both in the sacred and profane writers, which establish the general sentiment of mankind, concerning the inseparable union of a sacred and reverential awe, with our ideas of the divinity. Hence the common maxim, *Primus in orbe deos fecit timor.* ["Fear first created gods in the world." Statius *Thebaid* 661.] This maxim may be, as I believe it is, false with regard to the origin of religion. The maker of the maxim saw how inseparable these ideas were, without considering that the notion of some great power must be always precedent to our dread of it. But this dread must necessarily follow the idea of such a power, when it is once excited in the mind. It is on this principle that true religion has, and must have, so large a mixture of salutary fear; and that false religions have generally nothing else but fear to support them. Before the Christian religion had, as it were, humanized the idea of the Divinity, and brought it somewhat nearer to us, there was very little said of the love of God. The followers of Plato have something of it, and only something; the other writers of pagan antiquity, whether poets or philosophers, nothing at all. And they who consider with what infinite attention, by what a disregard of every perishable object, through what long habits of piety and contemplation it is that any man is able to attain an entire love and devotion to the Deity, will easily perceive that it is not the first, the most natural, and the most striking effect which proceeds from that idea. Thus we have traced power through its several gradations unto the highest of all, where our imagination is finally lost; and we find terror, quite throughout the progress, its inseparable companion, and growing along with it, as far as we can possibly trace them. Now, as power is undoubtedly a capital source of the sublime, this will point out evidently from whence its energy is derived, and to what class of ideas we ought to unite it.

A Philosophical Enquiry into the Origin of our Ideas of the Sublime and Beautiful (1757), Part II, sections 1–5. I, 130–45.

---

[8] *Psalms* cxiv:7–8.

Appendix: Leading Dates of Burke's Life

1729.	Born in Dublin.
1744–48.	Student at Trinity College, Dublin.
1750.	Entered at Middle Temple, London.
1756.	*A Vindication of Natural Society.*
1757.	*A Philosophical Enquiry into the Origin of our Ideas of the Sublime and Beautiful.*
1759.	Started the *Annual Register.*
1765.	Became private secretary to the Marquis of Rockingham and entered Parliament for Wendover.
1769.	*Observations on "The Present State of the Nation."*
1770.	*Thoughts on the Cause of the Present Discontents.*
1774–80.	Member of Parliament for Bristol.
1774.	*Speech on American Taxation.*
1775.	*Speech on Conciliation with America.*
1780–94.	Member of Parliament for Malton.
1783–88.	Leader in the case for the impeachment of Warren Hastings.
1790.	*Reflections.*
1791.	*Appeal from the New to the Old Whigs.*
1794.	Granted a pension by the ministry, which was attacked by the Duke of Bedford.
1796.	*Letter to a Noble Lord,* a caustic reply to the Duke of Bedford.
1797.	July 9. Death.

Suggestions for Further Reading

COLLECTED WORKS: Most easily available are the editions in Bohn's
"British Classics" (1853), and the Boston edition (1865–67),
12 volumes, which has been used for text and references in this
volume.

SELECTED WORKS: ed. Edward J. Payne, 3 volumes (Oxford, 1874–78);
in World's Classics, 6 volumes (1906–7); *Burke's Politics*, ed.
Ross J. S. Hoffman and Paul Levack (New York, 1949); H. V. F.
Somerset, *A Note-book of Edmund Burke* (Cambridge, 1957).

BIOGRAPHY: The brief biography by John Morley (1879), is a classic.
More recent biographies have been published by R. H. Murray
(London, 1931); Philip Magnus (London, 1939); and G. M.
Young (London, 1943). The first volume of an elaborate biog-
raphy by Carl B. Cone, *Burke and the Nature of Politics*, has
been published (Lexington, 1957).

CORRESPONDENCE: References in the present volume are to the edition
in four volumes published in 1844 by Charles William and Sir
Richard Bourke. A definitive edition of Burke's correspondence,
largely from unpublished sources, is in preparation by Thomas
W. Copeland. The first two volumes have appeared (Chicago,
1958, 1960).

COMMENTARY: John McCunn, *The Political Philosophy of Burke* (London, 1913). A. Cobban, *Edmund Burke and the Revolt against
the Eighteenth Century* (London, 1929); Russell Kirk, *The Conservative Mind* (Chicago, 1953); Charles Parkin, *The Moral
Basis of Burke's Political Thought* (Cambridge, 1956); Peter J.
Stanlis, *Edmund Burke and the Natural Law* (Ann Arbor, 1958).

Index

Abstract theory, dangerous in politics, 5, 7, 35, 38, 41, 84, 86, 89, 95, 98, 125–27, 190, 195, 205, 208, 212; *see also* Mathematical reasoning and Metaphysical politics.

Aesthetics, 256–67.

Agriculture, problems of, 27–31.

American Colonies, conciliation with, 36, 82–104, 176–78; spirit of liberty in, 79–81, 88–89; taxation of, 37–38, 82–93.

Analogies misleading in theory of state, 50, 166–67.

Arbitrary power, 17–20.

Aristocracy, 115–17, 139–41, 142, 144–46; natural, 49, 60–61, 220–21.

Aristotle, 38, 137.

Arnold, Matthew, 255.

Bedford, Duke of, 168–70, 228–30.

Body politic, 40, 49; *see also* Nation and People.

Bristol, letter to Sheriffs of, 93–101, 148–50, 175; speech at, 14, 47–48, 65–67.

Catholics, oppression of, 20, 65–67.

Change, and conservation, 118, 156–65, 177, 196; law of, 174, 196, 255; and reformation, 169, 173–74; *see also* Innovation and Reform.

Charters, kinds of, 67–70.

Church Establishment of England, 66, 75–78, 104–25.

Cicero, 13, 23, 24, 55, 56, 223–24.

Circumstances, importance of in political judgments, 41–42, 72, 89, 96, 102, 177, 179, 255.

Clergy in England, 114–18.

Commons, House of, corruption of, *see* Court faction; a deliberative body, 147–48; frequency of election of members, 150–55, 178–82; independence of, 138, 153–54, 156; taxation, right of, 88–89.

Compromise, 37, 48, 99–100, 162.

Conservation, 157, 162.

Constitution, English, 37, 67, 75, 95–96, 113, 139, 153, 165, 176–208, 210, 214–16, 228–30; and liberty, 64, 88, 91–92.

Constitutions, paper, 185.

Continuity, 109, 157, 206–8.

Contract theory, *see* Social contract.

Conventions, *see* Society.

Corporate bodies, *see* Institutions; church a corporate body, 119, 123.

Court faction under George III, 2, 138–41, 150, 182–87.

Declaration of Right (1689), 192–95, 205–6.

Democracy, 53, 108.

De Pont, letter to, *see* Dupont.

Despotism, 18–19, 183, 257.
Discontents, English, in 1770, 62–64, 81–87, 134–38, 182–87; *see also* Court faction.
Dissenters, English, 75–79, 188.
Dupont, letter to, 38, 70–71, 174.
Duty, principle of, 51, 53–56, 70, 133.

East India Company, 17–20, 67–70.
Economical reform, Burke's proposals for, 141–42, 169–73.
Education, 103, 246–47, 250–52; in England, 113–15.
Equity, *see* Justice.
Expediency, 85, 90, 95, 158, 165, 212–13; *see also* Prudence.
Experience, 36, 44, 48, 62, 162, 165; test of theory, 212–13.

Family, 54, 222, 237–38.
Feudalism and chivalry, 103, 125–26.
Freedom, *see* Liberty.
French Revolution, *see* Jacobinism.

George III, 2; *see also* Court faction.
Government, 27, 39, 52, 73–74, 80, 151, 158, 173–74; a human contrivance, 46–48, 50; and human nature, 14, 38, 90, 96, 81–131, 170, 211, 212, 235–37; legitimacy of, 158, 190, 216; must be supported by public opinion, 14, 15, 95, 97, 138, 172–73, 180, 186; *see also* People, supremacy of; simplicity of a defect, 48, 162–63.

Hastings, Warren, 17–20.
Helvetius, 104, 254.
History, lessons from, 6–7, 16–17.
Hobbes, Thomas, 13.
Homer, 262.
Horace, 127, 259, 266.

Human nature, 106, 126, 133, 137, 143, 156, 185, 211, 248, 252.
Hume, 164.

Inheritance, principle of, 157, 206–7.
Innovation, 166, 169, 206–7; *see also* Reform and Change.
Institutions, artificial and man-made, 43–47, 57; corporate in nature, 71, 122, 209–10, 218, 227–28; *see also* Nature and Society.
Ireland, 20.

Jacobinism, 4–10, 16, 31, 219, 231–55; atheism of, 234–35, 254.
Job, Book of, 261, 263–64.
Jurisprudence, 15, 109, 218, 228.
Justice, 12, 14, 46, 64–67, 71, 112, 168, 219, 225, 253.

Kings, 142, 189–90, 200, 234.

Law, basis in public faith, 195–96; a European bond, 102–3; international, 16, 31–34; and manners, *see* Manners and laws; moral, 5, 16, 17–19, 51–52, 111–12, 168, 219; of nature and nations, 13, 19, 44; needs supports, 184; opposition of reason to will, 14, 19, 44, 170, 195; superseded only by public necessity, 15, 192–93; *see also* Necessity; theory of, 13–31; *see also* Jurisprudence and Justice.
Liberty, 64–67, 70–73, 77, 98, 186, 241–43; English, an inheritance, 70–71, 206–8; spirit of, in Colonies, 79–81.

Majority rule, 51–53, 57–59, 222–23.

Manners, importance of, 102–4, 125–31, 234, 252; and laws, 31, 235, 238.

Mathematical reasoning in politics, 38, 41, 48–49.

Metaphysical politics, 41, 87, 93, 97, 98, 143, 196, 232; hardhearted, 233, 246.

Milton, 258.

Moral law, 5, 17–19, 44.

Morals, revolution in, 249–55.

Nation, what is a, 50, 211.

National Assembly, French, 74–75, 129, 158–61, 237, 247.

Natural rights, see Rights.

Nature, state of, 48, 57, 122; see also Rights and Society.

Necessity, recognition of, 14, 44, 111, 165, 201, 203, 216.

Parliament, power of, 93–96, 147–48; see also House of Commons.

Parties, political, 132–38.

People, the, 14, 39, 49, 51, 56, 62–63, 83, 101–2, 146, 150, 180, 211, 219, 241; accurate idea of, 49–64; control vested in, 22, 52, 56–57, 107–8, 118, 148, 174, 186; impossible to prosecute, 37, 108; and their representatives, 74, 88, 146–50, 152–53, 172–73.

Persius, 55.

Power, 14, 52, 73, 127, 216; arbitrary, 18–19; political, a trust, 107, 133, 187.

Prejudices, 106, 110, 158, 211, 231, 252.

Prescription, principle of, 109–10, 158–59, 210–11, 232; and British government, 197–216; and property, 208–30.

Price, Richard, 188–89, 191, 202.

Property, confiscation of in France, 104, 217–19, 223–25; place of in body politic, 221–23, 232, 244; rights of, 117, 217–25.

Prudence as a political virtue, 35–42, 90, 96–97, 156, 168, 176.

Psalms, 266–67.

Reform, danger of violent, 161–64, 173–74, 203–4; distinguished from innovation, 156–66, 169, 206–7, 215–17, 226; necessary to preserve state, 118, 171–74; see also Change.

Religion, abolition of in France, 234–35; see also Jacobins, atheism of; essential to society, 104–7, 110; in English state, 104–25.

Revolution, American, see American Colonies.

Revolution, French, 4–11, 187, 244; see also Jacobinism.

Revolution of 1688, English, 40, 187–208.

Revolution, Russian, 2, 4, 8–10.

Revolution Society, 187–90, 197–98.

Rights of Man, 36, 38, 42, 45–49, 64–67, 205; "chartered" rights, 67–70.

Rockingham, Marquis of, 67, 82, 143–45.

Rousseau, 164, 246–55.

Society, bonds of, 102, 112; a contract, 43–44; a convention, 45–49, 122; a heritage, 109, 128; is natural, 61, 146–47, 157, 207–8, 220; and natural rights, 44–49, 64–67.

Somers, Lord, 193, 195.

State, the, 39, 112, 218–19, 241–44; consecration of, 106–7; French and British compared, 241–46.

Sublime, theory of, 255–67.

Taxation, *see* American Colonies.

Theory, 40, 190, 212, 245–46.

Toleration, religious, 76–79, 118–25.

Tradition, 128, 156–65; in English Constitution, 176–208.

Tyranny, 65, 159, 222–23.

Virgil, 53, 160, 262.

Wisdom, 36, 109, 162–63, 173, 176, 227.

Of related interest

Peter J. Stanlis

EDMUND BURKE AND THE NATURAL LAW

This study reveals Edmund Burke's true position as a social philosopher—his principles of prudence, his distrust of abstract law, his appeals to nature, his concept of the law of nations.

"No one who hopes to understand modern politics will be able to ignore Dr. Stanlis' remarkable study."
                                —From the Foreword by Russell Kirk

T. H. Green

LECTURES ON THE PRINCIPLES
OF POLITICAL OBLIGATION

These lectures were delivered at Oxford in 1879 by T. H. Greene, one of the Oxford Idealists who were the critical successors to the Utilitarian School of John Stuart Mill. Green's thesis, that the law and the obligations imposed by it must serve a moral end, argues against the Utilitarian idea that political obligation has only the goal of attaining the most pleasure and the least pain for the greatest number.

Write for information on available editions and current prices.

THE UNIVERSITY OF MICHIGAN PRESS
Ann Arbor, Michigan 48106